Subterranean Politics in Europe

Subterranean Politics in Europe

Edited by

Mary Kaldor
Professor of Global Governance, London School of Economics and Political Science, UK

Sabine Selchow
Research Fellow, London School of Economics and Political Science, UK

First published 2015 by
PALGRAVE MACMILLAN

Palgrave Macmillan in the UK is an imprint of Macmillan Publishers Limited, registered in England, company number 785998, of Houndmills, Basingstoke, Hampshire RG21 6XS.

Palgrave Macmillan in the US is a division of St Martin's Press LLC, 175 Fifth Avenue, New York, NY 10010.

Palgrave Macmillan is the global academic imprint of the above companies and has companies and representatives throughout the world.

Palgrave® and Macmillan® are registered trademarks in the United States, the United Kingdom, Europe and other countries.

ISBN 978–1–137–44146–1

This book is printed on paper suitable for recycling and made from fully managed and sustained forest sources. Logging, pulping and manufacturing processes are expected to conform to the environmental regulations of the country of origin.

A catalogue record for this book is available from the British Library.

Library of Congress Cataloging-in-Publication Data
Subterranean politics in Europe / [edited by] Mary Kaldor (professor of global governance, London School of Economics and Political Science, UK), Sabine Selchow (research Fellow, London School of Economics and Political Science, UK).
     pages   cm
Includes bibliographical references.
ISBN 978–1–137–44146–1 (hardback)
 1. Europe—Politics and government—1989–   2. Europe—Social conditions—21st century.   3. Political activists—Europe—History—21st century.   4. Protest movements—Europe—History—21st century.
 5. Social movements—Europe—History—21st century.
 6. Radicalism—Europe—History—21st century.   7. Political culture—Europe—History—21st century.   I. Kaldor, Mary.   II. Selchow, Sabine.
D2024.S83 2015
322.4094—dc23   2014037981

Contents

Boxes, Figures and Tables

Boxes

Figures

Tables

Acknowledgements

This research would not have been possible without the generous support of the Open Society Foundations. In particular, we would like to thank Rayna Gavrilova, Heather Grabbe and Ellen Riotte at the Open Society European Policy Institute (formerly OSI Brussels) for their help and enthusiasm throughout. Jordi Vaquer, of the Open Society Initiative for Europe, also contributed significantly to the research process.

We would especially like to thank all those who gave their time to take part in the focus groups and interviews carried out by the field teams. It is also important to stress – partially on their behest – that their comments and our extrapolations do not necessarily reflect the views of all those involved in the loosely affiliated groups and movements that we see as characteristic of 'subterranean politics'. Indeed, the importance of avoiding the imposition of an overriding ideology on fellow activists is a core belief of many of those interviewed.

This book draws on the 'Subterranean Politics' research project. The full reports from the seven contextual case studies are available to academic researchers working on related topics; please see the website for further details: www.subterraneanpolitics.eu. In addition to the contributors to this volume, we would like to note the researchers who worked on the initial studies: Dr Bartolomeo Conti (CADIS, Paris), Maro Pantazidou (IDS), Erin Saltman (UCL) and Hajnalka Szarvas (Corvinus University).

We would also like to thank Dominika Spyratou, Pippa Bore and Jon Wiltshire (intern) of the Civil Society and Human Security Unit of the London School of Economics and Political Science (LSE) for their tireless assistance.

Contributors

Helmut K. Anheier is Professor of Sociology and Dean at the Hertie School of Governance. He also holds a chair in sociology at Heidelberg University and serves as Academic Director of the Center for Social Investment. He received his PhD from Yale University in 1986. From 2001 to 2009, he was Professor of Public Policy and Social Welfare at UCLA's School of Public Affairs and Centennial Professor at the London School of Economics. He founded and directed the Centre for Civil Society at the London School of Economics and the Center for Civil Society at UCLA. Before embarking on an academic career, he served as social affairs officer to the United Nations. He is currently researching the role of foundations in civil society and focuses on concepts and methods in civil society and globalisation studies. He is the founding editor of the *Global Civil Society Yearbook* and editor of the Cultures and Globalization series (with Raj Isar). His recent publications include *Foundations and American Society* (with David Hammack, 2009) and *Nonprofit Organizations: Theory, Management and Policy* (2005).

Ulrich Beck[†] was Emeritus Professor of Sociology at the University of Munich and Visiting Centennial Professor at the London School of Economics and Political Science. He was a prolific author; his most notable books translated into English include *Risk Society* (1992; originally published in German in 1986), *Reflexive Modernization* (1994, with Anthony Giddens and Scott Lash), *The Normal Chaos of Love* (1995, with E. Beck-Gernsheim), *The Reinvention of Politics* (1996), *Democracy Without Enemies* (1998), *World Risk Society* (1999), *Individualization* (2000), *Power in the Global Age* (2005), *The Cosmopolitan Vision* (2006), *Cosmopolitan Europe* (2007, with Edgar Grande), *World at Risk* (2008), *German Europe* (2013) and *Distant Love* (2014, with E. Beck-Gernsheim). Described as 'the most influential sociologist of his generation' by Lord Anthony Giddens, Beck died aged 70 on 1 January 2015, as this book went to press.

Jordi Bonet i Martí is Lecturer in Organizational Psychology at Pontificia Universidad Católica de Valparaíso (Chile). He completed his PhD in social psychology at Universitat Autónoma de Barcelona and his undergraduate studies at Universitat de Barcelona. His research interests lie in the area of community development, urban policies, minority rights and discourse analysis. In recent years, he has focused on feminist methodology through his participation in the creation of SIMREF (Seminari Interdisciplinar de Metodologia de Recerca Feminista; Seminar on Interdisciplinary Feminist Research Methodology).

Sean Deel is a researcher in the Department of International Development at the London School of Economics.

Donatella della Porta is Professor of Sociology in the Department of Political and Social Sciences at the European University Institute, where she directs the Center on Social Movement Studies (Cosmos). She also directs a major ERC project, Mobilizing for Democracy, on civil society participation in democratisation processes in Europe, the Middle East, Asia and Latin America. Among her very recent publications are *Can Democracy Be Saved?* (2013), *Clandestine Political Violence* (with D. Snow, B. Klandermans and D. McAdam, eds., 2013), *Blackwell Encyclopedia on Social and Political Movements* (2013), *Mobilizing on the Extreme Right* (with M. Caiani and C. Wagemann, 2012), *Meeting Democracy* (ed. with D. Rucht, 2012), *The Hidden Order of Corruption* (with A. Vannucci, 2012), *Social Movements and Europeanization* (with M. Caiani, 2009), *Another Europe* (ed., 2009), *Democracy in Social Movements* (ed., 2009) and *Approaches and Methodologies in the Social Sciences* (with M. Keating; translation into Spanish by Akal, 2008). In 2011, she was the recipient of the Mattei Dogan Prize for distinguished achievements in the field of political sociology.

Paolo Gerbaudo is Lecturer in Digital Culture and Society at King's College London. He has worked as a reporter for the Italian Left newspaper *il manifesto* and has been involved in anti-corporate, global justice and ecologist campaigns. His current research focuses on the use of new media and social media by social movements and emerging digital parties. He is the author of *Tweets and the Streets* (2012), a book analysing social media activism in the popular protest wave of 2011, from the Arab Spring to the indignados and Occupy Wall Street. He has a PhD from Goldsmiths College, where he worked under the supervision of Professor Nick Couldry. He has previously taught at Middlesex University and the American University in Cairo. He is currently the convenor of the Digital Culture and Political Protest module at King's College.

Jody Jensen is a research fellow at the Institute of Sociology and Institute of Political Science, Hungarian Academy of Sciences, and the Director of International Economic Relations, Institute for Social and European Studies, Hungary. Amongst other positions, she has been the regional director of ASHOKA Central Europe (1994–2002); director of the HCA Liaison Office for East Central European Cooperation (1994–1998); general secretary of the Consortium for the Study of European Transition (1991–1995); and co-convenor of the Helsinki Citizen's Assembly Commission on Nationalism and (Con)Federal Structures. Focusing on the Balkans, global civil society, transformation of the nation state and the governance of global markets, she contributes regularly to major journals and is also the English editor of the website Találjuk-ki Közepeuropát (Reinventing Central Europe; www.talaljuk-ki.hu) and editor-in-chief of English publications for Savaria University Press and ISES Publications.

Mary Kaldor is Professor of Global Governance, Director of the Civil Society and Human Security Research Unit at the London School of Economics and CEO of the DFID-funded Justice and Security Research Programme. She is the author of several books, including *The Ultimate Weapon Is No Weapon: Human Security and the Changing Rules of War and Peace* (2010); *New and Old Wars: Organised Violence in a Global Era* (1999; third edition 2012) and *Global Civil Society: An Answer to War* (2003). She was co-chair of the Helsinki Citizens Assembly, a member of the International Independent Commission on Kosovo and convenor of the Human Security Study Group, which reported to Javier Solana.

Lorenzo Mosca is an assistant professor at Roma Tre University, where he teaches new media, sociology of communication and public opinion. His research interests are mostly focused on political participation, communication and social movements. Recent research includes anti-austerity movements in Italy, the political use of the Internet in comparative perspective and the Movimento 5 Stelle.

Tamsin Murray-Leach is a research officer in the Civil Society and Human Security Unit at the London School of Economics and managing editor of *Global Civil Society 2012* and of this volume.

Anne Nassauer is a postdoctoral researcher at the Department of Sociology, John F. Kennedy Institute, Free University of Berlin. Her main research interests include collective behaviour, emotions and symbolic interaction. She completed her doctorate at Humboldt University, Berlin, on 'Violence in Demonstrations: A Comparative Analysis of Situational Interaction Dynamics at Social Movement Protests'. Currently, she is researching violence, social movements and crime from a micro-sociological perspective.

Louisa Parks holds a PhD from the European University Institute in Florence. She is the author of *Social Movement Campaigns on EU Policy: In the Corridors and in the Streets* (2015). She is Lecturer in the School of Social and Political Sciences at the University of Lincoln, where she is carrying out research within the Benelux project on the role of NGOs in the elaboration of norms on benefit sharing in global environmental law. This research, funded by the European Research Council, proceeds alongside continued work on social movement campaigning in the EU.

Mario Pianta is Professor of Economic Policy at the University of Urbino and is a member of the Centro Linceo Interdisciplinare of the Accademia Nazionale dei Lincei. His recent books include *Global Justice Activism and Policy Reform in Europe* (ed., with P. Utting and A. Elleskirk, 2012).

Geoffrey Pleyers is an FNRS researcher at the University of Louvain, Belgium. He holds a PhD in sociology from the Ecole des Hautes Etudes en Sciences Sociales (EHESS, Paris) and teaches sociology of globalisation and social movements at the EHESS and at the University of Louvain. He is the author of *Forums sociaux mondiaux et défis de l'altermondialisme* (2007) and *Alter-globalization: Becoming Actors in a Global Age* (2010) and has edited the books *Movimientos sociales. De lo local a lo global* (2009) and *Consommation critique* (2011).

Sabine Selchow is a research fellow in the Civil Society and Human Security Research Unit at the London School of Economics and in the Institute of Sociology at Ludwig-Maximilians-Universität, Germany. She holds a PhD in government from the London School of Economics. She is the co-editor of *Global Civil Society 2012*.

1

Introduction – In Search of Europe's Future: Subterranean Politics and the Other Crisis in Europe

Mary Kaldor and Sabine Selchow

Introduction

There is a growing body of research and commentary on the current global crisis and its social and political consequences. The majority of these studies take 'the crisis' to be a *financial* crisis that has been unfolding since 2007,[1] sometimes reading and analysing it as a crisis of capitalism as we know it. The outcome of these analyses is diverse and rich. Yet, they share the assumption that the financial crisis is the context that guides their research in terms of the questions that scholars ask and in terms of how they assess current political activism. In a subtle way, then, the financial crisis has come to serve as a key frame through which current socio-political developments and happenings are explored; socio-political phenomena, such as recent protests like Occupy, are analysed and, not least, evaluated with regard to their relationship to the financial crisis (and its consequences), or as a reaction against or a failure to react to it.

The starting point of this book is that when it comes to contemporary protests and the search for alternatives to existing political practices in Europe, the frame of the financial crisis predetermines analyses in an overly circumscribed way. It 'tames' both critical efforts to fully understand what is happening in the streets and squares worldwide, and the search for original ideas within these protests and collective activities that might form the basis for social transformation. A good example of this is the study of the impact of the financial crisis on British politics by Johal et al. (2012). In their study the authors observe that what they perceive as 'the most profound financial and regulatory crisis in

1

the United Kingdom since before the First World War' did not have a major impact on the underlying structures that led to the crisis and suggest that there won't be any substantial change 'until some means is found of linking programmatic action with civil society discontent' (ibid. p. 69).

In this book, we put forward an alternative conceptual and analytical frame for the critical exploration and understanding of the developments that are unfolding in Europe. Grounded in observations made within the context of a broader project on the future of Europe, and specifically building on the findings of seven empirical studies of recent protests and manifestations of collective activism across Europe that were conducted within our 'Subterranean Politics' project, we propose a shift in scholarly perspective, that is, in how we see and understand what is currently unfolding in Europe. To be clear, this is not a study of what is going wrong in Europe or how we should think about 'Europe' per se, rather about how the contemporary crisis is analytically treated and 'perceived' in Europe. There are two aspects to this alternative perspective.

First, we argue that the current protests and manifestations of collective activism that we see across Europe can be analysed as 'subterranean politics'. In this introductory chapter, we summarise the overall findings of our seven case studies and present five important features of subterranean politics: the fact that current protests strike a chord and have specific 'resonance' among the public, the relevance of *2.0 culture*, the fact that current public displays of subterranean politics are about democracy but not as usual, the observation that Europe is 'invisible' and, finally, the fact that protests and other manifestations of collective activism are to be seen, first and foremost, as being concerned about the state of politics and democracy in Europe, rather than simply and solely about austerity.

Second, we suggest that analysts and political decision makers need to understand that there is a crisis currently unfolding in Europe that is overshadowed by (the dominant and naturalised focus on and concern with) the financial crisis. This is the crisis of the legitimacy of political orders and practices across Europe. It is evident in the recent protests and manifestations of collective activism, such as Occupy and the 15-M, but also in the various *Wutbuerger* protests in Germany. It is this 'other' crisis that not only requires critical attention but that needs to be taken as the point of departure for social and political scientific analyses, as well as for the development of policies in the face of the current situation in Europe.

In what follows, we start by outlining the research project on which this book was based. We then describe the five features of subterranean politics in Europe that emerged from our research. Before concluding we summarise the main thrust of each of the case studies.

In search of Europe's future: Project background and approach

The arguments presented in this chapter arise out of the initial phase of a broader research project, based at the London School of Economics. Its critical interest is the future of Europe. At the heart of this initial phase were seven distinct, commissioned empirical studies that were conducted by European research teams between autumn 2011 and spring 2012. The chapter draws on empirical data from each of these studies.

In the face of the danger of a breaking apart of the European Union (EU), the project set out to investigate whether and which constructive ideas about the future of Europe as a political project are articulated 'on the ground'. Is there a trans-European movement (in formation) to rescue the (idea of) Europe? Which role does this idea of Europe actually play among those engaged in what might be termed politics from below? The original aim was to identify and analyse existing pro-European initiatives. What became clear from an initial exercise was that there are/were indeed a proliferation of conferences and workshops, appeals and petitions, articles and blogs proposing reform of the EU and a renewal of political Europeanism, but that these initiatives largely stem from what might be called mainstream politics – a trans-European elite that includes politicians and former politicians, think tanks and intellectuals as well as established NGOs and trade unions (see the listings of initiatives at www.subterraneanpolitics.eu). However, these multiple initiatives seemed to bear little relation to what might be described as 'politics from below' or, in other words, Europe 'on the ground'. Importantly, the exercise did not seem to capture a significant development unfolding across Europe.

Once we left this narrow question and adopted a wider vantage point, it became clear that what seemed to be actually happening was a 'bubbling up' of various kinds of socio-political phenomena, social mobilisations and collective activities, ranging from the 15-M in Spain, Occupy LSX (London Stock Exchange) in London, the Pirate parties across Europe to the German *Wutbuerger*. This initial observation led us to conclude that it was valuable to take these 'bubbling up' politics as the focus of research in the search for the future of Europe, rather than adopting an approach of focusing solely and narrowly on pro-European initiatives. This, however, seemed to require a novel concept because none of the concepts that are usually employed in studies with similar aims – such as 'social movement', '(advocacy) networks' and 'civil society', or even the more critical terms like counter-publics or resistance movements – would allow analysts to capture the diversity of politics that are currently 'bubbling up'. Or rather, most of these terms carry a conceptual history and genealogy that prescribes the kind of research that is undertaken and the choice of research tools employed. Our focus has less to do with the theory of social action and more to do with understanding the current crisis in Europe. Hence we invented the new term 'subterranean politics' which could be substantiated as a consequence of the research rather than as a starting point.

It is the above reasoning and stream of initial observations that account for the somewhat unusual experimental and explorative research design of the initial phase of the broader project on the future of Europe in general, and the commissioned case studies that constitute the core of this initial phase in particular. The concept of 'subterranean politics' was used as a relatively open frame to guide the empirical studies, and, at the same time, constituted the blank field to be filled with meanings in the self-reflective research process. That is, our ideas about subterranean politics fed into, and also grew out of, our research, positioning the concept of 'subterranean politics' in a dynamic relationship with the research about it. Interestingly, the only other application of the term that we have been able to identify is very similar to our approach. Simon Tormey, building on the work of Deleuze and Guattari, suggests that the term 'rhizomatic' can be used to describe

> 'subterranean' underground initiatives of this kind. The rhizome makes us to distinguish between the liminal and the subliminal, between what 'expert' commentary sees above, and what lurks beneath the surface. Even when 'nothing seems to be happening' rhizome-networks can be growing, developing, readying themselves for the next opportunity to push through the surface and emerge in unpredictable ways.
>
> (Tormey 2012: 66)

To start the exploration of 'subterranean politics' in Europe in this initial phase of the broader project, seven context-specific studies were commissioned. Four of them focused on national political cultures: Germany, Hungary, Italy and Spain. One analysed London as a global city and two looked at the trans-European context – one focusing on grassroots networks, the other on both alternative European initiatives and trans-European anti-austerity movements. Given the experimental nature of the research project with its explorative conceptual guiding frame of 'subterranean politics', the aim of these studies was not to capture a representative picture of protests across Europe but to explore 'subterranean politics' and to allow the concept to be filled with meaning through their respective research. The highly explorative and experimental nature of the project demanded that the empirical work had to be done by local research teams who were sufficiently familiar with the local socio-political context in order to be able to determine what were to be considered as public displays of subterranean politics in their specific contexts to begin with. Eventually, each research team engaged with and can be said to have filled in the concept of 'subterranean politics' differently. Likewise, each of them applied those social science research methods which they individually considered appropriate in their respective context. These included media content analysis, Protest Event Analysis (PEA), participant observation, surveys, focus group discussions and extensive ethnographic-style interviews with individual subterranean actors across Europe.

The result of this initial phase of the research project on the future of Europe was a set of empirical studies that each present context-specific arguments triggered by the experimental conceptual guiding frame of 'subterranean politics' and that, taken together and cross-examined, enabled us to develop broader arguments that contribute in an original way to the understanding of recent developments in and the critical search for where the future of Europe lies. These broader arguments are presented in this chapter. In addition to the observations developed in the project overall and the cross-examination of the data and findings gathered in the individual commissioned studies, it draws on existing data sets such as the survey data from protest demonstrations in seven European countries that the European Collaborative Research Projects (ECRP)-funded Protest Survey Project has been collecting (Protest Survey 2010) and European public opinion and demographics surveys including Eurobarometer (Eurobarometer 2011) and Eurostat (Eurostat 2011).

Five features of subterranean politics in Europe

What emerged from the research were five features of current protests and other manifestations of collective activism across Europe that seemed to be significant in terms of understanding the character of the European crisis. First, we noted that even though these political initiatives may not be new, what is new is the way that they strike a chord and have a particular kind of 'resonance' in the wider publics. This observation motivated us to conceptualise them as current displays of subterranean politics that have been 'bubbling up' to the surface. Second, we stressed the relevance of *2.0 culture*. We suggested that *2.0 culture* is at the heart of the changing nature of political activism. Third, we demonstrated that current public displays of subterranean politics are about democracy but not as usual; the prefigurative character of public displays of subterranean politics all have to do with emerging conceptions of democracy. Fourth, we observed that Europe is largely 'invisible' in current displays of subterranean politics. We suggested that it is oscillating between three poles: a widespread European cultural identity, especially among young people; an opposition to what is perceived as a neo-liberal bureaucracy; and a sense that the EU is abstract and remote. Finally, we argued that current protests and other manifestations of collective activism across Europe are to be seen, first and foremost, as being concerned about the state of politics and democracy in Europe, rather than simply and solely about austerity. In the following we will reflect on each of them in turn.

The 'bubbling up' of subterranean politics in Europe

On 15 May 2011 between 0.8 and 1.5 million people demonstrated all over Spain under the slogan 'Real Democracy Now'. Inspired by the Arab Spring, the demonstrations led to the idea of occupying squares in Spain, Greece and later cities across Europe, as well as in the United States, Israel and Chile. On 11 February 2012, Europe saw mass protests against the Anti-Counterfeiting Trade Agreement (ACTA), an international legal agreement seen to threaten Internet freedom and communication privacy. Numerous small and larger protests against austerity in the UK and Greece took place during 2011. In Greece, these protests appeared to be dominated by traditional social actors – the trade unions and far-left parties – but, as anecdotal evidence suggests, they also involved many people who called themselves *Aganaktismenoi* (indignant citizens). In the UK, new groups sprang up that distanced themselves from organised civil society groups such as trade unions or the National Union of Students, as well as from far-left parties. They included the student movement, which reacted against the Coalition government's decision to raise student fees, and UK Uncut (www .ukuncut.org.uk), which campaigns for alternatives to austerity using direct action or civil disobedience. In the German city of Stuttgart, citizens from all walks of life and ages demonstrated against a large-scale train station development project that had been in planning since the 1990s and which was officially launched in 2009. Italy, too, has seen protests against infrastructure projects during recent years, such as opposition to the high-speed train in Val Susa (No TAV), along with work protests and campaigns against cuts in education. In Hungary, both right and left took to the streets and the airwaves in unprecedented numbers: the largest include Jobbik, the new far-right party (see further Bartlett et al. 2012), Milla, which campaigns for freedom of the press and had almost 100,000 Facebook supporters at that time, and the Two-Tailed Dog Party, a mock political party that made fun of mainstream politics and had some 80,000 Facebook followers (see Chapter 6, p. 151). And during the same period national incarnations of the Pirate Party – standing for the strengthening of civil rights, direct democracy and participation (in the form of what they call 'liquid democracy' or delegated voting), reform of copyright and patent law, free sharing of knowledge, data privacy, transparency and freedom of information – conquered parliamentary seats across Europe (Appelrath et al. 2012).

Social mobilisations and manifestations of collective activism of the kind we are witnessing in Europe at the moment are, of course, not new. The entire past decade has been one of large-scale social mobilisation worldwide (see the Global Civil Society Knowledgebase and Kaldor et al. 2012). The anti-Iraq war protests in 2003 brought some 11 million people to the streets (see Kaldor et al. 2003: 26–27). The social forums, the main focal point of the alter-globalisation movement, have spread worldwide, and particularly in Europe, in the years since 2001, regularly mobilising hundreds of thousands of participants around issues of social and economic justice, labour rights, environmental sustainability and participatory democracy (Pianta 2002; Glasius and Timms 2005). Environmental campaigns like the Climate Change Action camps in the UK, Belgium, France, Australia, Canada, New Zealand and elsewhere took place during this period (see further Newell 2006), as did a blossoming of all sorts of online activism and forms of consumer activism (Bob et al. 2008). Viewed in relation to these mobilisations, the current manifestations of collective activism across Europe are smaller, less widespread and, arguably, less interconnected. Yet, there is something peculiar about them: they seem to have a specific 'resonance'. Unlike previous mobilisations and protests, contemporary protests and manifestations of collective activism are somehow striking a chord in the mainstream in a way that could not be said of earlier protests, causing ripples of discomfort in established institutions, challenging dominant ways of thinking and unsettling normal assumptions about how politics is done.

A good example of this 'striking a chord' is the way that the protests of citizens in Stuttgart triggered a new German term, *Wutbuerger* ('angry citizen'), a word which was eventually elected by the *Gesellschaft fuer die deutsche Sprache* (2010) as the 'word of the year 2010', singling it out as the word that shaped public discussions in a particularly important way during that year. *Indignados* is a similar word, which was employed by the Spanish press and not the activists themselves; it is a noun ('the Indignants', or 'the Outraged') rather than a verb or an adjective to describe the Spanish 15-M, identifying it with the bestseller *Indignez-Vous* written by the French World War II resistance hero, Stéphane Hessel (2010). The interest of the Spanish press reflected widespread popular support for the movement: according to a poll published in the newspaper *El Pais* on 26 June 2011, 64% of those polled backed the movement and 74% considered that it was a peaceful movement aimed at revitalising democracy (*El Pais* 2011), while a poll published by the Centro de Investigaciones Sociológicas (2011) at around the same time revealed that over half of those who voted for the *Partido Popular* (the ruling conservatives) expressed support for the movement.

Also exemplary is Occupy LSX, the occupation of the square in front of St Paul's Cathedral in the City of London from October 2011 until February 2012 by some hundred people. There had been similar camps in the UK previously, such as the Climate Camps or the long-running camp in Parliament Square in protest against the wars in Iraq and Afghanistan with, arguably, similarly prominent public displays and degrees of spectacle. What is particularly interesting about Occupy LSX, however, is the way in which it caught public attention and stimulated debate. Most significantly, it generated soul-searching within an institution that could hardly be more established: the Church of England – and led to the resignation of two high-ranking Church of England officials and a chaplain (BBC 2011a). In addition, Occupy LSX activists were invited to write an article for the *Financial Times*, an established bastion of the free market, as part of a series charting the pitfalls of capitalism (Dewhurst et al. 2012). What is more, academic analyses and commentaries of Occupy LSX were already being undertaken while the protest was still under way (see for example Couldry and Fenton 2011; www.possible-futures.org).

In Italy, the 2011 referendum concerning future development of nuclear power, the privatisation of water and the possibility of government ministers not appearing in court when accused of crimes marks another example of what we mean by increased 'resonance'. Italian civic groups not only collected sufficient signatures to hold a referendum according to the Italian constitution, they also managed to mobilise sufficient voters to turn out for the referendum (more than 50%) and then win (BBC 2011b; see further Box 3.2 in Chapter 3). The success of the 5 Star Movement, which won up to 10% of the vote in the municipal elections, is another example of the 'bubbling up' of subterranean politics in Italy (Bartlett et al. 2013). The 5 Star Movement is a populist, anti-corruption, eurosceptic, ecologist party started by the comedian and blogger Beppe Grillo, attracting voters who abstained from voting previously and candidates who had never before considered political careers (ibid.). And across Europe, national incarnations of the Pirate parties began to win parliamentary seats. In the case of the success of the Pirates in Saarland, not only did they 'suddenly' conquer the *Landtag* with an astonishing 7.4% of votes – overriding established parties like the liberals (Free Democratic Party), who lost 8.0% of their votes – but also 20% of their vote was based on previous 'non-voters' (Appelrath et al. 2012).

2.0 Culture

The second significant aspect about subterranean politics as it is currently 'bubbling up' across Europe relates to the role of the Internet or, more precisely, to the ethos of web 2.0, or, as we call it, *2.0 culture*. The growing everyday relevance of the Internet, in general, and of social networking applications such as Facebook and micro-blogging sites such as Twitter, in particular, is undisputed. There is also a growing body of studies that demonstrates the significance of these applications specifically in and for contemporary *political activism*, that is, their relevance for social mobilisation and collective action (e.g. Khondker 2011; Milan 2013). Whether it is useful to speak of Facebook and Twitter revolutions, as Clay Shirky (2010) does, or to claim that there is something different *in kind* about these tools and their use that actually determines the main nature of recent 'revolutions' is up for debate (see further Moore and Selchow 2012). Nevertheless it is clear that these tools are fruitfully used to mobilise and organise. In the current public displays of subterranean politics in Europe their significance is readily apparent. The 15-M in Spain, for instance, was started by a bloggers' network (see further Chapter 5). Similarly, Facebook was instrumental in the mobilisation that led to the occupation of the London Stock Exchange (LSX), while UK Uncut initially developed through Twitter (Chapter 7).

However, much more important than the widely documented use of various online applications as a tool for networking purposes is to understand the role of the Internet, more precisely, the *ethos of web 2.0*, as a 'culture' that evolves from, plays back into and is manifest in contemporary subterranean politics and its actors. David Gauntlett (2011) neatly explains the nature of web 2.0: instead of being about 'searching and reading', as was web 1.0 with its static web presentations, web 2.0 is about 'writing and editing' (also in Moore and Selchow 2012: 33). In this sense, web 2.0 is not simply about specific technological innovations or applications, but about an ethos of *how* to *do* things. It is about 'the disappearance of the signature', as Pierre Levy puts it (quoted in Lister et al. 2003: 17). That is, it blurs the distinction between authors and readers, bringing about the notion of collective production and reproduction.

It is this ethos that is a salient feature of subterranean politics in Europe. So, in addition to preoccupations with Internet-related issues such as Internet freedom and open content that ranks high on the agendas of actors such as the Pirate parties, the occupiers and, of course, the hacktivist group *Anonymous* that Nassauer and Anheier (Chapter 4, p. 101) identify as a distinct example of subterranean politics in Germany, the impact of the Internet, in the sense of web 2.0 ethos, is evident in broader organisational forms. In their analysis of subterranean politics in Germany, Nassauer and Anheier (ibid. p. 99) utilise the concept of 'swarm intelligence', with which they refer

> to actions by individuals based on simple rules. By these actions, groups fulfil tasks that would not have been achieved by the individual alone. Groups working with swarm intelligence are self-organised, adaptive and, when one individual drops out, another individual can take their place. Problems are solved by the group as a whole, without hierarchies or leaders. Every member can participate in the solution of a problem just as much as any other member.

A prime example of this kind of 'swarm intelligence' highlighted by Nassauer and Anheier was the GuttenPlag platform, an initiative through which activists revealed a total of 10,421 plagiarised lines in German Defence Minister Karl Theodor Freiherr von und zu Guttenberg's doctoral thesis, and, by doing so, played a key role in his 2011 resignation (Moore and Selchow 2012: 33).

While Nassauer and Anheier use the metaphor of 'swarm intelligence' in order to refer to collective efforts that focus on *quantitatively* large tasks, stressing the idea of getting something done – which would not have been possible alone – the logic of 'swarm intelligence' can also be found in more fundamental ways in the organisation of current displays of subterranean politics. The occupations of various squares are prime examples of 'swarm intelligence' in the sense of collective action that builds on horizontality, replaceability and leaderlessness. Of course, this does not mean that these principles were fully realised in practice and there was much (internal) debate about shortcomings in this respect (see for example, Chapter 7, p. 187). Yet the idea of horizontality constitutes an important ideal for many 'subterranean politics' actors, as they strive to achieve a culture of inclusion that places limits on the ability of individuals to use authority to dominate others or determine the group's priorities. The fact that these activities are shaped by what we call a *2.0 culture* of collectivity, openness and inclusion – a culture which then plays back into the broader mainstream culture with the potential of transforming it – is illustrated by the statement of the (then) secretary of the Pirate Party in Germany, Marina Weisband, who explained that the goal of the party is 'to make itself redundant' by having set into motion a cultural change towards openness and transparency (Spiegel Online 2012). This statement suggests that there is something specific about how 'subterranean politics' actors see their own political role and involvements. It seems to be about contributing to change without necessarily leaving a distinct and identifiable personal mark. Current displays of 'subterranean politics' are shaped by actors who come in and out of activism, whether online or in a square, taking seriously their contribution (sometimes based on their professional experience as designers, web developers, marketing specialists, as in the case of Occupy LSX) but being happy to have their contributions taken up and transformed by others, giving up 'their signature', coming back and again joining the rewriting of the new 'product'.

Democracy: But not as usual

Related to the point about *2.0 culture* is the significance of the subjective experience of participating in politics in a 'new' way. Underlying this is the idea of reconstructing democracy out of one's own actions. The campaign for the referendum in Italy, mentioned above, is a good example of this *practising* of democracy. Mobilising for the referendum (and, subsequently, winning it) showed how change can be achieved by citizens. As della Porta, Mosca and Parks (Chapter 3, p. 74) explain, it was seen as a form of direct democracy, the 'rebirth of civil passion'. In a different context, Geoffrey Pleyers (2010) uses the concept of 'prefigurative action' to describe this kind of action that attempts to practice the kind of democracy that the participants imagine should be practised in their societies. Arguably, it is this idea of 'prefigurative action' that was one of the primary attractions of Occupy LSX, which experimented with forms of participation like daily assemblies and consensus decision making and insisted on horizontality and leaderlessness (Chapter 7, p. 176). As Bonet i Martí (Chapter 5, p. 135) suggests, this experimentation was pioneered by the Spanish 15-M and taken up and displayed all over Europe, as well as in other parts of the world.

> ...the crucial innovation the 15-M repertoire was not the encampments, nor the fact of congregating at a city square, nor the organisation of meetings, but the combination of these three components: the gathering at a city square indefinitely to transform it into a permanent space for dialogue and enunciation. [...] The occupied squares became a 24-hour citizen agora where the exchange of ideas and their expression was possible. [...] non-violence contributed throughout to popularise its demands and increase the wave of sympathisers towards it.
>
> (ibid. p. 132)

The Spanish practice was replicated in other places, and new techniques for dialogue were developed, including the 'human microphone' technique, which allows people to communicate with a large group without the use of amplification equipment. More broadly, a repertoire of hand signs – adapted from sign language – came into use that allows an audience to indicate to a speaker 'approval' or 'disapproval' as well as to provide other feedback – such as 'out of frame', 'we understood your point – you are repeating yourself', 'what you are talking about belongs to a separate working group' – without interrupting the speaker. The aim of these novel techniques is to encourage debate and discussion without major interruption, while maintaining the possibility of intervening and preventing individual speakers from dominating the exchange (see Deel et al. 2012: 16).

It is the physicality of these practices, the sense of actually *practising* politics that is noteworthy as a significant aspect of the current display of 'subterranean politics' in Europe. It is also implied in the importance of occupying *physical* spaces. On the one hand, the occupation of physical spaces such as the square in front of St Paul's Cathedral in London can be seen as an act of reclaiming spaces 'in the name of the public' in environments that have come to be shaped by a wave of privatisation, as is the case in London,[2] as well as a key strategy in confronting government restrictions on public demonstrations, as

Jensen (Chapter 6) points out for Hungary. For the current manifestations of 'subterranean politics' in Europe, physical space also has an explicit importance both in terms of message and autonomy. As an occupier in London put it: 'The presence of the camp: the physical, the material and the symbolic has been so important – you can't ignore it; the bankers that pass by can't ignore it; it is already creating an alternative to the main system and demonstrating the alternative' (Chapter 7, p. 186). In this sense, the occupation of squares or temporary sit-ins are seen and practised as a way of constructing temporary autonomous zones where prefigurative politics can be practised.

In general, the idea of changing society by changing one's own practices of interaction must be acknowledged as a key aspect of 'subterranean politics' in Europe. 'Process is what this form of politics is all about', explained an 'occupier' in London (Deel et al. 2012: 16), and the Assemblea San Giovanni in Italy encouraged that 'doing the thing that you wish to say is the best way of saying it. In this case, thousands of citizens are calling for democracy by practising it in the first person in the square and sharing this practice with thousands of others who feel the same need' (Chapter 3, p. 80). This is why current displays of subterranean politics in Europe are about democracy – but not democracy as usual. As an *Indignada* – interviewed in Paris – made clear: 'We don't represent anyone. Everyone can come and bring her own ideas, her own expertise, as an individual. Actually, it's really the idea of questioning the authority' (Chapter 8, p. 206). Linked to this is a distancing from traditional social actors, such as trade unions, as well as a distancing from traditional forms of protest. Interviews in London suggest that the forms of 'attention-generating tactics', like sit-ins in high street shops or cyber attacks as well as the long-term appropriation of public spaces, are explicitly seen and practised as alternatives to 'classic' approaches, such as large-scale demonstrations like that against the Iraq war in 2003 and that have come to be perceived as inadequate (see Chapter 7, p. 185).

It is important to acknowledge the significance both of *2.0 culture* and the emphasis on democracy but not as usual, because this avoids misleading assumptions about the nature of the current public displays of subterranean politics. It is commonplace, especially but not only within policy circles, to dismiss current displays of subterranean politics as not being constructive and/or able to trigger social transformation. This critique usually runs along the lines that activists in the squares across Europe do not develop and articulate clear demands; David Cameron's critique of Occupy LSX is a prime example of this attitude (BBC 2011c), which can also be found in the various critiques addressing the Pirate parties or the 5 Star Movement in Italy (Bartlett et al. 2013: 27). In fact, this critique also comes from activists themselves, as evident in the following quote from an *Indignado* from Brussels:

> A general idea able to unite the movement was missing. We said 'Something is wrong', this was the first and fundamental idea. But then, 'What do we make to fix it?' There, there [sic] were so many different trends, so many ideas. There were people from everywhere and thus it couldn't work anymore.
>
> (Chapter 8, p. 207)

Yet, we need to be careful with such assessments, which are pre-committed to traditional conceptions of what politics is or, rather, what it should be. That is, we need to be open to understanding the (potential/emergent) cultural dimension of these current public displays of subterranean politics; the absence of a specific demand need not necessarily be regarded as a shortcoming. Rather, it can be seen as a manifestation of a different (2.0) culture that (potentially) transforms (the idea of) politics and the nature of political actors and that is about processes rather than outcomes.

Europe is 'invisible'

Our investigation of current public displays of subterranean politics suggests that, overall, 'Europe' does not play a significant role in the streets and squares across Europe; it is more or less 'invisible' (see Chapter 7, p. 189). In those displays of subterranean politics that we looked at, 'Europe' oscillates between three positions. First, it seems to play a role in terms of individuals' identities (i.e. it matters in a 'cultural' sense). 'I totally feel European. London is a European city; I feel more affinity with Europeans at activist meetings. Growing up in an open border EU has played a great role – [the] easyJet culture. This is what Europe means for me, and those ties are stronger than the political structures', explained a UK Uncut activist in London (Deel et al. 2012: 25; see also Chapter 7, p. 193). And an *Indignada* – interviewed in Paris – suggested that

> [b]eing European is something already incorporated by young people today [...] I have a feeling that young people are European in their mind. For my younger brother, the Euro is not a change; it is normal. To cross borders just like that, it is normal for him. It is amazing, he has friends in England, in Germany.
>
> (Chapter 8, p. 225)

As Pleyers observes in Chapter 8, there is a marked difference between older activists, who see Europe as a political project concerned with overcoming the legacy of twentieth-century wars and promoting the social model, and younger activists, who take Europe for granted. '[Young activists] are more critical to Europe because they grew up in an increasingly neo-liberal Europe, which contributed to their precarious conditions', explained an experienced, pro-European French activist (Pleyers and Conti 2012: 11). Younger activists, in contrast, seem to feel European but regard the EU in a much more problematic way. 'Europe is a given fact for my generation. We travel, we grew up in it. We don't have problems criticising European institutions and democracy in Europe as older activists may have. It's easier for us' (ibid. p. 10).

Second, in those instances in which the EU is *explicitly* 'visible', it tends to be regarded as part of the problem as much as part of the solution. There were European flags with stars replaced by swastikas to be seen in Syntagma Square (Chapter 2, p. 49). In the first declaration of the assembly of Syntagma Square, it was stated that 'we will not leave the squares until those who compelled us to come here leave the country: the government, the Troika, the IMF memoranda and everyone who exploits us', though actually this was a rather rare mention of the EU (ibid.). In Hungary, where pro- and anti-EU sentiments are sharply polarised, the EU is often described as a new form of colonialism following the tradition of the Hapsburgs and the Soviet Union; in one demonstration, the EU was represented as a wolf (Jensen et al. 2012: 6).

A third position has to do with the fact that the EU seems rather abstract and remote. While the idea of being 'European' in terms of life experience exists among activists, Europe as a political community or a public space seems to play an explicit and significant role only for a small 'expert' minority (see specifically Pleyers and Conti 2012); for many engaged in politics 'on the ground', Europe seems 'far away'. As an *Indignado* put it: 'Europe is something I don't know much about.... It's something that may be used and that can bring a lot of nice things. But the problem is that it is very remote from people. I don't feel at all concerned with Europe' (Chapter 8, p. 222). And an occupier in London explained: 'One of the difficulties of judging the EU is that a lot of its effects are not very visible. Some of the arguments would be different if you had a stronger empirical basis' (Deel et al. 2012: 24). Another noted: 'I think Occupy is thoroughly confused when it comes to Europe, and that's not very surprising given how little people know or care about Europe as an entity' (Chapter 7, p. 191). This detachment from the EU plays out in the difficulty that pro-European activists face in mobilising support for their initiatives. 'It has become impossible to develop a real discussion on Europe [...] In Germany, there are only a few small groups, who are really interested in working on European strategies and to develop alternative proposals, not only concerning protests', explained a German pro-Europe activist (Pleyers and Conti 2012: 10).

The 'invisibility' of the EU does, however, not mean that there are no expressions of solidarity beyond borders or that there is only concern with local and national issues. On the contrary, the slogan 'we are all Greeks now', used in many protests across Europe (Anheier and Nassauer 2012: 18) or shows of solidarity, such as in the Hungarian support for the No TAV campaign in Italy (Jensen et al. 2012: 12), are indications of concerns beyond the local. Yet, the point of reference is often more the global than the European. In his study of Spain, Bonet i Martí (Chapter 5, p. 135) emphasises what he describes as the multi-scalar character of the 15-M – global (with links to Chile), state, regional and local. Many of those interviewed in other contexts also emphasised the importance of the global. '[Occupy LSX is about] creating roots in the locality. [There is a] long lasting tension between the local and the global. [It is about] [t]argeting the City of London because it embodies the relationship between the local and the global', explained a UK Uncut activist in London (Chapter 7, p. 186). A French *Indignada* suggested:

> I care about the global level, the community level, the regional level [...] but Europe, does it still makes sense among all these levels? And even more, isn't it in some way a quasi-racist concept? Why should we care about Europe and not the Mediterranean region? [...] We have many links with French-speaking Africa for instance. Why shouldn't we be in solidarity with them? Why more with the Danes than with the Senegalese?
>
> (Chapter 8, p. 221)

and a Polish activist exclaimed: 'We may feel European, but people like me, we think of us as the global citizens' (ibid. p. 225).

It is all about politics

The fifth feature of the current public displays of subterranean politics in Europe is that what is shared across different types of protests, actions, campaigns and initiatives is extensive frustration with formal politics as it is currently practised. The terms 'angry', 'indignant' or 'disappointed' are an expression of this frustration. The case of Germany is particularly interesting in this respect. German society is far less affected by austerity measures than other European societies: its economy has recovered relatively quickly from the financial and economic crisis and it has experienced continued, albeit slow, growth and prosperity. Yet, despite the relatively positive situation in Germany, in 2011–2012 there was a striking public display of subterranean politics in Germany just as in other European contexts. This is because current protests are not so much simply about austerity but about *politics*. As Nassauer and Anheier (Chapter 4, p. 95) observe in Germany, protesters are 'driven by a general distrust in established political institutions and by deep-seated notions of scepticism and discomfort at the way political decisions are made'. Interestingly, a survey among protesters against 'Stuttgart 21', the large-scale infrastructure project in the city of Stuttgart, found that 80% of them expressed general dissatisfaction with the current political and social situation in Germany as one of their motivations for joining the protest, while the same percentage (80%) explained that they were satisfied with their own, personal social situation (Bebnowski et al. 2010; see also Chapter 4, p. 96). They objected to the nature of the planning process of this major project and the lack of acknowledgement of citizens' concerns. What needs to be kept in mind here is that there was nothing 'wrong' with the planning process of this *specific* project as such; rather, the dissatisfaction was about the *general* nature of how projects of this kind are handled in Germany, namely, as Nassauer and Anheier explain, as 'technocratic processes, in which at most juristic considerations interfere but citizens' concerns are sidelined' (ibid. p. 114).[3] The above-mentioned case of GuttenPlag, another public display of subterranean politics described in Chapter 4, illustrates how this frustration is not only about processes but also about the nature of the current political elite in general: this was arguably a reaction to a (perceived) corrupt political elite.

But even in other European contexts, which are much more affected by austerity than Germany, those who have engaged in the activities we have studied cite concern with the failures of democracy as the reason for engagement and protest rather than austerity per se. For instance, the 15-M in Spain, which triggered the spread of Occupy in Europe, was not simply a reaction to austerity policies. Rather, as Bonet i Martí (Chapter 5) highlights, it was inspired by the occupation of Tahrir Square, as the symbol of the Arab Spring. This concern with *politics*, that is, the general frustration with current political practices, was apparent in the symbols and the slogans that were used in the 15-M such as the widespread use of Egyptian flags and slogans such as 'Apolitical?

Superpolitical', 'A Cairo in each neighborhood' and 'It isn't the crisis, it's the system'. 'There's a lot to be said about frustrations with political processes', one of the occupiers in London said, '[...] this is a screwed up system in terms of allowing people to have a say, policies for the common good, informed debate [and] critical media coverage' (Chapter 7, p. 183). And the *Indignados*/Italian Revolution group put it as follows: 'We know very well that whoever has or will in the future be in government will never be on the people's side, nobody has ever listened to our needs, and in this system nobody ever will' (della Porta et al. 2012: 8). In Italy, the No TAV group, which campaigned to block the building of a high-speed rail link between Turin and Lyon, declared: 'it is a day of mourning for democracy in Italy. The caste (political elite) is deaf, blind and cruel: while the country goes bankrupt, political and economic oligarchies are inflicting contested choices on local populations and institutions, countering with heavy deployment of public forces' (ibid.).

Statistical data show a widespread frustration with formal politics beyond current displays of subterranean politics. Eurobarometer data for the autumn of 2011 show that, for the countries studied in this book, between 62% (Germany) and 80% (Italy and Spain) of their respective populations tend not to trust government. Lack of trust in political parties is even higher, ranging from 78% (Germany) to 86% (UK). Interestingly, trust in the Internet is considerably higher than trust in government or political parties. This is not to say that issues of austerity and banking regulation are not important concerns, as is the issue of anti-piracy. However, what is crucial to understand is that in protesters' analyses there is a clear link between politics and corporate and financial power as well as corruption. According to the manifesto of the 15-M:

> In Spain most of the political class does not even listen to us. Politicians should be bringing our voice to the institutions, facilitating the political participation of citizens through direct channels that provide the greatest benefit to the wider society, not to get rich and prosper at our expense, attending only to the dictatorship of major economic powers and holding them in power through a two-party system headed by the immovable acronym PP & PSOE.
>
> (Chapter 5, p. 124)

As della Porta, Mosca and Parks (Chapter 3) stress, Italian groups in particular are concerned about Mafia involvement and corrupt politicians, whom they blame, for example, for the waste disposal crisis in Campania and the failures to respond adequately to the earthquake in L'Aquila. According to the ARCI (Italian Cultural and Recreational Association), which is active in many of the Italian protests, Italian politics now represents: 'The authoritarian tendency that has overturned the constitutional principle whereby the popular will is expressed through elected assemblies and the constant relationship between institutions and intermediate societal bodies; the affirmation of an idea of power that sees institutions used for private purposes; distrust and disengagement where anti-politics thrives' (della Porta et al. 2012: 8).

Particularly interesting is that this kind of analysis applies not just to respective national governments but also to the political class in general, including politicians from both the left and the right. 'Some of us consider ourselves progressive, others conservative. Some of us are believers, some not. Some of us have clearly defined ideologies, others are apolitical', explained the 15-M (Chapter 5, p. 123). Or, as one of the activists at Occupy LSX said: 'Questioning the workings of parliamentary politics is not an anti-conservative, not an anti-liberal argument: it's a systemic argument' (Chapter 7, p. 184). Another stressed the deep distrust of mainstream political parties, including the left, when he explained that '[O]ccupy is a symptom that there is no real left anymore... Leftist politics and advanced late capitalism are not really compatible. So the political system we've got now is entwined with huge business and things that are at odds with Leftism' (ibid. p. 185). It is this distrust of the political elites and mainstream parties that is expressed by protesters and shared by the general public across Europe and that seems to explain the rise of new parties not only on the far right but across the political spectrum. A German activist describes the rise of the Pirate Party and the actions of Occupy and others as 'some sort of red light, something that is blinking' – a warning to the mainstream (Chapter 4, p. 114).

Even though trade unions and established NGOs have taken part in many events, especially in Italy and Spain, there was a certain wariness in the current displays of subterranean politics of what some saw as traditional civil society or, in the words of a 'trans-European' activists, interviewed in Paris, of 'pre-conceived labels, that would restrain the field of possibilities' (Chapter 8, p. 207). There was an emphasis on the (perceived) newness of what protesters and activists were doing, perceiving it as 'different from the communists, alter-globalisation activists, anarchists, bobos or greens', as another activist in Brussels put it (Pleyers and Conti 2012: 5). In both Spain and the UK, activists distance themselves from the World Social Forum (WSF), which they see as dominated by the traditional left. '[The] traditional left is involved in the WSF, which may explain the clash in process between the WSF and Occupy. WSF hasn't really taken on the assembly structures of Occupy; decisions [are] still made bureaucratically and behind closed doors' (Chapter 7, p. 188; see also Chapter 5, Table 5.2).

In Italy, Hungary and the UK, discourses about the systemic failures of democracy were often linked to concerns about the manipulation of the media. In Hungary, Milla (see above) is one of the largest grassroots groups, established to campaign against the new media law in Hungary (see Chapter 6. In the UK, the scandal concerning the way in which journalists hacked the phones of newsworthy people to discover details of their private lives exposed the both links between politicians and the media empire controlled by the press baron Rupert Murdoch, and the corruption at elite levels, particularly among police, journalists and politicians. In Italy, a number of groups, such as Articolo 21 and Valigia Blu, are devoted to defending journalists' rights and providing alternative sources of information. The No TAV movement is explicit about the threat to democracy from media manipulations:

> Between the real country, lived on the street and recounted on the web, and the virtual country lived in armchairs and recounted by newspapers and TV, is an abyss to the point of two antithetical universes with no contact between them. All the people who don't have the ability, the time or the wish to tap into the information battle on the internet, and who make up the vast majority of the population, remain relegated to a virtual world, built ad hoc to marginalise them from reality.
>
> (Chapter 3, p. 76)

The disaffection with political elites and how decisions are reached, that is, a sense of political blockage is something that is shared with populist parties on the right. Indeed, populists have joined demonstrations against austerity, for example. The Hungarian Party Jobbik explains:

> We are not communists, because our spiritual centre is not class domination. We are not fascists, because our spiritual centre is not state domination. We are not national socialists, because our spiritual centre is not racial domination. But it is also very important for everyone to understand this correctly: we are not democrats either, in the sense

[this word] has come to mean today, because money and profit are not in our spiritual centre either.

(Jensen et al. 2012: 13)

The specific practising of democracy discussed above is what distinguishes populist movements and parties from many of the groups described in this study.[4] Overall, we can speak of a shared trans-European concern among very disparate groups across Europe about the failure and indeed corruption of political elites, especially but not only at the national level, and about the lack of meaningful participation. Furthermore, there was something like a mismatch or chasm between what we describe as mainstream politics, elite trans-European policy-making circles, including what are sometimes depicted as 'expert' activists, and what we are calling subterranean politics – various forms of grassroots activism and protest.

Conclusion

The unique insights that are presented in this book demonstrate the value of adopting an explorative approach to empirical reality. By applying a different analytical frame, namely the frame of subterranean politics, we were able to detect nuances that might otherwise have been left uncovered. Our main conclusion is that what is unfolding in Europe is a political crisis rather than just a financial crisis. It needs to be understood as widespread public discontent with how politics is currently practised. Thus saving the euro will not solve current problems. Hence, it is not just that our analytical frame allows us to see a different reality, it also opens up an alternative way of imagining the future of Europe and its current challenges and how to deal with them.

Chapter overviews

European alternatives: Anti-austerity protests

In the first of two chapters that analyse subterranean politics in a trans-European context, Mario Pianta and Paolo Gerbaudo build on their previous work on global civil society events (summits, forums, protests and so on; cf. *Global Civil Society 2001* and *2012*), and look specifically at anti-austerity protests held across the continent since 2011. Their analysis begins with a survey of protest events that make claim to be at least partially international, transnational or global in nature, with the finding that the great majority of anti-austerity mobilisations have developed within a national context. The few truly pan-European events, they show, have been more limited in reach and impact. Narrowing their focus to the role that Europe plays as a political space in these events, they examine three different visions of the European project that have developed in anti-austerity mobilisations, trans-European networks of experts and major policy campaigns: a short-termist perspective advocating quick-fix adjustments and reforms of the Monetary Union and financial markets; a reactionary/retrogressive view that sees the reversal of European integration as the solution to the economic crisis; and a progressive outlook calling for the reduction of the power of finance along with greater democracy and sustainable growth policies. However, they conclude that currently the view from the grassroots is a predominantly sceptical and fractured one, far from united on the possibility of turning the European project towards progressive and equitable ends, with few social mobilisations directly and explicitly addressing European issues. The authors attribute this at least in part to the lack of a European political space with 'visible' power structures and an 'understandable' institutional setting, and contend that this leads to a lack of capacity to articulate a credible alternative to the status quo outside of national contexts – with potentially dangerous consequences both for individual nations and for Europe as a whole.

Italy

In Chapter 3, della Porta, Mosca and Parks set out to investigate two primary questions in relation to Subterranean Politics, the first specifically located in the Italian experience of recent protests, and the second grounded in Italy but applicable elsewhere, particularly in the South and in nations more recently absorbed into the EU. The first asks why, in a country with a rich history of contentious politics, did the wave of occupations that spread across Europe in 2011 in the wake of the Arab Spring have so little purchase? The second examines the relationship between two competing visions of Europe and EU: the former which has looked upon Europe as a positive, 'normalising' influence in comparison with the pathologies of Italian politics, and a more recent, post-financial crisis view that fears EU institutions as enforcers of austerity politics. Using Protest Event Analysis (PEA) of all articles covering protest events in *La Repubblica* during 2011, plus a frame analysis of documents on democracy and on Europe produced by the actors located in the PEA, alongside a comparative analysis of protest surveys carried out in Italy in 2011 and over the previous decade, the team found that subterranean politics did indeed bubble up in Italy in 2011, but in the emerging practices of and claims to democracy unfolding in groups that are familiar and long-standing. In particular, subterranean politics found expression in the referendum campaign, in citizens' movements against large-scale infrastructure projects and in the many labour conflicts – against factory closures, dismissals and worsening market and labour conditions. In sum, the authors argue that while the central organisations of Italian protest appear unchanged, the substance of beliefs and claims has shifted. Furthermore, although this process has been accompanied by a nosedive in trust in European institutions, Europe is still seen as the conduit best placed for bringing social justice back to the continent.

Germany

In Chapter 4, Nassauer and Anheier aim to understand how subterranean actors in Germany organise and mobilise. Having carried out initial media content analysis and a Google Trends search to map the contours of protest in the country, the researchers conducted interviews and carried out further media content analysis with selected emergent groups. They focus particularly on the actions of the German members of the international group Anonymous, on Occupy Germany and on the creators of GuttenPlag, bringing the concept of 'swarm intelligence' over from the biological and computer sciences to analyse and capture the way in which these groups organise and mobilise: these subterranean groups, they find, are collectively self-organised, adaptive, decentralised and non-hierarchical. Furthermore, their findings suggest three primary characteristics shared by all those studied: the engagement in a form of politics that is novel due to its emphasis on democratic decision making and political practices over content; with a strong focus on the Internet as both a tool and a topic of protest; and holding a perception of the EU as bureaucratic, non-transparent and hierarchic. The authors note that in one sense, the German chapter acts almost as a 'control group' for the book as a whole, given that Germany was barely affected by the financial crisis of 2008 and had already recovered and was on an upward economic trajectory by 2011. Hence the German protests indicate that the subterranean politics phenomena witnessed throughout that year were not necessarily phenomena driven by the economic crisis alone, but rather reflect a general discomfort with the way that political decisions are made, the lack of participatory possibilities, the threat of dwindling freedom of information and the lack of transparency in politics. The chapter closes with a number of suggestions for further avenues of research prompted by this initial study, both policy oriented and theoretical – notably the question of whether Occupy qualifies as a social movement in the tradition of that literature.

Spain

In his chapter on the 15-M (15 May movement), Jordi Bonet i Martí analyses the transformative impact of the euro crisis on the shape and content of social mobilisation in the Spain. He begins with a detailed examination of the contextual background to the emergence of the 15-M; notably to the conservative turn in politics at a time of increasing distrust in political parties and politicians in general, and increasing discontent in response to the impact of austerity measures introduced in the wake of the crisis. The chapter then explores the genesis and realisation of the 15-M, from the work of a handful of activists converging on social media platforms to 130,000 protesting in the central squares of 58 cities across the country on 15 May 2011. In his analysis of the ways in which this eruption of subterranean politics was different in kind to those that preceded it, he focuses particularly on the coalitions of actors that took part, comparing the complexity of their relative and intertwining roles to the more simplistic assignations found in some social movements analysis. He also examines the role played by anonymity, finding that 'de-identification' is a defining feature of these forms of politics in emergence, a finding that calls into question theories on the importance of identity posited by other social movement scholars. The chapter considers the impact of ICT on the action repertoires of the group and on the resonance of their actions with the wider public, resonance which Bonet i Martí in part assigns to the way in which the protests were framed both by participants and the press: notably a diagnosis frame of disappointment, and a prognosis frame of radical democracy. All the above factors, he concludes, both differentiate the 15-M from other recent protests in Spanish history and also contributed to its sizable impact within the public arena of Spanish politics. However, he concludes by noting that although another strength was the multi-scalarity of the protests, in the sense that the target of the 15-M changed according to its local, regional or global application, while the form and essence remained the same, there was scant evidence for the existence of the European scale during this protest period.

Hungary

The Hungarian chapter (Chapter 6) takes as its starting point not the economic crisis, but the protests that erupted in 2006 following the revelations of deceit by the then Prime Minister Gyurcsány. Noting that in the Hungarian setting it is 'too early' to talk about 'social movements' that underpin the notion of a democratic civil society, and that the concept of 'subterranean politics' thus enables a broader analysis of dissatisfaction with politics and civil dissent, author Jody Jensen sets out to examine in what ways such phenomena demonstrate an interconnectedness of the Hungarian political and economic crises that emerged in 2006 and the broader economic and political crises of the EU (and beyond) in 2011–2012. Her research maps the landscape of protests and actors in that latter period, and includes both online and face-to-face interviews with protestors attending pro- and anti-government marches. She finds a profound disillusionment with politics in all groups, with Hungary at the bottom of the *Active Citizenship Composite Indicator* and bottom but one in the *Representative Democracy Index*. However, her findings indicate a split in the attribution of blame for economic hardship: anti-government protestors blame Hungarian politicians and government, while government supporters criticise the austerity measures and the 'Hungary-bashing' that they perceive as being carried out by the EU. The chapter also examines the impact and role of the press regarding subterranean politics in Hungary, and concludes with an analysis of generational change in both attitudes towards Europe and in political process amongst Hungarian protestors, finding that younger protestors are more likely to be connected to Europe-wide actions and receptive to the possibilities of opening space for civil discourse.

London

Rather than a country-specific study, in Chapter 7 Sean Deal and Tamsin Murray-Leach take for their unit of analysis London, a 'global city' in Sassen's definition (Sassen 2000). Understood as a point of convergence for local, national and transnational identities, home to activists from across Europe and beyond, the aim of the research was to explore the nature of the relationship of subterranean political actors to 'Europe' beyond the national context. Through semi-structured interviews with participants in four political 'groups' active in 2011 – Occupy LSX, UK Uncut, London Citizens and student fees protestors – the authors examine two primary aspects of these participants' motivations. Firstly, they find that participants' views and actions tally with the notion of 'political blockage': each set of interviewees complained of an inability to affect politics either through the formal channels of representative democracy or through well-worn repertoires of contestation. This diagnosis extended across party political lines and beyond specific national contexts. Furthermore, contrary to the prevailing notion presented in the media at the time of protestors failing to offer an alternative to the status quo, each group experimented with alternative democratic forms and practices, modes of contention and conceptions of politics in an attempt to address this 'blockage'. Secondly, the chapter reveals an absence of Europe as a political space in the minds and actions of participants – despite the fact that half of those interviewed were citizens of non-British EU nations, living in London under EU regulations, and acknowledging a self-professed 'easyJet' European identity, in which Europe is viewed as a shared social and cultural space. In fact, while the authors are concerned that the interviews showed little evidence that the crisis has thus far stimulated specific reflection on the future development of EU institutions and practices at the grassroots level, they argue that Europe is present politically in an implicit sense of respondents' notions of their own legitimacy and responsibility in trans-European contexts – and that this potentially offers leverage for the implementation of a progressive approach to the future of the European project.

Alter-Europe: Progresssive activists and Europe

The last case study in the volume (Chapter 8) examines subterranean politics across Europe from an agency-centred perspective. Geoffrey Pleyers, whose previous work has examined the ways in which activists find/express their agency in our globalised age (Pleyers 2010), applies his approach here in an attempt to answer two 'paradoxes': the first, a question which runs throughout the book, is why the European crisis, which has dominated the European press and the concerns of public intellectuals since its start, has such little traction for the continent's progressive actors. The second makes a suitable conclusion – or jumping-off point, depending on your perspective – for the book as a whole. Pleyers notes that, in Western Europe at least, the squares are now empty and the camps gone, while austerity policies and socio-economic hardship remain. Was 2011's eruption of subterranean politics merely an ephemeral outcry? His interviews and focus groups with progressive activists in France, Belgium, Spain, Finland, Poland and Germany lead him to define four dominant Weberian ideal-type 'cultures of activism' in subterranean politics: those who take part in camps and assemblies; belief in 'critical consumption' and transition movements; 'expert' activists; and mobilisers for mass demonstrations and policy change. The motivations and potential to affect political change are analysed for each group. Pleyers finds that only the 'expert' activists see Europe as the main scale of action and advocacy. While mobilisers may work transnationally, they regard national governments as the primary policymakers; and while the identities, claims and networks of camp occupiers span the globe, their actions are rooted primarily in the local. Transition activists strongly focus on the local level, and are suspicious of national and European institutionalisation. The research also reveals the deep and pervasive influence of the national context, and also highlights a generational divide, with older activists more likely to evidence pro-EU sentiments. Pleyers concludes by noting that the research suggests that a sense of social agency at the European level is key to understanding attitudes towards the European project: the more activists believe that they can have an impact on EU policies, the more they feel European. On the contrary, those who are convinced that the European institutions pay no attention to civil society and will stick to their neo-liberal agenda whatever happens do not feel particularly European, nor consider Europe as an important scale of action. As with other authors in the volume, his research highlights a growing crisis of democracy of which these eruptions of subterranean politics are but an early warning/the tip of the iceberg, calling for the need to rethink democracy and re-politicise Europe as one of the most urgent challenges for the EU and its citizens.

Notes

1. But see Calhoun (2013) who traces the crises back several decades and finds a deeper history.
2. See Kaldor and Selchow (2012: 37, Figure B.1) for a map of Occupy LSX that shows how public space is being eroded in the City of London under the impact of neo-liberal policies. The occupiers originally planned to establish their camp in Paternoster Square in front of the London Stock Exchange. However, because the square is privately owned, it was closed off to them. In the end the camp was established on the border between space owned by the corporation of London and space owned by the Church of England, which could be negotiated by the protestors.
3. In Berlin and Frankfurt large-scale projects were planned to further develop the airports, which affect surrounding neighborhoods. While the airport development in Berlin had been planned for years, German flight control announced in September 2010 that the development of two parallel runways to increase the capacity of the airport would not be possible. As a result, deviating air routes were necessary, and airplanes now fly over previously unaffected neighborhoods.

(Anheier and Nassauer 2012: 8)

4. For a recent study of populist movements and politics in Europe see Bartlett et al. (2012); Fieschi et al. (2012).

References

Anheier, H.K. and Nassauer, A. (2012) 'The "Swarm Intelligence": Mapping Subterranean Politics in Germany', Draft Report for the Subterranean Politics Project, London School of Economics and Political Science, Accessed online at http://www.gcsknowledgebase.org/europe/draft-reports/.

Appelrath, A., Hebel, C., Patalong, F. and Pfaffinger, C. (2012) 'Darum waehlen wir die Piraten', Spiegel Online, 29 March, Accessed online at http://www.spiegel.de/politik/deutschland/0,1518,824369,00.html.

Bartlett, J., Birdwell, J., Krekó, P., Benfield, J. and Gyori, G. (2012) 'Populism in Europe: Hungary', Demos Report, Accessed online at http://www.demos.co.uk/publications/populismineuropehungary.

Bartlett, J., Froio, C., Littler, M. and McDonnell, D. (2013) 'New Political Actors in Europe: Beppe Grillo and the M5S', Demos Report, Accessed online at http://www.demos.co.uk/files/Beppe_Grillo_and_the_M5S_-_Demos_web_version.pdf.

BBC (2011a) 'Bishop of Blackburn Backs St Paul's Cathedral Protests', 6 November 2011, Accessed online at http://www.bbc.co.uk/news/uk-england-lancashire-15613442.

BBC (2011b) 'Italy Nuclear: Berlusconi Accepts Referendum Blow', 14 June 2011, Accessed online at http://www.bbc.co.uk/news/world-europe-13741105.

BBC (2011c) 'David Cameron Opposes St Paul's Protest', *BBC News*, Accessed online at http://www.bbc.co.uk/news/uk-politics-15643596.

Bebnowski, D. Hermann, C., Heyne, L., Hoeft, C., Kopp, J. and Rugenstein, J. (2010) 'Neue Dimensionen des Protests? Ergebnisse einer explorativen Studie zu den Protesten gegen Stuttgart 21', Report of the Göttingen Institute for Democracy Research, Accessed online at http://www.demokratie-goettingen.de/studien/neue-dimensionen-des-protest.

Bob, C., Haynes, J., Pickard, V., Keenan, T. and Coudry, N. (2008) 'Media spaces: Innovation and activism', in M. Albrow, H. Anheier, M. Glasius, M. Price and M. Kaldor (Eds.) *Global Civil Society 2007/8: Communicative Power and Democracy*. London: Sage, pp. 198–223.

Calhoun, C. (2013) 'Occupy Wall Street in perspective', *British Journal of Sociology*, 64(1), pp. 26–38.

Centro de Investigaciones Sociológicas (2011) 'Barómetro de Junio: Tabulación por recuerdo de voto y escala de ideología', Accessed online at http://datos.cis.es/pdf/Es2905rei_A.pdf.

Couldry, N. and Fenton, N. (2011) 'Occupy: Rediscovering the general will in hard times', *Possible Futures*, 22 December 2011, Accessed online at http://www.possible-futures.org/2011/12/22/rediscovering-the-general-will/.

Deel, S., Murray-Leach, T. and Pantazidou, M. (2012) 'Politics, Process and the Absence of Europe: Subterranean Politics in London', Draft Report for the Subterranean Politics Project, London School of Economics and Political Science, Accessed online at http://www.gcsknowledgebase.org/europe/draft-reports/.

della Porta, D., Mosca, L. and Parks, L. (2012) '2011: A Year of Protest on Social Justice in Italy', Draft Report for the Subterranean Politics Project, London School of Economics and Political Science, Accessed online at http://www.gcsknowledgebase.org/europe/draft-reports/.

Dewhurst, D., Dombi, P. and Colvin, N. (2012) 'How Hayek helped us to find capitalism's flaws', *Financial Times*, 25 January.

El Pais (2011) 'Majority of Spaniards Support 15-M Movement', 27 June, Accessed online at http://elpais.com/elpais/2011/06/27/inenglish/1309152044_850210.html.

Eurobarometer (75, Spring 2011) 'Europeans, the European Union and the Crisis. Brussels: European Commission', Accessed online at http://ec.europa.eu/public_opinion/archives/eb/eb75/eb75_cri_en.pdf.

Eurostat (2011) *Demography Report 2010*. Luxembourg: Publications Office of the European Union.

Fieschi, C., Morris, M. and Caballero, L. (2012) 'Recapturing the Reluctant Radical: How to win back Europe's populist vote', *Report*. London: Counterpoint.

Gauntlett, David (2011) *Making is Connecting: The Social Meaning of Creativity, from DIY and Knitting to YouTube and Web 2.0*. Cambridge: Polity Press.

Gesellschaft fuer die deutsche Sprache (2010) Accessed online at http://www.gfds.de/aktionen/wort-des-jahres/.

Glasius, Marlies and Timms, Jill (2005) 'The role of social forums in global civil society: Radical beacon or strategic infrastructure?' in M. Glasius, M. Kaldor and H. Anheier (Eds.) *Global Civil Society 2005/6*. London: Sage, pp. 190–238.

Global Civil Society Knowledgebase (2001–2012) Accessed online at www.gcsknowledgebase.org.

Hessel, S. (2010) *Indignez-Vous!* Montpellier: indigène éditions.

Jensen, J. with Saltman, E. and Szarvas, H. (2012) 'Hungary at the Vanguard of Europe's Rearguard? Emerging Subterranean Politics and Civil Dissent', Draft Report for the Subterranean Politics Project, London School of Economics and Political Science, Accessed online at http://www.gcsknowledgebase.org/europe/draft-reports/.

Johal, S., Moran, M. and Williams, K. (2012). 'The Future has been postponed: The great financial crisis and British politics', *British Politics*, 7(1), pp. 69–81.

Kaldor, M., Anheier, H. and Glasius, M. (2003) 'Global civil society in an era of regressive globalisation', in Kaldor, Mary, Helmut Anheier and Marlies Glasius, (Eds.) *Global Civil Society 2003*. Oxford: Oxford University Press.

Kaldor, M., Moore, H.L. and Selchow, S. (2012) *Global Civil Society 2012*. Basingstoke: Palgrave Macmillan.

Kaldor, M. and Selchow, S. (2012) 'The "Bubbling Up" of Subterranean Politics in Europe', Report, London School of Economics and Political Science, Accessed online at www.subterraneanpolitics.eu.

Khondker, H. H. (2011) 'Role of the new media in the Arab Spring', *Globalizations*, 8(5), pp. 675–679.

Lister, M., Dovey, J., Giddings, S., Grant, I. and Kelly, K. (2003) *New Media: A Critical Introduction*. London: Routledge.

Milan, S. (2013) *Social Movements and Their Technologies: Wiring Social Change*. Basingstoke: Palgrave Macmillan.

Moore, H. L. and Selchow, S. (2012) 'Global civil society and the internet 2012: Time to update our perspective', in M. Kaldor, H. L. Moore and S. Selchow (Eds.) *Global Civil Society 2012: Ten Years of Critical Reflection*. London: Palgrave, pp. 28–40.

Newell, Peter (2006) 'Climate for change? Civil society and the politics of global warming', in M. Glasius, M. Kaldor and H. Anheier (Eds.) *Global Civil Society 2005/6*. London: Sage, pp. 90–119.

Pianta, Mario (2002) 'Parallel summits of global civil society: An update', in M. Glasius, M. Kaldor and H. Anheier (Eds.) *Global Civil Society 2002*. Oxford: Oxford University Press, pp. 35–53.

Pleyers, G. (2010) *Alter-Globalization: Becoming Actors in the Global Age*. Cambridge: Polity.

Pleyers, G. with Conti, B. (2012) 'Subterranean Politics: European Progressive Activists: Obstacles on the Road Towards an "Alter-Europe"', Draft Report for the Subterranean Politics Project, London School of Economics and Political Science, Accessed online at http://www.gcsknowledgebase.org/europe/draft-reports/.

Protest Survey (2010) 'Manual for Data Collection on Protest Demonstrations. Caught in the Act of Protest: Contextualizing Contestation (CCC-Project)', Accessed online at www.protestsurvey.eu.

Sassen, S. (2000) 'The global city: Strategic site/new frontier', *American Studies*, 41(2/3), pp. 88–90.

Shirky, C. (2010) 'The Twitter Revolution: More than Just a Slogan, Prospect, 166', 6 January, Accessed online 29 March 2012 at http://www.prospectmagazine.co.uk/2010/01/the-twitter-revolution-more-than-just-a-slogan/.

Spiegel Online (2012) 'Marina Weisband: Ober-Piratin will Partei u¨ berflu¨ ssig machen', 22 January, Accessed online 1 March 2012 at http://www.spiegel.de/politik/deutschland/0,1518,810638,00.html.

Tormey, S. (2012) 'Occupy Wall Street: From representation to post-representation', *Journal of Critical Globalisation Studies*, Issue 5, pp. 132–137.

2
In Search of European Alternatives: Anti-Austerity Protests in Europe

Mario Pianta and Paolo Gerbaudo

Introduction

Europe has been an object of constant scrutiny and criticism since the beginning of the economic crisis of 2008, and more so with the explosion of the sovereign debt crisis in 2010. Recurrent news media expressions such as 'euro-crisis' have popularised the idea that there is something irremediably wrong in the project of the European Union (EU), which threatens its very existence as a political entity. The economic crisis – turned by austerity policies into a long and deep depression of Europe's periphery – has shown the rising power and increasing lack of legitimacy of the current technocratic institutions of the EU, including the European Council, the European Central Bank (ECB) and the European Commission. Yet, the protest movements which have developed in the old continent in response to the crisis, and in particular the 'subterranean politics' of the *Indignados* and Occupy groups, have shown little interest in a transformation of European governance structures and policies. Anti-austerity protests have largely developed at a national level with limited transnational coordination and vision. While rightly criticising neo-liberal policies pursued at the European level, protests have mostly ended up seeing Europe only as the culprit and not also as the space where a political alternative to neo-liberalism could be developed.

In this chapter we analyse anti-austerity protests in Europe, exploring their nature of 'subterranean politics' and the way they relate to the European political space. We argue that anti-austerity movements, as well as more institutional forces like European trade unions, have fallen short of making European institutions and policies the main target of their campaigns, despite the fact that they had a pivotal role in dictating austerity policies on the continent. Most campaigning efforts have focused on the implementation of policies at the national level, instead of challenging decision power at the European level.

We begin by surveying protest events, inquiring as to their national or transnational character. The great majority of anti-austerity mobilisations have developed within a national context, associated with struggles of resistance against plant closures, unemployment, cuts in public services or to youth protests in schools and universities. In comparison, truly pan-European anti-austerity events have had a more limited reach and impact. Such events included the Global Change protest on 15 October 2011; the Blockupy Frankfurt protests in May 2012 and 2013; the Florence 10+10 Forum in November 2012; the European strike/day of action called by the European Trade Union Confederation on 14 November 2012; the Brussels demonstration against the Spring meeting of the European Council in March 2013; and the AlterSummit in Athens in June 2013.

The lack of interest for Europe as a political space is visible in the different political visions emerging from anti-austerity movements, where scepticism towards the possibility of turning the European project towards progressive and equitable ends dominates. Different visions of Europe have developed within anti-austerity mobilisations, in experts' networks and in major campaigns, driving actions and policy initiatives. First, short-term proposals for change emphasised the need for a European adjustment, with reforms of the Monetary Union and financial markets that included the introduction of the Financial Transaction Tax, the creation of Eurobonds, an extended role of the ECB and a less restrictive view of fiscal integration within Europe. A second perspective pointed to the reversal of European integration, reviving national political processes, responding to the financial crisis with some debt repudiation, considering a break-up of the euro and the return to domestic currencies. Third, a longer-term view of a Europe beyond neoliberalism argued that greater European integration should not be based on the dominance of the single market and currency, but on a vision of greater democracy, sustainable and more equal growth, with the drastic reduction of the power of finance, the elimination of tax havens, reduction of the burden of debt, protection of welfare and labour rights and the introduction of coordinated fiscal policies capable of avoiding a new Great Depression.

On the limited occasions when social mobilisations have directly and explicitly addressed European issues, a variety of positions have emerged, ranging from trade unions arguing for a European adjustment to *Indignados* and radical grassroots groups demanding a reversal of European integration, while the question of a post-neo-liberal Europe has influenced public opinion and activists but has not yet been associated with large-scale mobilisations.

This lack of a shared European vision in anti-austerity mobilisations reflects the absence of a pan-European democratic space and of a clear set of European political institutions that social movements can confront in pursuing their goals. Without a legitimate and visible 'site' of democratic politics in Europe, mobilisations against neo-liberal policies may increasingly retreat to the context of national politics, with dangerous consequences both for the individual countries and for Europe as a whole.

Subterranean politics and the European space

In the aftermath of the financial crisis of 2008, new actors have appeared on the European scene as part of a common anti-austerity 'protest wave' (Tarrow 1994: 153). Besides activism from established organisations, including trade unions, this protest wave has been marked by the appearance of the 'subterranean politics' of the *Indignados* and Occupy groups, which have been particularly active in Spain, Greece, Portugal and the UK, where a number of occupations of public spaces and protest encampments have taken place since 2011.

The activism associated with 'subterranean politics' – examined in detail in other chapters of this book – has shown many similarities to the anti-globalisation movement, including the emphasis on consensus-based decision making and direct action. Yet, there have also been significant differences as seen in the adoption of the square occupation tactic and in the attempt to defuse antagonism so as to appeal to large sectors of the population. *Indignados* and Occupy groups have configured subterranean politics as fundamentally a 'civic politics', a politics of citizens who do not feel represented by existing political institutions, including parties and trade unions, as expressed by recurrent slogans like *no me representan* (they don't represent me) (see Gerbaudo 2012).

The extent to which these forms of subterranean politics can constitute a means for a democratic renewal in Europe, capable of addressing the current crisis of legitimacy of democratic institutions, remains to be established, and it lies beyond the scope of our discussion. In this chapter we focus instead on the extent to which this type of activism –

alongside other, more traditional, anti-austerity protests – has engaged with Europe as a political space. Is Europe seen as an enemy only, or does it possibly represent a way towards an alternative politics? And how did the European space of protest sit alongside national spaces in their mobilisations? Are these movements a symptom of a 'return of the national', as some have suggested (see for example Gerbaudo 2012: 10), or do they articulate a coherent transnational vision?

The activism wave of the anti-globalisation movement demonstrated the increasingly transnational character of social mobilisations in a globally interconnected world. In mobilising against global institutions like the International Monetary Fund (IMF), the World Trade Organization (WTO) or the G7/G8, activists built complex transnational alliances, acted across borders and aimed to construct a new democratic space at the global level (della Porta 2007; Pianta and Marchetti 2007). In this context of transnational protests, Europe acquired importance as an intermediate space between the national and the global, where common mobilisations could emerge. Europe became a crucial terrain for many activists intending to escape the narrow confines of a nation state increasingly weakened by global markets. This effort to construct a radical European space is shown by the experiences of the European Social Forum, and by the 'Europeanization of public discourses and mobilization' (della Porta and Caiani 2007).

The anti-globalisation movement perceived Europe as a new centre of power to be targeted, but also as a new political space in which to construct new forms of democracy and collective action. But is this still the case for contemporary anti-austerity protests, and in particular for the subterranean politics of *Indignados* and Occupy groups? We answer these questions through an analysis of various movement documents, including manifestos, assembly resolutions, position papers and publications, as well as a mapping of relevant anti-austerity protest events in Europe.

What emerges from the trajectory of mobilisation and from the agenda of contemporary anti-austerity movements is that Europe as a political space has, by and large, lost the relevance it had during the time of the anti-globalisation movement. In spite of a common understanding of the nature of the crisis and of neo-liberal policies, European mobilisations up to 2013 have mostly framed their campaigns within national political contexts, leaving little room for the development of a truly continental mobilisation. Moreover, markedly different positions have emerged on how to address the crisis, leaving no room for the building of a clear alternative to the European status quo.

Trajectories of mobilisation

Anti-austerity mobilisations in Europe between 2009 and 2013 were characterised by a national – rather than transnational – character. While the recession and austerity measures have been common to most EU countries, protests and activism have developed along autonomous lines in different European countries, with limited cross-border coordination. Anti-austerity mobilisations have tended to reflect the rhythm of national politics. Calls to protest have been made in response to national government measures, such as the announcement of budget cuts, as well as in reaction to major effects of the crisis at the national level, such as high unemployment, job losses and youth and student dissatisfaction. Since 2012, protests have also addressed the heavy police repression used by governments in Southern European countries.[1]

In order to analyse the trajectory of Europe-wide anti-austerity mobilisations since the start of the crisis in 2008, in this chapter we adopt the methodology and definitions used in the analysis of parallel summits and global civil society events (Pianta 2001; Gerbaudo and Pianta 2012). We identify only a limited number of events with clear cross-border coordination and European ambition, amongst which a handful of events stem from experiences of subterranean politics.

Table 2.1 reports the main European protest events from 2008 to June 2013. Few protests have been recorded, although with increasingly frequency since 2012; their trajectory is discontinuous, with no persistence of particular mobilisations – with the exception of trade union actions. The range of actors involved is rather limited; the European content of mobilisations is uncertain.

The scarcity of pan-European protests is made particularly baffling by the fact that there was no shortage of events that could have constituted a target for protest. Many important decisions which have influenced the way in which the crisis has been managed have been taken at high-profile EU meetings, including European Council meetings, EU finance ministers' meetings and EU summits like the one in March 2012, where the 'Fiscal Compact' was decided; or at meetings between heads of state, such as those frequently held between the French president Nicolas Sarkozy and the German chancellor Angela Merkel. Each of these events offered a clear 'political opportunity' (Tarrow 1994: 15) for protest activity. Yet only sporadically did people mobilise in protest against them and the policies put forward. And on no occasion did we witness anything comparable to the counter-summit protests of the anti-globalisation movement, such as those in Prague in 2000 or Genoa in 2001. While

Table 2.1 Major Europe-wide anti-austerity protests

Title	Organisers	Description	Type	Locations	Date
Anti-G20 protest	G20 Meltdown + TUC + other groups	First big counter-summit protest since the beginning of the economic crisis. Big union march on March 26 and direct actions April 1–2	Protest	London	26/03/2009–2/04/2009
Fight the crisis put people first	ETUC	Tens of thousands of protesters take part in decentralised protests all over Europe	Protest	Madrid, Brussels, Berlin, Prague	14–16/05/2009
European Social Forum	ESF	A few thousand attend the smallest European Social Forum to date, which earns almost no media coverage	Forum	Istanbul	1–4/07/2010
European Trade Union Protest	ETUC	100,000 workers from all over Europe march on Brussels in a large Europe-wide labour demonstration	Protest	Brussels	29/09/2010
No to austerity for everyone and bonuses for the happy few	ETUC	The decentralised day of action sees tens of thousands protesting in France, Luxembourg, Denmark and the Czech Republic	Protest	Paris, Luxembourg City, Prague, Copenhagen	14/12/2010
European Day of Action	ETUC	Ten of thousands of trade unionists march in Brussels; minor clashes with police, who use tear gas and water cannon to disperse protesters	Protest	Brussels	24/03/2011
Day of Action for Global Change	*Indignados* and Occupy groups with specific coalitions in each country	A total of over 1,000,000 people march in different European cities	Protest	Madrid, Rome, Barcelona, Athens, Brussels, London and dozens of other cities	15/10/2011

Event	Organisers	Description	Type	Location	Date
European Day of Action Against Austerity	ETUC	Over 100,000 workers participated in demonstrations across Europe in advance of a Council of Ministers meeting on the economy	Protest	Paris, Marseille, Lille, Barcelona, Athens, Brussels and several other cities	29/02/2012
Blockupy Frankfurt	German coalition of grassroots groups, Attac Germany, Occupy activists	Protest against the European Central Bank in Frankfurt, with around 10,000 protesters	Protest	Frankfurt	17–19/05/2012
Florence 10+10	Coalition of groups, social movements and European networks	4,000 activists representing 300 European networks and organisations meet for 4 days, 10 years after the first European Social Forum	Forum, Alternatives	Florence	8–11/11/2012
European Strike/day of action of ETUC	ETUC, national unions	General strike in Italy, Greece, Spain, Portugal; trade union demonstrations in the rest of the EU	Protest	25 EU countries	14/11/2012
Protest against the EU Council Spring meeting	Groups present in Florence 10+10. AlterSummit, national groups	Demonstration in Brussels	Protest, Alternatives	Brussels and other EU cities	14/03/2013
Blockupy Frankfurt	German coalition of grassroots groups, Attac Germany, Occupy activists	Protest against the European Central Bank in Frankfurt with a few thousand protesters	Protest	Frankfurt	31/05/2013–01/06/2013
AlterSummit in Athens	AlterSummit	Meeting and demonstration	Protest, Alternatives	Athens	14–16/06/2013

European elites carried out neo-liberal policies that contributed to worsening the crisis, European social movements appeared unable to build a continent-wide opposition.

In analysing the trajectory of anti-austerity mobilisations, we look separately at the two main actors that have been involved in anti-austerity protests in Europe: the subterranean politics of the *Indignados* and Occupy groups and the more institutionalised politics of European trade unions and the European Trade Union Confederation (ETUC).

The former represent the main novelty of the anti-austerity protest cycle. Using the format of the protest encampment, like those established in Puerta del Sol in Madrid and in Syntagma Square in Athens, these movements have found powerful ways to give voice to the widespread popular opposition to austerity policies (Gerbaudo 2012). They have created new spaces of democratic decision making and grassroots participation. However, these movements have not managed to scale up anti-austerity protest to the European level. The *Indignados* movement, as it has developed in Spain and Greece, has mainly focused on rejecting the politics of austerity at the national level, opposing the implementation of deep cuts to public spending and protesting its dramatic consequences on employment and public services. It is true that some sections of these movements, especially the more politicised groups stemming from the anti-globalisation protest cycle, harboured the hope that the movement would transcend national boundaries and would blossom into a European Spring. However, such transnationalisation attempts have had limited success.

The *Indignados* movement emerged in Spain in 2009 – see Chapter 5 for a detailed account – and had a limited diffusion in other countries. Only in Greece did a local *Indignados* movement – established in late May 2011 and called, in Greek, Αγανακτισμένοι (to be transliterated as *aganaktismenoi*) – come to be recognised in the spring and summer of 2011 as a powerful social actor. Despite several attempts and efforts, other countries, like France and Italy, have not proven fertile ground for the *Indignados* (see Chapter 3, p. 61), reflecting the strong specificity of this movement. The primary occurrence of transnational coordination of protest events was in October 2011, when the movement launched a coordinated day of protest; under the slogan 'United for Global Change', demonstrations took place in dozens of European cities on 15 October 2011, with the biggest ones in Madrid and Rome. In Rome the demonstration ended in violent clashes with the police – and with deep divisions within social movements. The demonstration in Brussels, originally planned to be the major event of the day with a march of Spanish protestors arriving in the European capital, ended up attracting only few thousand participants. While overall turnout for the protest across Europe was large, totalling around one million people, the event did not seem to produce any lasting results in terms of organisational capacity and political influence.

A second attempt to turn the wave of anti-austerity protests from a series of disconnected national efforts into a coordinated pan-European campaign was 'Blockupy Frankfurt', in which local autonomous groups and Attac Germany played a significant role. The days of action took place between 16 and 19 May 2012 in the German city and targeted the ECB, considered the decisive institution responsible for directing austerity policies at the European level. Tens of thousands of activists, mostly Germans with some Italians and few French, converged on Frankfurt. Nevertheless, the protest did not spark broader pan-European actions. Harsh repression by the German police, with authorities imposing a strict protest ban, contributed to its relative failure. However, its limited degree of success was also down to the difficulty in creating a sense of common purpose among different sections of the European anti-austerity movement, as seen in the difficulty involved in mobilising participants from outside – in particular from Spain and Greece – and the perception that the event was managed by German activists alone. A second 'Blockupy Frankfurt' took place in May 2013, with similar outcomes (see Box 2.1).

Other attempts to build Europe-wide mobilisations against austerity rooted in the experiences of the *Indignados* have also had limited success. The Spring Days of Action against austerity, and in particular the 14 March 2013 protests against the Spring meeting of the European Council, were attended by only a few thousand people and had little resonance in the press, particularly when compared with national events like the protests against the crisis in Cyprus around the same period. All in all, the subterranean politics of the *Indignados* has proven very difficult to scale up to the European level.

Similar problems in developing Europe-wide mobilisations can be seen in trade union activity. The main actor here is the ETUC, established in 1973, which represents 60 million workers all over Europe and is an obvious candidate to lead a pan-European campaign against austerity. However, the divisions among members of ETUC – which includes both more militant and more moderate unions, and unions from both 'centre' and 'periphery' countries of Europe, with starkly different economic and social conditions – have made it difficult for the organisation to develop a major wave of cross-border activism and to commit

Box 2.1   Blockupy Frankfurt!

Call for Action
Resistance in the Heart of the European Crisis Regime,
31 May and 1 June 2013

Once again Blockupy calls for European days of protest in Frankfurt am Main against the crisis regime of the European Union. On 31 May and 1 June 2013, we want to take the resistance against the poverty policy of the German government and the Troika – consisting of ECB, EU Commission and IMF – into one of the centers of European crisis management: to the residence of the European Central Bank (ECB) and of many German banks and corporations – the profiteers of these policies.

The programs of austerity and privatizations, which already have been imposed on the countries of the Global South decades ago, are now arriving in Europe. The German Agenda 2010 was just an archetype for what now is enforced especially in Southern Europe to an even more dramatic extent. If we do not defend ourselves, this pauperization will keep intensifying – also here, in the centre of Europe: the ongoing cuts of social and democratic rights. These measures shall secure the ability of payment for the return-assumptions of large fortunes, while at the same time the 'economic competitiveness' of Germany and (Central) Europe in the capitalist world market is to be enhanced through the price reduction and precarization of waged-related labour.

Together with the people in Southern Europe we say: 'Don't owe, don't pay!' and resist the rehabilitation of capitalism on the backs of employees as well as unemployed, retirees, migrants and the youth. We reject any cooperation with the German crisis politics, which not only has catastrophic consequences for people in Southern Europe, but also here, where the social division is continued permanently. Therefore we also fight against the still ongoing worsening of the living and working conditions just here, already implemented and imminent to an even larger extent. Moreover, its effects are gender-specifically unequally distributed and thus intensify gender injustice. We consider initiatives against rising rents, communal impoverishment, systematic harassments against unemployed people, deportations, isolation camps and mandatory residence as parts of ourselves.

Again and again there are several attempts to divide us, e.g. by claiming that 'enough has been paid for the Greek'. No Greek person has been saved at all, in fact the yields of banks and corporations have been assured. We oppose any effort spent on agitating employees, unemployed and precarious in Germany and Greece, in Italy, Portugal, France or other countries against each other by activating such nationalist slogans. Especially, we fight against all (neo-)fascist tendencies, marches and events. We also oppose any form of reactionary or racist crisis interpretation – no matter whether from 'below or above', no matter if anti-Semitic, anti-Muslim or antiziganistic.

We are part of the international movements who have been resisting the attacks on our life and our future, fight for social rights and alternatives, develop new forms of organization and solidarian economy for years. We oppose the authoritarian execution of austerity-measures, which stand in blatant contradiction to democratic principles, and stand up for the democratization of all aspects of life. We defy the imposition of economic interests through war and exports of weapons. We do not accept at all the capitalist economic model which is based on global exploitation, necessarily produces poverty as well as social injustice and systematically destroys nature.

We carry our protest, our civil disobedience and resistance to the residence of the profiteers of the European crisis regime to Frankfurt am Main. We will not let ourselves be intimidated neither by police nor by judicial repression – which globally affects movements on many places including ourselves – but we will react with transnational solidarity.

Let's practice our solidarity against the politics of austerity terror! Let us make clear: We will not permit the crisis continuously being loaded on the backs of wage-related employees, unemployed, retirees, precarious, students, refugees and many others – neither here nor anywhere else. The days of protest in Frankfurt thereby join last year's global protests, the protests in this year's spring in Brussels and other places as well as the movements for an Alter Summit in Athens in the summer of 2013.

We will demonstrate against the policies of the German government and the really great 4-party-coalition, against the policies of ECB, EU Commission and IMF. We will block the ECB. We will

---

Box 2.1   (Continued)

occupy public squares in the economic and financial metropolis Frankfurt – we are Blockupy!

Blockupy is a German-wide coalition in which numerous groups, organizations and individual activists take part and work together. We are active in different social and political collectives or currents. So far the following structures take part: Attac-activists, unions, antiracist networks, parties like 'Die Linke', Occupy-activists, unemployed initiatives, student groups, North–South, peace and environmental initiatives, the leftyouth ['solid], the green youth, as well as radical left associations like Interventionist Left and...Ums Ganze!-Alliance.

http://blockupy.org/en/call-for-action/

---

significant resources to Europe-wide mobilisations. Overly focused on the national level, trade unions have had only a minimal impact on the policy agenda at the continental level.

The most prominent anti-austerity protest organised by the ETUC thus far has been the European strike/day of action called for 14 November 2012, which saw general strikes in Italy, Spain, Portugal and Greece, and national demonstrations across the rest of the EU. The event was historically important as the first true attempt at a general strike in Europe, and included a strong participation of *Indignados* and similar groups in several countries. Its outcomes, however, were highly uneven: in Spain there was a very large participation with mass demonstrations; 80 local demonstrations were held in Italy, where also students took to the streets; in Greece the protest ended with clashes in the streets of Athens; a more limited outcome emerged in Portugal; and in the rest of the EU, trade union demonstrations were organised but with no strike action (see Box 2.2).

This day of action built upon a number of prior protests organised by the ETUC in Brussels and in other European cities. The most notable example of these events was the ETUC march organised on 29 September 2010, when about 100,000 people, representing all the countries of the European Union, marched in Brussels. Other noteworthy events included the 'Euro-demonstration' in Wroclaw on 17 September 2011, the 'No to Austerity' demonstration in

Box 2.2   The first European strike – European Trade Union
Confederation (ETUC)

*ETUC day of action and solidarity for a Social Compact
for Europe*
*Declaration adopted by the ETUC Executive Committee at their
meeting on 17 October 2012*

The ETUC Executive Committee meeting on 17 October 2012 call
for a day of action and solidarity on 14 November 2012, including strikes, demonstrations, rallies and other actions, mobilising
the European trade union movement behind ETUC policies as set
down in the Social Compact for Europe.

They express their strong opposition to the austerity measures
that are dragging Europe into economic stagnation, indeed recession, as well as the continuing dismantling of the European social
model. These measures, far from re-establishing confidence, only
serve to worsen imbalances and foster injustice.

While supporting the objective of sound accounts, the Executive Committee consider that the recession can only be stopped
if budgetary constraints are loosened and imbalances eliminated,
with a view to achieving sustainable economic growth, and social
cohesion, and respecting the values enshrined in the Charter of
Fundamental Rights.

Fiscal consolidation had a sharper effect than originally esti-
mated by Institutions, including the European Commission and
the International Monetary Fund (IMF). Indeed the IMF now
admits that they grossly miscalculated the impact austerity measures have on growth. This miscalculation has an unmeasurable
impact on the daily life of workers and citizens the ETUC represents, and brings into question the whole basis of austerity policies
advanced by the Fiscal Treaty and imposed by the Troika.

The Executive Committee note mounting opposition among
citizens and workers in the countries concerned and reaffirm
their support for affiliated unions fighting for decent working
and living conditions. This situation results from the lack of
coordination of economic policies and the absence of minimum
social standards throughout Europe. In the context of free movement of capital, this gave free rein to competition between states,

Box 2.2   (Continued)

in particular in the field of taxation, labour costs and social conditions.

They reiterate that social dialogue and collective bargaining are central to the European Social Model. They strongly oppose the frontal attacks on these rights, at national and European level. The ETUC Executive Committee urgently calls for immediate adoption and transposition of the European social partners agreements currently before Council.

They recall that the Union is treaty-bound to 'work for the sustainable development of Europe based on balanced economic growth and price stability, a highly competitive social market economy, aiming at full employment and social progress, and a high level of protection and improvement of the quality of the environment'. They further recall that the ETUC's support for the Lisbon Treaty was mainly predicated on the full application of those objectives.

They note that discussions are currently under way among Institutions and governments about the desirability of further treaty changes. A change of direction is necessary and priority should be given to resolving the crisis in line with the three pillars of our proposed Social Compact for Europe, which is gathering increasing support. This is articulated around social dialogue & collective bargaining, economic governance for sustainable growth & employment, and economic, tax & social justice.

They insist that active solidarity, social progress and democratic accountability must be an integral part of the European project. They consider as essential that a social progress protocol to be included as an integral and operative part of any new treaty. The ETUC will evaluate any new step in European integration on this basis.

http://www.etuc.org/IMG/pdf/EN-ETUC-EC-Declaration-17-10 -2012-2.pdf

Budapest on 9 April 2011 and the European Day of Action on 24 March 2011, which featured a number of small protests around Europe.

The limited impact of these protests reflects the reduced power of organised labour and the lack of a common strategy for responding to the crisis, as well as the weakness of the ETUC compared with the ability of business groups and lobbies to influence European policies (Hyman 2005). Trade unions have responded to national governments' austerity plans mainly through industry-specific and general strikes at the country level. Plant closures, job losses, the precarisation of work and record youth unemployment have deeply divided the unions' base, making the construction of effective social alliances more difficult. The challenge to extend such alliances across countries with very different conditions – from the crisis-ravaged European 'periphery' to those countries of the 'centre' largely shielded from economic problems – has proved to be out of reach for Europe's trade unions, as well as for labour-based political strategies.

Anti-austerity protests, both those taking the form of the subterranean politics of *Indignados* groups, and at the more institutional level of trade unions, have thus been characterised by a high national fragmentation and an incapacity to construct a coordinated campaign at the continental level, commensurate with the governance structures directing austerity policies. This failure comes just few years after a strong wave of anti-globalisation protest agitated Europe (Pianta and Marchetti 2007), leading to a significant impact on the political process in major European countries and to some changes in national policies, such as debt cancellation for developing countries, trade liberalisation and the introduction of the financial transaction tax (Utting et al. 2012). For several years the European Social Forum, launched in Florence in 2002, was a gathering point for all those opposed to neo-liberalism and served as a platform for coordinating continental campaigns. However, its structure relied on inter-organisational relationships that led to a progressive loss of relevance and participation, ending with the 2010 European Social Forum in Istanbul.

An effort to 're-create' this space of grassroots dialogue among activists was made with the Florence 10+10 November 2012 meeting, 'Uniting forces for another Europe'. It was organised ten years after the first European Social Forum, with the goal of looking ten years into Europe's future. Four thousand activists from 300 networks, and organisations from 28 European countries participated in the event, including representatives from well-established EU civil society networks, trade unionists, grassroots militants, 'older' anti-globalisation veterans and 'younger' activists from the *Indignados* and Occupy experiences. The gathering of such a wide range of forces was a significant success and led to the organisation of protests on 14 March 2013. However, the debates on the way forward out of Europe's crisis remained rather fragmented, failing to result in a shared framing of European mobili-sations that could lead to widespread coordinated actions. Ultimately, Florence 10+10 was unable to overcome the difficulty in articulating a coherent vision for an alternative, post-liberal Europe. The same weak-ness emerged in June 2013 at the AlterSummit organised in Athens by a similar range of forces; participation, the involvement of Greek move-ments and the overall impact were limited, despite the overt intentions of the organisers to create a pan-European movement.

Visions and alternatives

Besides the lack of international coordination of anti-austerity protests, the incapacity of movements to articulate a clear Europe-wide strategy is rooted in the different visions of Europe that have emerged and in widespread euro-scepticism. Anti-austerity mobilisations have, by and large, failed in converging on one common vision that might consti-tute the vehicle for developing a credible alternative to the European 'status quo'.

Three different visions of Europe have emerged as major frames of anti-austerity protests. A first perspective, focusing on short-term changes needed to respond to Europe's crisis, is that of a *European adjustment*, which envisages limited reforms of the Monetary Union and financial markets – including the introduction of the Financial Transac-tion Tax, the creation of Eurobonds, an extended role of the ECB and a less restrictive view of fiscal integration within Europe – without altering the existing framework of European integration. Second is the frame of a *reversal of European integration*, which sees the revival of national political processes, a response to the financial crisis with some debt repudiation, consideration of the break-up of the euro and a return to domestic cur-rencies, a reversion to less open and less integrated economies, and the recovery of some degree of national policy sovereignty. Third is the frame of a *Europe beyond neo-liberalism*, which argues that greater European integration should not be based on the dominance of the sin-gle market and currency but on a vision of a democratic Europe with sustainable and more equal growth – a vision that includes a drastic reduction in the power of finance, the elimination of tax havens, a reduction in the burden of debt, the protection of welfare and labour rights and the introduction of coordinated fiscal policies capable of avoiding a new Great Depression.

These three frames are less mutually incompatible than might be thought, and the importance attached to them also depends on the gravity of the crisis in different countries. The proposals for reform of the Monetary Union and the ECB, the 'easiest' to implement, are widely shared and, if enacted earlier, would very likely have been successful in preventing the vicious circle of austerity and crisis in Southern Europe. Now that the depression in the 'periphery' is more dramatic, more drastic measures to curb the freedom of action of finance are necessary – the Cyprus banking crisis in 2013 has been addressed by introducing controls on capital movements. The proposals for a different model of European integration, reversing austerity, with less power for the markets and an enhanced role for democracy, are much harder to insert into the EU policy agenda, but become more urgent as the recession worsens. If the crisis gets out of hand, in a perilous scenario of disintegration of the euro and of Europe, this could necessitate a return – amidst great difficulties – to national economies with their own currencies and lower external openness.

Adjusting Europe?

A clear statement of the need to adjust European institutions and policies has come from the ETUC. At its May 2011 congress in Athens, ETUC denounced the deepening spiral of debt, austerity and unemployment. Its emergency resolution read: 'To get out of the crisis, Europe must help countries in crisis such as Greece with an ambitious investment and development programme to generate growth and employment and with that income and tax revenue. However, anybody sticking to the one-sided austerity plan, accepts the collapse of the Eurozone.'

The need for addressing the debt crisis through European solidarity and for reversing austerity policies are at the centre of the work of the European Trade Union Institute (ETUI), which has produced two volumes on policy alternatives: *After the Crisis* (Watt and Botsch 2010) and *Exiting from the Crisis* (Coats 2011, with a preface by Joseph Stiglitz). They include contributions from dozens of American and European economists and trade unionists on themes ranging from the tax on financial transactions to policies to stimulate demand, from controls on capital movements to protection of labour rights and wages.

These proposals were discussed – among several trade union initiatives – at the conference 'Beyond the Crisis: Developing Sustainable Alternatives', organised at the European Parliament by the Socialist, Democratic and Green MEPs (9 February 2012). The discussion was an encounter between economists, unions and politicians of various extractions on how to deal with the crisis, reduce inequality, change the growth model and develop the green economy. A common critique emerged on the rules of European economic governance and on the 'Fiscal Compact' later adopted by the euro-area, two issues on which the euro-parliamentary groups of Socialists & Democrats, Greens and European Left (GUE-NGL) were united in opposing the decisions of the Council and Commission.

The criticism of the effects of the European policy of austerity – budget balance written into constitutions, repayment of a portion of the public debt – has been further developed in a volume by Hoang Ngoc (2011), a French Socialist MEP and an economics professor at the Sorbonne. The proposals include a different role for the ECB, Eurobonds, a public investment programme, a tax on financial transactions, and European harmonisation of corporate taxes.

These criticisms have widely informed the positions of social-democratic parties in Europe, but they have failed to build a common front for change and could not prevent the European Council launching the Fiscal Compact in the spring of 2012. Even the election victory of the socialist François Hollande in May 2012 did not reverse this course of European policy, in spite of his efforts to emphasise the need for growth as well as austerity.

Yet despite this, even within the establishment, an understanding of the need for adjusting European policies has become evident. 'Founding fathers' of the European Union like Romano Prodi, former President of the Commission, and Giuliano Amato, former Vice-President of the European Convention responsible for preparing the draft Constitution, have advocated a federal model for a 'United States of Europe' with fiscal and political integration; they want Europe to impose the Tobin tax on financial transactions, contend that the 60% ceiling on the debt/GDP ratio be guaranteed collectively by the Monetary Union as a whole, and call for the issue of Eurobonds (EU securities to fund development projects) and a larger EU budget no longer dependent strictly on member state transfers. They also propose a constitutional convention for the revision of the European treaties, granting observer status to representatives of employer and labour organisations, civil society and local and regional governments.

However, the decisions of the European Council in 2012 and 2013 have not changed the trajectory of policy for addressing the crisis; the only novelties have come from the new leadership of Mario Draghi at the ECB, who has clearly stated that he will protect the euro 'by whatever means necessary' and has managed to introduce new policy tools that have limited – to some extent – financial speculation on the public debt of countries of Europe's periphery.

In spite of an increasing understanding of the need for a new course for Europe, official policy has not changed. The battle over the prospects for 'adjusting Europe' seems to be mainly played within the ranks of Europe's elite, with little opening for the demands of civil society, the trade unions and/or to progressive political forces such as social-democratic and green parties.

Reversing European integration?

As documented in the country-specific chapters of this book, most mobilisations of 'subterranean politics' paid little attention to Europe and gave priority to a return to national political processes. Some grassroots protests and more radical groups have reacted to the crisis with a fundamental critique of European integration and the power of finance. Such a euro-sceptical position appeared to be dominant within the *Indignados* movement, with Europe primarily seen as a problem to dispose of, rather than as a means towards the solution of the economic crisis.

Both in Spain and in Greece, some actors within the *Indignados* movement, including constituent groups and local assemblies, have taken positions that come close to the idea of a reversal of European integration. In May 2011, for example, the group Democracia Real Ya (DRY), one of the key organisations of the Spanish *Indignados*, included among its proposals for political and economic renewal 'compulsory referenda on laws imposed by the European Union'.[2] In 2012 one of the factions that emerged from the internal fighting within DRY, which took the name Asociacion DRY, explicitly discussed the possibility of an abandonment of the euro and a return to the peseta, and argued for forms of national protectionism.[3]

The attitude of the Greek *Indignados* has been similar. Since the birth of the movement in late May 2011, Europe has often been seen as just an enemy to be kept at bay. This perception is captured well by the presence of a flag of Europe in which the stars had been replaced by swastikas, as one of the authors of this chapter witnessed during his research visit to Athens. In the first declaration of the assembly of Syntagma Square, protestors were casting European institutions as invaders that had to be sent back home: 'we will not leave the squares until those who compelled us to come here leave the country: the governments, the Troika (EU, ECB and IMF), the IMF Memoranda and everyone who exploit us'. Many *Indignados* activists, as well as some trade unions, have asked for a return to the drachma. Conversely, the rising Greek Party of the left, Syriza – which, under the leadership of Alexis Tsipras, received 26% of the votes in the 2012 second general elections in June[4] – has adopted a more favourable position towards Europe and the common currency, stating its intention to remain within the euro as long as it was possible and feasible.

Euro-scepticism has also been present in the anti-austerity protests in other countries. In Italy, a distancing from Europe and the euro has been advocated by small groups of activists and an anti-European stance has been typical of the populist 'Five Star Movement' of the former comedian Beppe Grillo, which obtained 25% of the votes in the general election of February 2013.[5] In the French debate, voices critical of European integration have often emerged from radical grassroots and left groups, questioning the euro and advocating protectionist policies. In 2013, arguments for reducing European integration and a break-up of the eurozone have emerged in France from Bernard Cassen, long involved in the World Social Forums, and in Germany by Oskar Lafontaine, former leader of the left party Die Linke. Such views, however, remain far from dominant in the broad anti-austerity movements of these countries.

A post-liberal Europe?

The combination of demands for a radical departure from current policies and a view of Europe as a key arena for political action has been slow to emerge in the mobilisations we have examined. Only since 2012 have these elements started to characterise major initiatives, such as the launch of the AlterSummit – a network of trade unions and civil society groups – the protest of 'Blockupy Frankfurt', European strikes such as the one on 14 November 2012 and a range of national initiatives, some of them involving parts of the *Indignados* and Occupy movement.

The large participation of activists' networks – including all the above groups – in the Florence 10+10 meeting, 'Uniting Forces for Another Europe' held in November 2012, was a significant development in activists' ability to address the European question. In spite of the fragmentation of perspectives and initiatives, recognition of the need for a 'post-liberal Europe' has started to emerge, but has not yet resulted in wide-ranging coordinated protests at the European level.

Yet while these efforts have fallen short of a shared framing for contestation, and different views on Europe are present in mobilisations, a growing number of initiatives by experts' networks, civil society groups and social movements in several EU countries have put on the agenda a radical critique of European policies and proposals for an alternative Europe.

Much effort has focused on the need for alternatives to Europe's economic policies. The 2013 edition of the annual Euromemorandum (2012), backed by 350 European economists, called for limiting the freedom of action of the financial sector and enhancing the role of the ECB as lender of last resort, replacing austerity with policies of increasing public demand, wage support, full employment and shorter working hours. In France, the Manifeste des economistes atterrés (Economistes atterrés 2011) became a hugely popular denunciation of financial excesses – and a surprise bestseller. The manifesto dismantles the 'false certainties' of the virtuous functioning of markets and proposes severe restrictions on those financial activities that brought speculation and crisis. In a second book, the same group denounced the Fiscal Compact (the latest European Treaty, introduced in spring 2012). With its requirements for balanced budgets and the reimbursement of the public debt in excess of 60% of GDP, the French economists argue that the Fiscal Compact is contributing to the depression of Europe's economy (Economistes atterrés 2012). A new book by Michel Aglietta (2012) suggests that only a federal Europe can make the euro a sovereign currency and end the crisis. He calls for making the ECB a lender of last resort, integrating fiscal policy at European level, issuing Eurobonds and narrowing the gap between the production capacity of the European 'centre' and the 'periphery'. Detailed analysis and proposals on the public debt problem are brought together in the volume produced by the Attac campaign (2011).

In Germany, a thorough analysis of the mechanisms of the crisis and the missteps of European policy was set out by one hundred academic advisors to Attac Germany, the German affiliate of the international network that for years now has been urging the taxation of the financial industry and the abandonment of free-market policies. They denounced the spread of the crisis from private banks to sovereign debt, pointed to the risk of a crisis of hegemony that could bring new conflicts, and called for an end to the logic of growth, for managed default to reduce the debt, and for the taxation of capital assets and finance.

In Italy, Europe's crisis has been at the centre of a debate on 'Europe's course', started by the civil society campaign Sbilanciamoci! (Rossanda and Pianta 2012), and in Europe the debate was hosted by openDemocracy (www.opendemocracy.net/can-europe-make-it) and other European groups. A Forum on 'The Way Out' of Europe's crisis was attended by 800 people in Florence on 9 December 2011, at which the idea of a European appeal was first discussed. The Appeal 'Another Road for Europe' was then launched in May 2012 by a large number of European intellectuals and activists (including one of the authors, see Box 2.3). The Appeal called for a debate on these issues at the European Parliament, which was subsequently held on 28 June 2012, at the same time as the European Council meeting. The Forum 'Another Road for Europe' saw many of the signatories discuss the alternatives to Europe's crisis with civil society networks, trade unions and MEPs from the Socialist and Democrats, Green and United Left groups in the European Parliament, as well as with national politicians. The demands that emerged then were common to a number of other policy documents produced by civil society and political initiatives. A new development in the European links among groups active on economic alternatives has been the creation at the Florence 10+10 meeting of the European Progressive Economists Network (Euro-pen) that launched there a 'Common Call for Another Economic Policy for Europe' (see Box 2.4).

Conclusion: In search of European politics

The mobilisations against austerity in Europe highlight a paradox. While European institutions – the European Council, the European Commission and the European Central Bank – are responsible for the responses to the financial crisis and the austerity policies imposed on Europe, social movements have rarely challenged these institutions directly. Truly continental campaigns have been slow to emerge and have yet to develop a shared alternative to current policies.

This paradox is the result of two major factors. First, what we are witnessing looks like a European contention in search of framing, with mobilisations absorbed by the immediate challenge of resisting at the national level the economic and political effects of the European crisis. This is the level where the political process is most structured and visible, where the political system and civil society are ready to frame social responses to the crisis in well-tested forms – trade unions protests and negotiations about lay-offs and unemployment protection; political protests by opposition parties; anti-government protests by radical groups. What these responses are missing is the European nature of the crisis and of the political process leading to austerity policies; no common frame is yet available for defining this as an issue of European-wide contention, where mobilisation can develop and have an impact on policies.

The second factor is the lack of a European political space with 'visible' power structures and an 'understandable' institutional setting that can

Box 2.3   The European Appeal: 'Another Road for Europe'

Europe is in crisis because it has been hijacked by neo-liberalism and finance. In the last 20 years – with a persistent democratic deficit – the meaning of the European Union has increasingly been reduced to a narrow view of the single market and the single currency, leading to liberalisations and speculative bubbles, loss of rights and the explosion of inequalities.

This is not the Europe that was imagined decades ago as a space of economic and political integration free from war. This is not the Europe that was built through economic and social progress, the extension of democracy and welfare rights.

This European project is now in danger. Facing the financial crisis, European authorities and governments have acted irresponsibly; they saved private banks but refused to contain the difficulties of indebted countries using the tools of the Monetary Union; they imposed on all countries austerity policies and cuts in public budgets that will now be enshrined in European Treaties. The results are that the financial crisis has extended to more countries, the euro is in danger, a new great depression and the risk of disintegration of Europe are looming.

Europe can survive only if another road is taken. Another Europe is possible. Europe has to mean social justice, environmental responsibility, democracy and peace. This is what the larger part of Europe's culture and society yearns for. This is the way indicated by justice movements, mobilisations for dignity and against austerity policies. But it is the sort of Europe that has been ignored by dominant political forces in Europe.

This other Europe is not a new superstate nor is it another intergovernmental bureaucracy. A form of democratic governance for Europe is needed if we are to address the global challenges that nation states are not able to manage.

Along the road to another Europe, visions of change, protest and alternatives have to be woven into a common framework. We propose six objectives.

- a smaller finance (...);
- more integrated economic policies (...);
- more jobs and labour rights, less inequality (...);

Box 2.3 (Continued)

- protection of the environment (...);
- practising of democracy (...);
- peace making and upholding of human rights (...).

We propose to bring this agenda for another Europe to the European Parliament and to Europe's institutions. This new meaning of Europe is already visible in cross-border citizens' mobilisations, civil society networks and trade union struggles; it has now to shape Europe's politics and policy making.

Thirty years ago, at the start of the 'New Cold War' between East and West, the Appeal for European Nuclear Disarmament launched the idea of a Europe free from military blocs and argued that 'we must commence to act as if a united, neutral, pacific Europe already existed'. Now, in the midst of the crisis of finance, markets and bureaucracies, we must commence to practise an egalitarian, peaceful, green and democratic Europe.

The initiators of this appeal included, among others, Rossana Rossanda, Mary Kaldor, Susan George, Elmar Altvater, Samir Amin, Philippe Askenazy, Zygmunt Bauman, Seyla Benhabib, Donatella della Porta, Trevor Evans, Nancy Fraser, Monica Frassoni, Paul Ginsborg, Rafael Grasa Hernandez, Dany Lang, Maurizio Landini, Giulio Marcon, Doreen Massey, Chantal Mouffe, Heikki Patomäki, Mario Pianta, Kari Polanyi Levitt, Wolfgang Sachs, Saskia Sassen and Peter Wahl. The Appeal was signed by more than one hundred personalities of European culture, politics and society.

The Appeal led to the international forum 'Another Road for Europe', held on 28 June 2012 at the European Parliament in Brussels, where participant organisations included Attac France, Attac Germany, Attac Finland, Corporate Europe Observatory, Economistes Atterrés, Euromemorandum, European Alternatives, European Anti-Poverty Network, European Federalist Movement, Fiom-Cgil, Green European Foundation, il Manifesto, Joint Social Conference, New Economics Foundation, OpenDemocracy.net, Red Pepper, Rete@sinistra, Rosa Luxembourg Stiftung, Sbilanciamoci!, Transform! Europe and Transnational Institute. Political forces were represented by 20 MEPs and national politicians from the Greens/EFA Group and the European United Left – who cooperated in the organisation of the event – as well as from the group of the Socialists and Democrats.

www.anotherroadforeurope.org

provide the context for European mobilisations. The lack of a European public space as an arena for common discussion and deliberation on shared problems is a well-known weakness of the European construction, and this has certainly influenced the inability of mobilisations to develop a common framing. But what may be more important today is the lack of a democratic politics at the European level that could provide an 'entry point' for contestation; European contention appears to be in search of the very 'site' of politics where contestation can take place. The 'dispersed' nature of European authority is a clear factor, with power distributed between the European Council, the Commission and the ECB and with a marginal role played by the European Parliament. The emphasis on intergovernmental decision making during the crisis has put national governments (apparently) at the centre of the European stage, where they have found themselves heavily constrained by supranational European authority – such as the 'independent' ECB – by the rise of German influence on EU policies and asymmetries in intergovernmental processes, and by the unchallenged power of finance in key areas.

With no 'site' of European contention, Europe-wide mobilisation has been limited. Social movements share a common 'diagnostic' (Snow and Benford 2000) analysis of the causes of the crisis: the power of finance and in the neo-liberal policies which for the last two decades have dominated Europe's economic governance. But the different groups that have been at the forefront of campaigns at the European level – from the trade unions to the new subterranean politics of the *Indignados* – do not share a common alternative vision, nor do they agree on possible solutions.

In this chapter, we have painted a rather grim picture of the state of European mobilisations against austerity and their capacity to articulate a credible alternative to the neo-liberal 'status quo'. However, to be fair, the discussion on how an alternative could be achieved through political processes – at both the European and national levels – was intensified with both the acceleration of social mobilisations in 2012 and preparations for the European elections of 2014. This development is the result of activists' efforts to rebuild cross-border connections among civil

Box 2.4   European Progressive Economists Network (Euro-pen)

A Common Call for Another Economic Policy for Europe
Florence 10+10 Forum, 9 November 2012

The European Progressive Economists Network brings together groups of economists and other researchers, institutes and civil-society coalitions who are critical of the dominant economic and social policies that have brought Europe to the current crisis. We seek to promote a European wide debate on policy alternatives based on the following six points.

1. Austerity policies should be reversed and the drastic conditionality imposed on countries receiving EU emergency funds must be radically revised, starting with Greece. The dangerous constraints of the 'fiscal compact' need be removed, so that countries can defend public expenditure, welfare and wages, while the EU assumes a greater role in stimulating demand, promoting full employment and taking a new course of sustainable and equitable progress. European policies should reduce current account imbalances by obliging surplus countries to also adjust.

2. Policies must favour a redistribution that reduces inequalities and move towards fiscal harmonization, putting an end to tax competition, with a shift of the tax burden away from labour and towards profits and wealth. Policies must favour public services and social protection. Labour and collective bargaining have to be defended; labour rights are a key part of Europe's democratic rights.

3. Facing Europe's financial crisis – marked by the interaction between a banking crisis and the public debt crisis – the European Central Bank must act as a lender of last resort in the government bond markets. The public debt problem has to be solved with a common responsibility of the eurozone; debt should be assessed by a public audit.

4. A radical downsizing of the financial sector is needed, with a financial transaction tax, the elimination of speculative finance and the control of capital movements. The financial system must be brought under social control; it must be transformed so that it promotes socially and environmentally sustainable productive investment and employment.

5. A fundamental ecological transition provides a way out of Europe's crisis. Europe must reduce its ecological footprint and its use of energy and natural resources. Its policies must enhance new ways of producing and consuming. A major investment programme promoting sustainability can provide high-quality jobs, expanding capabilities in new innovative fields and enlarging possibilities for action at the local level, especially on public goods.

6. Democracy has to be expanded at all levels in Europe. The European Union has to be reformed and the concentration of power in the hands of few states and unaccountable institutions that has taken place during the crisis has to be reversed. The aim is to achieve greater citizens' participation, a major role for the European Parliament and a much more significant democratic control over key decisions.

Facing a risk of collapse, Europe's policies need to change course. An alliance between civil society, trade unions, social movements and progressive political forces is needed to lead Europe out of the crisis created by neo-liberalism and finance. The European Progressive Economists Network seeks to contribute to this change.

The European Progressive Economists Network (Euro-pen) was launched at the Florence 10+10 forum by Euromemorandum, Another Road for Europe, Economistes Atterrés from France, Sbilanciamoci! from Italy, Econosphères from Belgium, Econonuestra from Spain, the Transnational Institute, Critical Political Economy Network, Transform! and other organisations.

The above document is the launch document.

http://www.euro-pen.org

---

society groups and shared proposals among experts' networks. In the coming years it is foreseeable that the search for a common framing and the construction of a common continental political space will constitute a crucial task for anti-austerity movements in their struggle to shape the future of a post-liberal Europe.

Notes

1. The other chapters in this book provide extensive evidence on the national specificities that have shaped the framing of contention, the mobilisation of

particular actors and the forms of action that have been adopted, leading to widely different patterns of activism.

2. 'Propuestas' (Proposals) document published on 16 May 2011. Last retrieved on 15 September 2013 at http://www.democraciarealya.es/documento-transversal/.

3. These policies are proposed in the organisation's document, 'Nuestra propuesta social, economica e politica' (Our social, economic and political proposal). Last retrieved on 14 September 2013 at http://www.asociaciondry.org/wp-content/uploads/2012/11/Asociaci%C3%B3n-DRY-Programa-desarrollado-y-objetivos-pol%C3%ADticos1.pdf.

4. In 2012, Greece witnessed two general elections. In the first, held in May, Syriza obtained over 16% of the vote and the elections produced a hung parliament, and new elections were called.

5. The figure refers to the Chamber of Deputies elections where the 5 Star Movement obtained 25.55% of the votes among Italian voters (excluding overseas voters). This put the party in second position, less than one percentage point away from the centre-left Partito Democratico.

References

Aglietta, M. (2012) *Zone euro. Éclatement ou fédération.* Paris: Michalon.

Attac (2011) *La piège de la dette publique. Comment s'en sortir.* Paris: Les liens qui libèrent.

Coats, D. (Ed.) (2011) *Exiting from the Crisis.* Brussels: European Trade Union Institute ETUI.

della Porta, D. (Ed.) (2007) *The Global Justice Movement. Cross-National and Transnational Perspectives.* Boulder, CO: Paradigm Publishers.

della Porta, D. and Caiani, M. (2007) 'Europeanisation from below? Social movements and Europe', *Mobilization*, 12(1), pp. 1–20.

Economistes atterrés (2011) *Manifeste des economistes atterrés.* Paris: Les liens qui libèrent.

Economistes atterrés (2012) *L'Europe Mal-Traité.* Paris: Les liens qui libèrent.

EuroMemo Group (2012) 'The Deepening Crisis in the European Union: The Need for a Fundamental Change', Euromemorandum 2013, Accessed online at http://www.euromemo.eu.

Gerbaudo, P. (2012) *Tweets and the Streets. Social Media and Contemporary Activism.* London: Pluto Press.

Gerbaudo, P. and Pianta, M. (2012) 'Twenty years of global civil society events: The rise and fall of parallel summits, the novelty of global days of action', in M. Kaldor, H. L. Moore and S. Selchow (Eds.) *Global Civil Society 2012. Ten Years of Critical Reflection.* Basingstoke: Palgrave, pp. 190–193.

Hoang Ngoc, L. (2011) 'L'Europe dans le piège de l'austérité. Bruxelles', *Group of Socialists and Democrats in the European Parliament.*

Hyman, R. (2005) 'Trade unions and the politics of the European social model', *Economic and Industrial Democracy*, 26(1), pp. 9–40.

Kaldor, M. and Selchow, S. (2015) 'Subterranean Politics in London', Chapter 1 of this volume.

Pianta, M. (2001) 'Parallel summits of global civil society', in H. Anheier, M. Glasius and M. Kaldor (a cura di) *Global Civil Society 2001*. Oxford: Oxford University Press.

Rossanda R. and Pianta M. (Eds.) (2012) 'La rotta d'Europa. 1, L'economia, 2', *La politica. Roma, Sbilanciamoci!, sbilibri*, pp. 2–3.

Snow, D. A. and Benford R. D. (2000) 'Framing processes and social movements: An overview and assessment', *Annual Review of Sociology*, 26, p. 611.

Tarrow, S. (1994) *Power in Movement: Social Movements, Collective Action, and Politics*. Cambridge: Cambridge University Press.

Utting, P., Pianta, M. and Ellersiek, A. (Eds.) (2012) *Global Justice Activism and Policy Reform in Europe. Understanding How Change Happens*. London: Routledge.

Watt, A. and Botsch, A. (Eds.) (2010) *After the Crisis*. Brussels: ETUI.

3

2011: Subterranean Politics and Visible Protest on Social Justice in Italy

Donatella della Porta, Lorenzo Mosca and Louisa Parks[1]

Introduction

Subterranean Politics (SP) was the initial idea behind the studies presented in this volume – but what does this really mean in the Italian context? The idea was to go beyond the study of 'civil society' or 'social movements' in order to focus on all that was extra-institutional in the recent protests that have swept across Europe. Rather than look at particular movements or themes, we therefore decided to focus on protest. For us this general term is key to our understanding of SP as essentially all extra-institutional manifestations of politics, expressed by any one of a variety of informal or formal actors, but all united in some form of dissatisfaction with institutional politics and its outputs. Protest, in its most encompassing sense (protest denoting anything from a letter to the editor to a mass demonstration) was what we singled out as a common activity for SP, and forms the basis of our search for SP in Italy (see the methodology section below). Our work leads us to conclude that SP in Italy is to be found in the practices of democracy unfolding in what are, for the most part, familiar and long-established formal and informal groups, but groups which are at the same time challenged by new events. In labour marches, for example, trust in political institutions and even trade unions fell sharply between the beginning of the new century and 2011. Social movement organisations continued to dominate the protest scene in Italy (while new actors were springing up in other countries, namely Occupy and the *Indignados*). However there was no business as usual. Rather, several of their claims resonated with those expressed by the newer groups, namely their calls for substantive and meaningful politics free from the tyranny of markets, and radical changes in the conception and practice of democracy. In sum, while the central organisations of Italian protest appear unchanged, the substance of beliefs and claims has shifted, and many new campaigns and networks are living out the kind of participatory democracy they call for in their actions and everyday organisation. This is how SP is now bubbling up in Italy: the organisational channels may be old and well worn, but the substance has a decidedly new hue.

Italy has long been recognised as a country with a rich history of contentious politics, and it was for this reason that we expected the new wave of square occupations in Europe, inspired by the events of the Arab Spring and indeed the protests seen in Iceland, would take hold and be reproduced in Italy. Yet when the *Indignados* movement did spread from Spain to Greece it saw a weak following in Italy. Some camps were set up in Italy's main cities, but they usually remained small in proportion. The global day of action on 15 October 2011 saw hundreds of thousands of demonstrators in Rome, but the day ended in violent outbursts that neither the protest organisers nor the police were able to control (della Porta and Zamponi 2013). A first puzzle we wanted to address in our research was therefore why Italy appeared to be so quiet in 2011. Was this a true social peace, or, as we indeed found, did the convergence of attention on the *Indignados* hide other contentious forms of actions on the issues of the financial crisis and the policies adopted to address it?

Attitudes towards Europe and the European Union (EU) formed another focus for our study. Given the specific pathologies of the Italian political system (magnified under Silvio Berlusconi's governments), Europe and the EU have been seen by collective actors and public opinion alike as potential sources of 'normalisation' and therefore regarded with more sympathy than in other European countries. At the same time, however, the financial crisis of 2011 was a 'European' crisis, and the EU institutions were feared (as in Spain and Greece) as the enforcers of austerity policies. How these two visions clashed, and/or were bridged, is another important question for understanding the emerging conceptions of democracy within Italian civil society. As we will see, trust in Europe and the EU has indeed taken a nosedive, with discourses framing the European Central Bank (ECB) as responsible for austerity and cuts, and 'Europe' as generally in thrall to its economic mission and actors alone. Europe, however, is still seen as the conduit best placed for bringing social justice back to the continent.

The chapter begins with a brief overview of our methodology, followed by a brief historical summary of protest time in Italy and a breakdown of the types and actors of protest in Italy in 2011. We then focus on democracy, then on Europe, drawing on the results of our frame analysis and survey data. Our conclusions develop the idea introduced above of the ideals and practices of the *Indignados* and Occupy movements finding their expression via different groups in the Italian context, in particular the referendum campaign, citizens' movements against large-scale infrastructure projects but also the many labour conflicts – against factory closures, dismissals and worsening market and labour conditions taking place throughout the year.

Introducing the research design

Our research on SP in Italy followed a research design structured in different phases (see Figure 3.1).

First, we employed Protest Event Analysis (PEA) – a methodology often used in social movement studies – and selected all articles covering protest events published by the Italian newspaper *La Repubblica* between 1 January and 31 December 2011. We decided to focus on *La Repubblica* as a source for protest event reports for two main reasons:

- accessibility – the full database of articles published since 1984 is publicly accessible from its website (www.repubblica.it);
- diffusion – it is one of the most widely read Italian newspapers.[2]

Notwithstanding its centre-left leaning – which means potentially more space devoted to protests and social movements than in centre-right oriented newspapers – it is worth noting that *La Repubblica* was one of the sponsors of the new government led by Mario Monti. We expect this to have affected its reporting of protests. This means that many underground and invisible actions, actors and events that occurred in Italy that year are likely to have been ignored. However, we decided to use PEA for the analysis of SP in Italy as we wanted to limit our focus

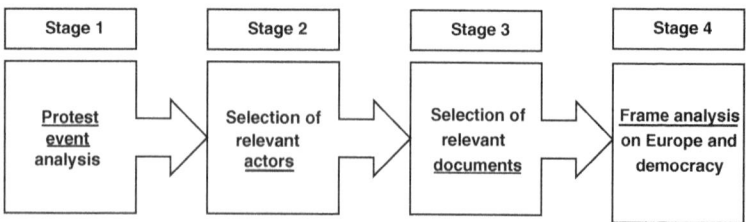

Figure 3.1   The different phases of the research design

to those social and political phenomena which attract public attention, bubbling up from SP to the public sphere. Other methodologies could be triangulated with PEA in order to understand how and how much subterranean and visible forms of politics from below are related. As we will see, protest is not only an instrument of well-organised actions, but is rather used by informal groups that from time to time bubble up and become visible.

Second, the PEA was useful not only to depict the characteristics of protest in Italy in 2011, but also allowed us to single out the main actors organising such protests. On the basis of this information we were able to compile a list of 95 actors. After further research the list was limited to 58 actors that we considered most relevant, ranging from trade unions to social centres, from women's groups to environmental organisations, from networks of precarious workers to anti-crisis groups (see Appendix). We then searched for these actors on the Internet, detecting their online presence. As we wanted to focus on online platforms describing the official position of the group on democracy and the future of Europe, we only selected websites, avoiding social network profiles for the following part of the analysis.

Third, we collected documents focusing on democracy and Europe from the websites of the groups involved in the protest events. The search was carried out using a function available on the Google search engine which allows the user to look for specific keywords within websites. The keywords used for searching for relevant documents were democracy 2011; Europe 2011; democracy 2012; and Europe 2012. On the basis of this research we located 797 documents. Because of time and resource restrictions, a random sample of documents was chosen from each of the organisations for a total of 140 documents, on which we performed a frame analysis. The codebook we elaborated aims at investigating conceptions of democracy among groups analysed as well as their framing linked to Europe and economic crises. We pay particular attention to diagnostic frames (what's wrong with Europe?), prognostic frames (what Europe do these groups want?) and mobilisation frames (how should social movements mobilise to struggle at the EU level?).

In addition, we draw on the results of surveys administered to Italian demonstrators involved in protest events during 2011, and compare them to similar surveys carried out over the past decade. The aim of these surveys was (amongst other aims) to understand their relationship with democracy and representative institutions, and with processes of Europeanisation and globalisation. These surveys were conducted within the research project 'Caught in the Act of Protest: Contextualizing Contestation' (CCC) (della Porta and Reiter 2012) on three marches that took place in Italy during 2011:

- Labour Day (LD): trade union march in Florence (1 May 2011);
- a protest on precarity issues: EuroMayDay (EMD) march in Milan (1 May 2011);
- an anti-austerity protest: national general strike (GS), Florence (6 May 2011).[3]

All three events took place in May 2011, and all focused on demands for social justice. These three cases represent different types of march. The first belongs to the long tradition of the May Day celebration, organised jointly by the three main Italian trade union confederations; the second involved young people facing precarious work conditions mobilising in a 'parade'; the third was the march that accompanied a general strike against austerity measures, called by the main Italian trade union, the Cgil (traditionally communist–socialist), but also joined by activists from other social movement organisations. While the issues are similar, we assume that the different characteristics of the demonstrators created different contexts that are interesting to compare.

Italian protest in 2011

In its recent and more remote history, Italy has been quite a contentious country. It produced one of the largest communist parties in Western Europe and a strong and politicised labour movement, often ready to join forces with other social movements on broad concerns of social justice. In the late 1960s and early 1970s, the Italian 'long autumn' was contrasted to the 'short French May' as the student movement was accompanied by a widespread cycle of protest (Tarrow 1989; della Porta 1995). In the 1980s and, especially, the 1990s, the collapse of 'real socialism' and the gradual strengthening of neo-liberal views had obvious repercussions on the Italian Left, but in the 2000s Italy harboured an extremely vital movement for global justice – the strength and influence of those mobilisations was testified to by the hosting of the first European Social Forum in Italy (della Porta et al. 2006; della Porta 2007, 2009).

What type of protest that took place in Italy in 2011 acquired visibility in the media, thereby emerging from the hidden domain of SP? PEA is a quantitative methodology which has been used to study the dynamics of protest in time and space. It was first employed, among others, by Charles Tilly and his colleagues during the 1970s to shed light on repertoires of collective action. Later on, PEA inspired other important studies on the American civil rights movement (McAdam 1982, 1999), the Italian cycle of protest during the 1970s (Tarrow 1989), new social movements in Western Europe (Kriesi et al. 1995) and the transformations of environmental activism in Europe (Rootes 2003). As observed by Koopmans and Rucht, 'it is a method that allows for the quantification of many properties of Protest, such as frequency, timing and duration, location, claims, size, forms, carriers, and targets, as well as immediate consequences and reactions (e.g., Police intervention, damage, counter protests)' (2002: 231). PEA has often been criticised for being based on newspaper reports of protests which are biased both in terms of their selection of events and their descriptions. Although we do not consider the sample of cases we collected as either complete (far from this, we know from previous research that less than 5% of protests are reported in the press) or representative of the broad range of protest, we think our mapping of protests reported in the press provides useful information on those protests which attracted public attention. Our interest is in fact in those protests that became visible in the press, 'bubbling up' from the underground domain of SP, as we assume that they had a greater influence on the public discourse.

In our study, PEA was carried out using a codebook to record the following information for each protest event: date and location of the event, actors participating in the protest, the issue of the protest, forms of protest, number of participants, targets of the protest event and their territorial levels, the main claims of the protest, and police reactions.[4]

At the end of the coding process we had detected 172 protest events for the year 2011 from the 215 articles located using the above-mentioned keywords (see Figure 3.2). First, we note a peak in contentious events in March, when protests mainly addressed the situation of North African immigrants on the small island of Lampedusa, the *ad personam* laws[5] passed by the Berlusconi government, and a government decision to cut incentives for renewable energies. Another peak in protest is noted for May, when government efforts to introduce evaluations of lower secondary schools (teaching quality and student ability in Maths and Italian) via a test was strongly opposed by rank-and-file unions and students themselves. It is also clear that after Berlusconi's resignation (12 November) and the formation of a government headed by Mario Monti supported by most political parties in parliament (Pdl,

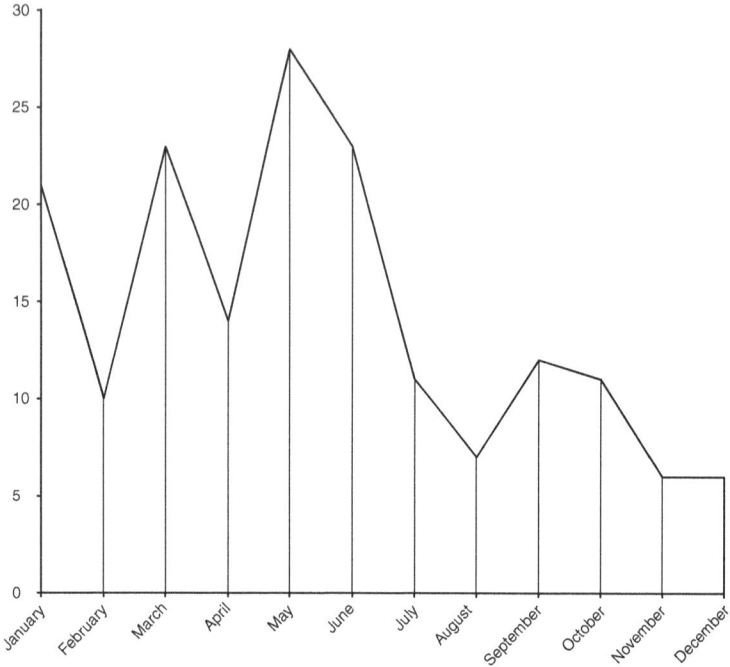

Figure 3.2   Protest events in Italy by month, year 2011 (absolute values)
Source: La Repubblica.

Pd, Udc), opportunities for protest strongly decreased in terms of both organisation and mobilisation in the streets and media coverage. Supported by a large coalition with the centre-left as minority partner, the Monti government was firmly backed by the president of the Republic and some media, which helped spread an image of a 'technical government'. Notwithstanding strong continuity between the Monti and Berlusconi governments in terms of the development of neo-liberal policies, the lack of potential allies in government initially thwarted protest.

As shown in Figure 3.3, informal groups are particularly numerous among the actors which attracted media coverage using protest. They can be considered the core of SP that bubbled up into the public sphere. In fact, the presence of traditional unions and formal groups – also relevant – can hardly be defined as belonging to this domain. Institutional actors and parties tend to avoid the use of protest, but when they do employ it they generally intervene in partnership with other actors, providing them with public visibility and recognition.

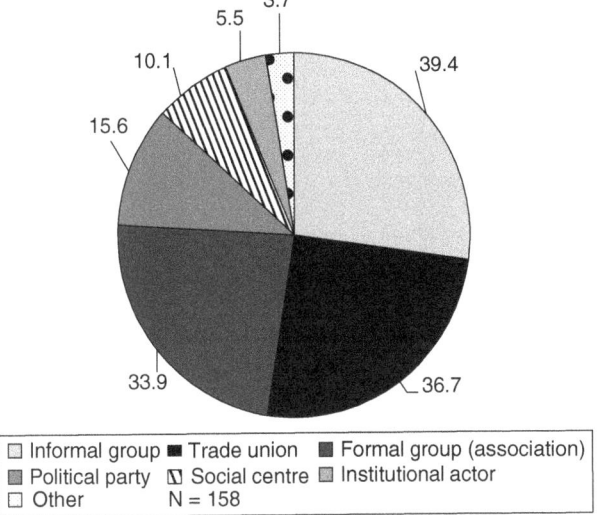

Figure 3.3 Type of actor involved in protest events (multiple responses, % of cases)

Table 3.1 Types of union involved in protest events (multiple responses, % of cases)

Union	%
Rank-and-file	67
Social democratic (Cgil–Fiom)	49
Catholic and socialist unions (Cisl–Uil)	6
Right-wing union (Ugl)	3
Other	9
Total (N)	44

Trade union protests covered by the print media (Table 3.1) are mostly promoted by underground groups (rank-and-file) which are present in both firms and new professions (i.e. call centre workers) that are generally ignored by traditional unions. However, among the latter both the leftist grouping (Cgil) and in particular its metalworkers' branch (Fiom) tend to be present in a significant share of events where a union intervened.[6]

As for the social groups most represented in the protest events covered by the newspaper (Table 3.2), we found that almost half of events

Table 3.2 Type of social group involved in protest events
(multiple responses, % of cases)

Social group	%
Workers	47.3
Students	21.8
Citizen(s) (in general)	13.6
Women	10.9
Precarious workers	10.0
Immigrants or ethnic minorities	10.0
Intellectuals/artists/journalists	10.0
Other	10.0
Total (N)	147

were initiated by workers, circa one-fifth by students, and one-tenth by
citizens in general and women. This comes as no surprise: as we have
seen, unions are one of the most common actors present in protest
events covered by the print media. Protests by students and women
are generally promoted by informal groups that are also very much
present among the groups which gain media coverage. The presence
of other marginal social groups such as precarious workers and immigrants is lower than expected, as is the presence of more influential
social groups such as intellectuals/artists/journalists. For the former
groups at least this is probably due to the fact that immigrants and
precarious workers tend to lack the resources needed to attract media
attention.

In regard to the repertoire of protest (Table 3.3), the different forms
of action were aggregated into macro-categories. While demonstrative
forms (marches, strikes and other symbolic forms of action) concern
almost 75% of the cases, perturbative (sit-ins, road blocks, disturbance of
public events), conventional (public letters, petitions, leafleting, assemblies) and violent forms (against property or persons) comprise between
18% and 24% of the cases. As tents in the streets and the occupation
of public squares represent a partial innovation in the repertoire of
collective action imported from the Arab Spring through the Spanish
acampadas and the Occupy movement, we coded this form as distinct
from the others. In around one-tenth of the cases protest took the form
of squatting buildings and occupying squares.

If we cross the repertoire of action with the type of groups protesting,
informal groups are more likely to resort to perturbative and violent
action while formal associations and institutional actors, parties and
unions tend to prefer demonstrative actions. This means that in order

Table 3.3 Repertoire of action (multiple responses, % of cases)

Forms of action	Institutional actors, parties and unions	Formal groups (associations)	Informal groups (including social centres)	All groups
Conventional	14	36	11	19
Demonstrative	84	77	62	74
Perturbative	27	13	30	24
Violent	19	7	27	18
Squat/occupation	14	0	16	11
Other	0	7	5	4
Total (N)	37	31	37	105

to emerge from the underground domain of SP, informal actors have to adopt radical forms of action.

Regarding the issue of protest events (Table 3.4), the most frequent concerns are work, the environment (both small-scale infrastructure and the opposition of large-scale infrastructure projects like the high-speed train in Val Susa), the economic crisis and gender (the dignity of women and Europride), as well as protests related to the laws of the Berlusconi government, perceived as threatening the freedom of information, the balance of power (justice reforms), the Constitution and democracy.

Some protests were specifically organised against Berlusconi because of sexual scandals, conflicts of interest and laws passed by his government. Around 10% of the protests were related to cuts to education and funds for culture, immigration and against war. There are interesting differences among the diverse groups: institutional actors, parties and unions are mainly mobilised on labour issues and the economic crisis, while fewer differences are found between formal and informal groups which focus mostly (albeit with different emphases) on freedom of information, democracy, justice and defence of the Constitution, as well as environmental issues, and mobilise against Berlusconi, on gender issues and against war. Emerging protest as represented by informal groups springing from the domain of SP tends to address a variety of issues beyond the economic crisis and labour.

According to our data, protests generally target the national government (Table 3.5). Also frequently targeted (especially by unions) are firms – in most cases the Italian car manufacturer Fiat, which imposed harsh conditions on its workers in 2011. Formal groups direct their action mostly towards the government. Only in a limited number of

Table 3.4   Issues of protest (multiple responses, % of cases)

Targets	Institutional actors, parties and unions	Formal groups (associations)	Informal groups (including social centres)	All groups
Environment	0	20	35	18
Work	41	0	8	17
Economic crisis	27	10	5	14
Freedom of information, democracy, justice, defence of the Constitution	5	29	11	14
Gender	5	16	11	11
Against Berlusconi	5	16	8	10
Education (school/university)	8	0	5	5
Against war	0	7	3	3
Immigration	3	0	3	2
Culture	3	0	0	1
Other	8	3	14	9
Total (N)	37	31	37	105

Table 3.5   Targets of protest (multiple responses, % of cases)

Targets	Institutional actors, parties and unions	Formal groups (associations)	Informal groups (including social centres)	All groups
Government	73	97	72	80
Firms	32	0	8	14
Police	0	3	11	5
Banks	3	3	6	4
Church	0	3	3	2
Parties	3	0	6	3
Other	5	7	0	4
Total (N)	37	31	36	104

cases did protests address the police (targeted especially by informal groups), banks, the church or political parties.

The main territorial level of the targets, as reported in the press, tends to be national in most cases (Table 3.6). However, the subnational

Table 3.6 Level of protest targets (multiple responses, % of cases)

Territorial level of targets	Institutional actors, parties and unions	Formal groups (associations)	Informal group (including social centres)	All groups
National	105	74	78	87
Subnational	8	13	17	12
Supranational	3	22	8	11
Unclear	0	3	3	2
Total (N)	37	31	36	104

Table 3.7 Selected actors (absolute values)

Type of actor	N
Environmental groups	11
Single-issue platforms	6
Social centres	6
Women's groups	5
Trade unions	5
Groups against the economic and financial crisis	4
Groups for the freedom of information and democracy	4
Groups against cuts to culture and entertainment	3
Groups mostly active online	3
Other groups	11
Total	58

(especially addressed by informal groups) and the supranational levels (particularly targeted by formal groups) are also addressed in around 10% of the cases each.

On the basis of the results of the PEA we created a list of actors that gained visibility in the press and emerged from the realm of SP, focusing in particular on informal groups (see Appendix for more details). As Table 3.7 shows, most deal with environmental issues (mostly mobilised against small-scale infrastructure). Among the selected groups we included both squatted, self-managed social centres (which engage in a variety of protests) and platforms focused on specific issues (peace, war, water, opposition to large-scale infrastructure) and on the organisation of specific protest events (i.e. the national demonstration organised for the global day of action on 15 October 2011). Women's groups and unions were also selected, along with groups against the effects of the financial crisis and related policies (the Italian incarnation of the

Indignados) and for the freedom of information and democracy (mostly mobilised against the policies of the Berlusconi government). During 2011 groups against cuts on culture and entertainment were also visible, as well as groups which are mostly active online. In the category 'other' we included groups of precarious workers, groups of students, groups against the Mafia, etc.

Claiming democracy

A great deal of the frames found in the documents we analysed focus on themes reflecting the idea introduced elsewhere in this volume that *it is all about politics*. These views are expressed in distrust of representative democracy and the politicians it produces. When speaking about democracy, all of the groups included in our frame analysis share a basic belief that representative democracy has failed at the national, European or indeed the global level. Italy's democracy comes in for particularly strong criticism, and feelings of near-complete alienation and animosity towards the country's politicians (of all colours, although the most vitriolic judgements are reserved for Berlusconi) are often expressed. In this vein, the views of the *Indignados*/Italian Revolution group are often expressed: 'We do not represent any party or association, and nobody represents us! And we say ENOUGH, ENOUGH of there being no way for the active and direct participation of citizens in decisions [...] BE OUTRAGED TOO!!! LESS POLITICIANS AND MORE DEMOCRACY!!!'[7] The No TAV group (see Box 3.1) is equally despairing:

> This leads us to understand that the State is no longer (or perhaps never was) that democratic institution in which many want to believe but only a fascist police-state seeking to silence the people who still have the courage to hold their heads high and demonstrate against something they disagree with using physical and legal repression![8]

The campaign for the referendum (see Box 3.2) is also linked to the wider crisis of democracy. For the 'vota sì per fermare il nucleare' committee:

> The referendum campaign thus constituted a formidable chance to reclaim debate and elaborate on national and global strategic questions on the ground: today, this makes it possible for us to weave local experiences into a more collective arena and in a perspective of a new national scale social and cultural mobilisation.[9]

Box 3.1   No TAV

The No TAV movement has been actively fighting against proposed high-speed train lines (Treni ad Alta Velocità – TAV) for nigh on 20 years in Italy. The most well-known and ongoing of these campaigns has unfolded in the mountains near Turin, against a line between Turin and Lyon in France. Originally, the arguments of the movement were framed in mostly environmental terms focusing on the damage that would be caused by the drilling of tunnels through the Alps. However, after being ignored by successive governments and dubbed troublemakers following increasingly violent protests, these arguments have in recent years been joined by frames focusing on the undemocratic exclusion of citizens from decisions surrounding the high-speed line, as well as on the economic consequences of the project in a context of deep financial crisis.

The positive outcome of the abrogative referendum has shown citizens that change can be achieved through direct democracy.

In addition to these frames, a substantive dimension of democracy is also stressed: democracy is not only participation, but the provision of public goods. A point made, among others, by Arci: 'To save Italy from crisis [...] large investment in common goods, in culture and in democracy, is needed. And only participation can restore dignity and value to a new politics, capable of carrying the country out of the disaster. All this is possible.'[10] Focusing attention on a democracy based on the common ownership of common goods is thus an important theme in encouraging democratic participation and decision making in the Italian context.

Corruption is also a recurring theme emerging in the frame analysis, and is seen as the reason behind growing anti-political feeling in the country. Claims about corruption are quite an innovation in left-wing social movement discourses, as it was previously considered a populist topic. The emerging evidence of Berlusconi's conflicts of interest, as well as accusations of *ad personam* laws, went a long way in sensitising the left to the social inequalities in which corruption is embedded. The *Indignados* movement also converged then in spreading anti-corruption claims in the left, pointing to the growing entanglement of politics and business. So, according to the Arci group, for example Italy was unable to rid itself of a discredited government because of the deep-seated

Box 3.2   Common goods

Common goods (*beni comuni*) was the main issue at stake in the abrogative referendum campaign that occupied Italian social movements in the first half of 2011. A first campaign focused on collecting enough signatures to trigger the referendum, and a second on securing four '*sì*' answers to the questions, which concerned the future of nuclear power, the privatisation of water and the possibility that government ministers might not be obliged to appear in court when accused of crimes. The referendum was seen both as an example and a chance to practice direct democracy by many groups, one that was all the more successful in the light of the government's attempts to scupper the vote (either by temporarily withdrawing the offending legislation or refusing to hold the vote on the same day as administrative elections and, according to a great number of groups, by ensuring scarce media coverage. The Monti government, as well as many local governments, including those led by the centre-left, now stands accused of ignoring the outcome of the referendum regarding the privatisation of water). The Arci group (the Italian Cultural and Recreational Association, founded in 1956 as a satellite of the communist party, but gaining autonomy since the 1990s), one of many involved in the campaign, described the referendum as an exercise in popular education, an experience that reinvigorated words such as rights, common goods, democracy. It wrote in fact that 'Defending the result of the referendum for public water will allow us to strongly state that only the value of participation can return dignity and value to a new politics, capable of guiding the country out of disaster.'[11] The rank-and-file trade union, Cobas, saw too the wide participation in the referendum as the 'rebirth of civil passion and participation from below. The revolution of common goods'.[12] Similarly for Libertà e Giustizia, direct democracy was a corrective for a representative system that had degenerated:

> In a system of representative democracy, the danger that the citizen will remain too distant from the palaces of government, that the citizen becomes a passive and ever more sceptical observer, always exists. Referenda are one of the few mechanisms outside of elections that allow citizens to make their voice heard.[13]

degeneration of its political system. Mentions of Mafia involvement in political decision making also fit into this discourse, especially among anti-Mafia groups, groups active on the waste disposal crisis in Campania, and citizens' groups from the earthquake-struck L'Aquila who lay the blame for bad decisions on corrupt politicians and contract-seeking Mafiosi. Generally, the diagnosis is that 'Corruption pollutes the processes of politics, threatens the standing and the credibility of institutions, pollutes and seriously distorts the economy, sucks resources destined for the good of the community, corrodes civic responsibility and democratic culture itself.'[14]

Extensive campaigns against *ad personam* laws proposed by the Berlusconi government also brought to the fore accusations of government corruption and attacks on the Italian Constitution and thus democracy (from the association Libertà e Giustizia in particular). Defending the Constitution, characterised as the ideal form of Italian democracy, is a recurring theme for a majority of the groups in this case, as exemplified in the text of this typical call for participation by the anti-Mafia group Agende Rosse, which refers poignantly to the principle of equality before the law, flaunted by Berlusconi: 'For years we have witnessed attacks on the principles of the Constitution born of the Resistance, on the rights it sanctions, on the principle of equality for all before the law that is at the foundation of a democratic State'.[15]

These themes raised in the frame analysis find confirmation in the results of the surveys among demonstrators which highlight a sharp dip in levels of trust among citizens in both institutions and politicians. Trust is lowest for the national government, and only very slightly higher for the national parliament (only 2.4% for EMD, 5.9% for GS and 10.7% for LD). Trust in political parties is also extremely low. While participants in all three of the demonstrations where surveys were administered equally mistrust the national government, for all other institutions and collective actors trust declines from the LD, to the GS, to the EMD participants. This is all the more true for political parties and trade unions. The percentage of activists that trusts political parties 'quite a lot' or 'very much' rises from 1.6% for the EMD parade to 15.2% for the LD march; it is significant that even GS participants, traditionally attributed to the Old Left, express minimal trust in parties (5.9%). Trust in trade unions is higher, but still low considering that these demonstrations were called by the unions themselves. Here too the three demonstrations present different images: only in the LD march is trust in unions expressed by slightly more than half of participants (52.3%), while in both the other demonstrations it remains well below

---

Box 3.3   Freedom of information

Strongly linked to all diagnoses of what is wrong with Italy's democracy are discourses about the manipulation of the media and information. Ex-Prime Minister Berlusconi, an owner of countless private media outlets and the ultimate power over the state broadcaster Rai, is obviously the target for (usually well-founded) accusations of media bias, manipulation or straightforward silencing. Indeed, the representation of women in the media and its repercussions for democracy was one of the triggers behind the widespread women's protests in the country (combined with the sexual scandal 'Ruby-gate') seen with the emergence of the new *Se non ora, quando?* (If not now, when?) movement.

In a wider perspective of ideas of democracy, Italian groups saw the provision of complete and unbiased information as a central theme of their struggle. Two groups, Articolo 21 and Valigia Blu, are exclusively devoted to defending journalists' rights and providing alternative sources of information.[16] The threat to democracy constituted by media manipulation is clear in the view of the No TAV movement:

> Between the real country, lived on the street and recounted on the web, and the virtual country lived in armchairs and recounted by newspapers and TV, is an abyss to the point of two antithetical universes with no contact between them. All the people who don't have the ability, the time or the wish to tap into the information battle on the internet, and who make up the vast majority of the population, remain relegated to a virtual world, built ad hoc to marginalise them from reality [...].[17]

Most groups claim that, without information, democracy cannot be achieved in the country.

---

that mark (18.7% for EMD and 34.7% for GS). However, this mistrust is not uniformly applicable (marchers did express their faith in the judiciary, for example, and to a great extent the EU as we will see below).

Comparing these data to those collected on the same battery of questions at other marches in Italy since 2001 allows us to understand whether levels of trust have changed over time among Italian demonstrators. The comparisons show that trust in national institutions and traditional actors (parliament, parties and trade unions) is lower than registered at the demonstrations surveyed at the beginning of the decade (della Porta et al. 2006). The decline of trust in political parties and parliament is the most striking, with those trusting it to either a large extent or broadly dropping from about a quarter of marchers to just 7% for political parties and from about one-fifth to just 6% for parliament, if we compare the 2011 data with that recorded during the anti-G8 protest in 2001. The data on the Italian participants in the first European Social Forum (ESF) in Florence in 2002 and in the Global Day of Action against the war on Iraq on 15 February 2003 (especially compared with data on the Peace March from Perugia to Assisi which took place after 11 September 2001) had already registered this declining trend. In contrast, there is an increase in trust in the EU, which rises from a quarter to almost half of the demonstrators, while trust in the UN tends to oscillate between the various demonstrations.

Another battery of questions confirms the low level of confidence in parties and representative institutions. Politicians are considered to fail to fulfil their promises, and voting in elections is seen as (much) less useful than unconventional forms of participation. There is in fact broad agreement that 'most politicians make a lot of promises but do not actually do anything'. If confidence in politicians is extremely low, there is nevertheless confidence in the capacity of citizens to make an impact on political decisions, especially if they organise and do so transnationally. Here too, looking at the two items for which we have comparative data for past protests (in particular to the Global Day of Action in 2003), we note a strong increase of mistrust in politicians (from 66.9 to 95.1%) but a decline in mistrust in elections (from 35.9 to 22.9%).

This mistrust does not however bring about either a lack of commitment or mistrust in politics. Not only do protestors trust citizens to influence political decision, they also ask for power to be handed back to political institutions. Protestors address a multi-level system of governance and, as we will see in the following, they ask for the strengthening, at all geographic levels, of politics over markets.

Alongside more specific accusations about the Berlusconi-induced decline of democratic quality of public institutions lies a more general disillusionment with representative democracy. Resonant with the discourse of the *Indignados* movement, representative democracy is in particular seen as not representative of people, but of banks and financial power. A number of groups, including the Italian Indignati,

Anonymous Italy and Comitato No Debito thus refer to powers outside the country as responsible for a degradation in democracy. The Draghi Ribelli group (a play on the surname of the Italian president of the ECB, Mario Draghi, meaning 'rebellious dragons') described an 'economic dictatorship' in their call for participation in an Anti-banks Day,[18] for example, while the *Indignados* group in Rome, Assemblea San Giovanni, offered the following analysis:

> The will and the aim of the system is the accumulation of wealth, which takes precedence over the efficiency and wellbeing of society. It wastes resources, destroys the planet, creates unemployment and unhappy consumers.

> The citizens are gears in a machine designed to enrich a minority who are entirely unaware of our needs. We are anonymous, but without us none of this would exist, it is us that moves the world.[19]

This 'anti-banks' discourse also leads to the argument that 'those who created the debt should pay it' (*La crisi va pagata da chi l'ha provocata*), often claimed by Cobas, among many others, and which is in turn one of the strongest justifications for many groups' proposals as to what a radical new democracy *should* be. The Assemblea San Giovanni group is very eloquent in describing what democracy is and is not in their eyes. The following citation from the manifesto of the group 'Real democracy now' makes their views clear:

> The priorities of any advanced society must be: equality, progress, solidarity, freedom of access to culture, ecological sustainability and development, wellbeing and people's happiness.

> There are fundamental rights that should be protected in these societies: the right to housing, work, culture, health, education, political participation, free personal development and consumers' rights to access to those goods necessary for a healthy and happy life.

> The current functioning of our economic system of government is not able to face up to these priorities and constitutes an obstacle to human progress [...].[20]

The survey evidence bears out this lack of patience with the results of neo-liberal globalisation, seen not as an opportunity for economic growth, but rather as the main cause of increased inequality which requires the building of global governance institutions. The demonstrators at the three marches display very little difference in this aspect. Between 11% (for GS) and 26% (for EMD) only believe that neoliberal globalisation can provide opportunities for economic growth, while more than 80% (over all demonstrations) think that globalisation increases inequalities, and even more (86%) believe it requires institutional control through the building of institutions of global governance (79% for EMD, 87% for LD and 90% for GS).

The condemnation of current systems, accused, in a nutshell, of no longer representing the majority of ordinary citizens but instead a minority of financially powerful actors thus leads groups to reflect on what kind of democracy they want to develop. Their visions can be loosely summarised as a wish for more participatory and direct democracy, and for citizens to hold more decision-making power. A common theme is bringing decision making and power back down to local levels, to bottom-up democracy. Some groups speak of rejuvenated and empowered local government (Action-diritti in movimento, citizens' committees from L'Aquila, environmental committee 'no tubo'), self-determination (citizens' committees in Campania) and subsidiarity (Libertà e Giustizia) and the world social forum (Arci), but all groups share the general view that (non-violent) participation is an essential component of true and direct democracy. For Libertà e Giustizia, among others, citizen participation is sparked by their wish to look after 'common goods' and is seen as the best way of interacting with institutions that should fulfil that role. For other groups including Arci, Assemblea San Giovanni and the *Indignados*, participatory democracy is built on the model of assemblies held in squares, where citizens deliberate decisions. Common goods and citizens' assemblies form the bases of two main sources of inspiration for practising these democratic ideals in a concrete manner. We shall look at each in turn.

Living democracy

As hinted at above, more telling than descriptions of an ideal democracy are these groups' efforts to experiment and live out those democratic ideals (della Porta 2009, 2013). Many of the groups convey the idea that the crisis is not all doom and gloom, but also an opportunity to invent alternatives and for creating happiness. Participation and protest in this view are seen as transformative, as a means of living out 'real' democracy. For example, the Coordinamento Regionale Rifiuti Campania seeks to

---

Box 3.4   The influence of the *Indignados*

The Spanish *Indignados* (in turn seen as inspired by the Arab Spring and events in Iceland) and their method of open and democratic meetings in public squares based on rules of mutual respect and inclusion, have great influence on the democratic experiments practised by the Italian movement of the same name as well as others, and are cited as an admirable example by yet more. The Italian Revolution or Indignati group eloquently sums the idea up, stating that 'doing the thing that you wish to say is the best way of saying it. In this case, thousands of citizens are calling for democracy by practicing it in the first person in the square and sharing this practice with thousands of others who feel the same need'.[21] By organising their movement on the basis of non-violence, participation and inclusiveness, with no leaders or flags (no matter how slow this may be), an important point is demonstrated and those that become involved are transformed by their experience: the change towards real democracy must first take place within each citizen through participation, then at the societal level. Thus, despite the relatively limited spread of the *Indignados* by name, the nature of this movement can be said to have influenced Italian SP in 2011.

---

redefine the waste crisis in the Naples region by labelling it a resource, an opportunity for the area to begin a new economy based on valorisation of the land and recycling.[22] The No TAV movement is also supported and cited for its experiments in democracy, the protection of common patrimony and resistance to state violence.

The more or less permanent occupations of squares and other spaces are seen in the light of creating a new agora in a publicly owned space ('Because the squares belong to us and they are location of a new communitarian and participatory democracy')[23], and experiments with 'new democracy' are seen not as rehearsals but as the beginnings and the foundations of the solution to problems of democracy all the way up to the global level. The argument is compelling and solidarity and support is widespread from the constellation of Italian movement groups. Even Anonymous Italy, a hacker group based on anonymity, cites inspiration by the rules of Spanish *Indignados* assemblies for active participation and coming up with proposals and collaborations.

In sum, those groups involved in Italian SP share a general feeling of indignation and disgust towards their national politicians and institutions, seeing them as corrupt, distant, manipulating, money-grabbing and in any case controlled by banks and shady figures from the worlds of finance and the Mafia. Europe, although seen as less inherently bad, is also described as a Europe of the banks, based solely on the logic of the single currency and the stability pact, in thrall to its central bank and supranational financial institutions. This bleak picture is contested not only through words and ideals of a new democracy, but also through the practice of the participatory and direct democracy they wish to see both within Italy and throughout the world, most notably in the campaign for the 2011 referendum on public goods, the No TAV movement and to a lesser (but more wordy) extent in the occupied squares and public assemblies of the *Indignados* movement. The movement organisations we have investigated therefore show themselves to be promoters of 'another politics', against the degeneration of institutional politics, rather than anti-political.

Changing Europe

In line with other findings on the invisibility of Europe in this volume, Europe is generally less of a pressing subject in its own right for Italian groups involved in SP: just under half of those groups that 'bubbled up' to the surface and thus included in the frame analysis (20 out of 44) refer to Europe in any way (Table 3.8). Of those that do talk about Europe, 36% do so to criticise what Europe (or rather, the EU) is (diagnostic framing), 23% to talk about what Europe should be (prognostic framing) and 22% refer to the forms of action needed to change Europe from below (mobilisation framing).

Among the groups that do talk about Europe, we decided to investigate potential effects of organisational age on framing – would older

Table 3.8   Visions of Europe by age of the organisations (mean values)

Year founded	Talking Europe	Diagnosis	Prognosis	Mobilisation
Before 2008	0.3339	0.2829	0.2065	0.1871
After 2008	0.5367	0.4070	0.2409	0.2405
Total	0.4584	0.3590	0.2276	0.2199
(N)	44	44	44	44

Note: all variables concerning Europe are dummies.
Average values can vary between 0 and 1.

Table 3.9   Diagnostic frames on Europe

Diagnostic frame	%
Europe of the market/neo-liberal Europe	40
Europe of banks, financial power	33
Europe of the elites/bureaucrats/from above	20
Fortress Europe	10
EU democratic deficit	8
Intergovernmental Europe (i.e. too much power to the member states)	8
Other	31
Total (N)	20

groups be more likely to refer to the historical reasons for and potential of Europe, while younger groups see it exclusively in terms of cuts imposed during the economic crisis? We distinguished between those groups created before the economic crisis (2008) and those created afterwards. The groups that were founded or created during and after the economic crisis refer to Europe in their documents more than the older ones. However, this concerns only half. While the younger groups are more keen to criticise Europe (diagnostic frames), only one out of four made suggestions as to how Europe should change by engaging in prognostic framing, or explained how should they mobilise to achieve such goals by using mobilisation frames.

We now turn to talk about the actual content of the frames produced by the organisations. The percentages quoted here are calculated referring only to those groups that talk about Europe, while those that remained silent were excluded from the analysis.

Generally, our frame analysis shows that the idea of the EU is not in itself widely condemned. As Table 3.9 demonstrates, frames condemning the fabric of the EU, such as those attacking the democratic deficit or the intergovernmental nature of the organisation, are much less widespread than those condemning the perceived neo-liberal direction of its policies, something that may be corrected (Europe together with the banks and neo-liberalism).

Democracy (or the lack thereof) is a central concern here as well. The content of these frames stigmatising a market-oriented Europe often uses the word 'impose' – Europe is mentioned as the body imposing austerity cuts on its unfortunate members. The group Action-diritti in movimento provides a good summary of the arguments leading to this frame: ' ... the only form the European Union has historically given itself: that defined by the single currency. Since its beginnings, the construction sanctioned by the Maastricht agreements has shown itself to be the steel cage within which national policies cutting transfers to local bodies have been placed and justified ... '.[24] Yet the same document also goes on to talk about the development of a political and social Europe, thus confirming the interpretation that Europe as a vehicle for government in itself may be salvaged. Much as the Italian Constitution is seen as a source of true democracy and something to be protected, so is the idea of Europe.

This view is also expressed by the marchers surveyed in the 'Caught in the Act of Protest: Contextualising Contestation' (CCC) project, already mentioned. They demonstrate scepticism that the EU presents an alternative model to neo-liberalism or mitigates the most negative effects of neo-liberal globalisation. Rather, they see the EU as an institution that promotes neo-liberalism – as did many groups in the frame analysis. The percentage of those who believe that the EU strengthens neo-liberalism is around 60, rising to 73 among the EMD protestors. In parallel, 37% believe that the EU mitigates the most negative effects of neo-liberal globalisation (including 31% of EMD participants); 35% that it defends an alternative and more solidarity-based social model (but only 18% of EMD marchers).

Reflecting and indeed surpassing the findings of the frame analysis (in that they demand more power for all territorial levels), and reflecting the previously noted themes of politics and democracy, while extremely critical of the workings of existing institutions, our activists expressed a very strong search for politics – to the point of demanding increased power for the very institutions they mistrust. Mistrust and disappointment in neo-liberal Europe among the survey respondents does not, therefore, mean that they write off Europe all together as it may first appear. When moving from the assessment of responsibility to potential solutions, they agree that it is necessary to strengthen all levels of governance. On the national level in particular, positions are rather different from those expressed by ESF activists in 2002, and the national level is the only one that registers virtually no difference between the three demonstrations. On average, among the three demonstrations in 2011, 73.3% of the protestors called for the EU to be strengthened (compared with 43% at the first ESF in Florence) and 70.5% for the local level of government to be strengthened, while 53.9% favoured strengthening at the national level (compared with 22% in Florence) and 51.3%

Table 3.10   Prognostic frames on Europe

Prognostic frame	%
Europe of the citizens/from below	15
'Open' Europe	10
A democratic Europe	10
A social Europe	8
A political Europe	7
EU control of banks and finance	3
EU citizenship to residents	3
A federal Europe	3
Other	32
Total (N)	20

supported the building of institutions of world governance (compared with 65% in Florence) (della Porta and Giugni 2009: 94).

Strengthening the EU is not mentioned as such by the groups talking about Europe in our frame analysis. Instead, as Table 3.10 shows, they make more reference to a Europe of the citizens, an open Europe and a democratic Europe, although it may well be that these ideas were in the minds of the survey participants when they spoke of strengthening the European level. In this vein, the groups underline the importance of their role in developing new practices of democracy, thus giving substance to their wish of spreading their new practices of democracy to other levels of government. The role of civil society in an eventual participatory European democracy is spelled out most clearly by the Arci group in its capacity as a leading member of the European Civic Forum: 'Participatory democracy responds to the current demands of European governance, completing and reinforcing representative democracy. The participation and involvement of organised civil society in the processes of policy formation and decision-preparation reinforces the democratic legitimacy of public institutions, their work and activities.'[25] Although this is rather institution-friendly language, other more radical groups express similar ideas. The Italian indignati groups, for example, are very critical of Europe, yet state that they 'want to be responsible protagonists of a new Italy, and new Europe and a new world based on solidarity and the respect of all'.[26]

As noted for the activists of the ESF a decade ago, the 'subterranean groups and protestors' we analysed here 'do not seem to be Eurosceptics, wanting to return to an almighty nation state, but rather "critical Europeanists" (or "critical globalists"), convinced that transnational

Table 3.11 Mobilisation frames on Europe

Mobilisation frame	%
To protest in the street	29
To form loose alliance	18
To assemble in European forums	6
Other	16
Total (N)	20

institutions of governance are necessary, but that they should be built from below' (della Porta and Giugni 2009: 94).

Finally, Table 3.11 shows that among the groups talking about Europe in our frame analysis, mobilising in order to change Europe means protesting in the streets – at the national level – and in some cases forming loose alliances. Mobilising transnationally does not then seem to be an option coming to the fore in the repertoire of these groups, at least from the reading of their documents. Rather, each country or locality must mobilise alone, albeit in loose solidarity with the efforts of those in other contexts. Additional support for this comes from some anecdotal advice on the end of the ESF cycle of mobilisation, with just 6% of the groups speaking of European forums as a venue for mobilisation.

This seems markedly different to the previous wave of protests that grew at the turn of the millennium on issues of global justice (della Porta et al. 2006). When main concerns move from global inequalities to national austerity politics it seems that protests also 'scale down' to the national level. While both waves of protest talk a cosmopolitan language, claiming global rights and blaming global financial capital, the global justice movement moved through the transnational to the national (and the local), while the new wave has taken the reverse route. In fact, protests followed the geography of the emergence of the economic crisis, which hit European countries with different impacts and at different times. For the most recent wave of protest too, research has already singled out numerous examples of cross-national diffusion of frames and repertoires of action from one country to the next. Direct, face-to-face and mediated contacts have contributed to bridging the protest in various parts of the world in a sort of upward scale shift. Suffice it to say that on 15 October 2011, a Global Day of Action launched by the Spanish *Indignados* produced demonstrations worldwide: protest events were registered in 951 cities in 82 countries, reflecting the wired nature of ties between the different SP groups across the continent. As one of us recently wrote:

> The degree of transnational coordination of the protest seems however lower than for the Global Justice Movement at the turn of the millennium, for which the World Social Forum and then the macro-regional Social Forum had represented a source of inspiration and offered arenas for networking. At the same time, surveys carried out in various European countries indicated a growing importance given to the national level of government. The forms of transnational brokerage in the newest social movements emerged as, if not weaker, at least different: more grassroots and mediated through new media. Faced with different timings and depths of the financial crisis, mobilizations were also more sensitive than the global justice movements – mobilized on common transnational events – to national political opportunities (or the lack thereof).
>
> (della Porta 2012)

Conclusion

To address the first puzzle mentioned at the beginning of this chapter, we can state that even though the *Indignados* as such were less visible in Italy than in other Southern European countries, this does not entail that there was no contention on social issues. On the contrary, 2011 saw the development of many protests, mainly addressing issues of work and other social rights. Protests were organised by unions, but also by social movement organisations, and used a variety of forms. We also noted a surge in the numbers of small, informal groups protesting in Italy in 2011 – groups that appear from our analysis to be most indicative of SP in the country outside more established types of organisations that have historically dominated contentious politics in Italy. SP has also found its way into more established organisations through the changed priorities and claims of individuals, however. Focusing on protest as a trait common to all extra-institutional organisations in its widest sense therefore proved a fruitful beginning to identifying SP. Despite drawbacks related to journalistic bias, this allowed us to gain a good overview of those SP groups that did bubble up to the surface, thereby having greater impacts.

According to the newspapers analysed, the protests we uncovered mainly addressed the national government. If we look at the data from the frame analysis of organisations involved in the protest and at survey data on protest participants, we see that issues of democracy are key. Here we can note an apparent paradox. The activists and their organisations are very critical of existing representative institutions, which they mistrust and disagree with. Nevertheless, they ask for those institutions to be strengthened. In order to surmount the financial crisis they believe the world needs more democracy (rather than a government of experts) and more politics (rather than the market). This is true also for the European level, which is perceived at the same time as a source of problems and one of potential solutions. In this sense, social movement activists emerge as 'critical Europeanists', criticising the EU policies as neo-liberal and its politics as lacking democratic legitimacy, but also asking for a social Europe and another democracy (della Porta 2009).

Our frame analysis also helps to explain the apparent lacklustre performance of the *Indignados* movement. Two main focal points for discourses on democracy were identified from the documents authored by groups active in SP in Italy: the June 2011 referendum on public goods and the inspiration drawn from the Spanish *Indignados* movement. The referendum campaign documents uniformly denounced attempts at boycott from the national government, as well as a general silence in the country's media – a situation which may have spilled over into a comparative lack of coverage in the print press.[27] To boot, the referendum campaign generally involved collecting signatures to trigger the vote, and information campaigns to convince citizens to vote, neither of which involved large levels of attention-grabbing protest. Second, and in common with the *Indignados* movement (and indeed the No TAV movement), the referendum campaign was also identified as about living out experiments in democracy at least as much as about demanding democracy in large-scale protests. Judging from the minutes of lengthy assemblies of *Indignados* camps and the much more common daily assemblies in various cities in Italy, engaging in deliberative processes, made up of the exchange of arguments in an open and participatory environment, formed the core of the agenda. In sum, while visible protests and large occupations seem indeed to be missing from the Italian context, a 'quieter' focus on the practice of democracy at the micro, local level with a view to networking towards a national, European or global democratic goal seems to be very much present in a variety of contexts. SP in Italy thus appears to be gently simmering rather than exploding through cracks.

To conclude, concepts such as localists, nationalists and cosmopolitans have often been used in the social sciences. In particular, the young and highly educated seem more and more cosmopolitan, both in their life practices and in their values. At the same time, the 'losers' of globalisation seem to have returned to nationalist (and populist) identities (Kriesi et al. 2008). Previous research has also indicated that dimensions such as identification with a territorial level and assessments on the performance of that level of governance can be discrepant. In fact, research on the ESF has singled out the presence of critical Europeanists: social movements emerged as very critical of the policy and politics of the EU, but at the same time identified themselves as Europeans, developed projects for 'another Europe' and mobilised transnationally in their support (della Porta 2009; della Porta and Caiani 2009). While the trend towards cosmopolitanism seemed to be linked to growing economic globalisation as well as worldwide social exchanges, the recent wave of protest on financial crises emerged as very much focused on the national level (Kriesi 2011). While cross-national diffusion did take place (della Porta 2011), the development of broker institutions such as the ESF continues to be lacking. *Indignados* and the Occupy Wall Street demonstrators are very concerned about democracy: disappointed by the bad performances of representative democracy, they propose and practice alternative (participatory and deliberative) conceptions that do, however, seem to address more a local than a supranational level (della Porta 2013). This story holds in Italy according to our investigations into SP in 2011 – practising democracy is the main focus, while its transfer to European and global levels is seen through some kind of 'trickle-up' process.

If this was the picture in 2011, the following year seemed to have brought some innovations. After the initial decline of protests (or at least, protest visibility) during the grand coalition government, led by Mario Monti, attempts at bridging the thousand underground rivers of SP are under way. The many, if fragmented, protests of workers, students and other actors calling for social rights and democracy have succeeded in breaking the wall of silence around the 'political' nature of a government that pretended to be 'just' technical. Faced with the government implementation of drastic austerity measures within a neo-liberal policy agenda and the bipartisan support they received, the mobilisations of 2012 seem to be moving towards some aggregation at both national and European levels, joining the broad contention in Spain, Greece and Portugal. If and how this will happen is a topic that deserves further research.

Appendix

Type of actor	N
Environmental groups	11

- Comitati campani contro gli inceneritori
- Comitati cittadini di Riano e Corcolle
- Comitato cittadini per l'ambiente Sulmona
- Comitati di lotta contro la discarica di Terzigno
- Comitato 'No Tubo'
- Greenpeace Italia
- Legambiente
- Sos Rinnovabili
- Zero Waste

Platforms 6

- Coordinamento 2 aprile
- Coordinamento 15 ottobre
- Forum dell'acqua
- No Dal Molin
- No TAV
- Tavola della

Social centres 6

- Centro sociale Askatasuna (Torino)
- Centro sociale Bottiglieria (Milano)
- Centro sociale Cantiere (Milano)
- Centro sociale Pedro (Padova)
- Centro sociale Rivolta (Venezia)
- Centro sociale 'Zero81' di Napoli

Women's groups 5

- Associazione Filomena
- Comitato 'Pari o Dispare'
- Di Nuovo
- Se non ora quando
- Usciamo dal Silenzio

Trade unions 5

- Cgil
- Cobas
- Cub
- Fiom
- Usb

(Continued)

Type of actor	N
Groups against the economic and financial crisis	4
– Assemblea di San Giovanni	
– Comitato nazionale 'No Debito'	
– Draghi Ribelli	
– Indignati	
Groups for the freedom of information and democracy	4
– Articolo 21	
– Libertà e Giustizia	
– Popolo Viola	
– Valigia Blu	
Groups against cuts in culture and entertainment	3
– Movimento centoautori	
– Teatro Valle Occupato	
– ZeroPuntoTre	
Groups mostly active online	3
– Anonymous Italia	
– Avaaz Italia	
– MoveOn Italia	
Other groups	11
– Action	
– Agende Rosse	
– Arci	
– Collettivo Senza Tregua	
– Emergency	
– EuroPride	
– Grillini/Movimento 5 stelle	
– Il nostro tempo è adesso	
– Libera	
– Movimento artigiani e commercianti liberi	
– Radio Aut	
Total	58

Notes

1. Although the authors share responsibility for the whole article, Louisa Parks wrote Sections 1 and 4, Lorenzo Mosca wrote Sections 2 and 3 and Donatella della Porta wrote Sections 5 and 6.
2. The keyword used in searching for relevant articles in the newspaper database is 'protest' for the year 2011.
3. For information on the methodology see della Porta and Reiter (2012). The surveys were organised with the collaboration of Massimiliano Andretta, Stefania Milan and Federico Rossi.

4. The coding, performed by Louisa Parks, was preceded by two tests in order to check the validity of the indicators included in the codebook as well as to adjust it to international standards.
5. Essentially these laws were seen as designed purely for the purpose of helping Berlusconi out in the large number of legal proceedings to which he is subject.
6. While often present in protest events, major conflicts have arisen during the past decade between Cgil and Fiom. The former is often accused by the latter for its subalternity towards Confindustria (employers' association) while the latter of maximalism. In Table 3.1 we treat them together because Fiom forms part of the Cgil confederation.
7. http://www.italianrevolution.org/tag/siamo-qui-per-prendercelo, accessed 30 March 2012. All quotations are taken from Italian documents translated by Louisa Parks.
8. http://www.notav.eu/article-print-5564.html, accessed 28 March 2012.
9. http://www.fermiamoilnucleare.it/?p=4961, accessed 5 March 2012.
10. http://www.arci.it/speciale/iniziative/il_26_novembre_in_piazza_per_lacqua _i_beni_comuni_e_la_democrazia_difendiamo_lesito_referendario_per_una _politica_nuova/index.html, accessed 7 March 2012.
11. http://www.arci.it/area_riservata/notizie_dallinterno/26_novembre_manife stazione_nazionale_acqua_pubblica__beni_comuni_e_la_democrazia/index .html, accessed 15 March 2012.
12. http://www.cobas.it/Acqua-e-Nucleare/Nucleare/VITTORIA-REFERENDARIA -DEL-12-13-GIUGNO-2011, accessed 2 March 2012.
13. http://www.libertaegiustizia.it/2011/05/27/giu-le-mani-dai-referendum/, accessed 6 March 2012.
14. http://www.libera.it/flex/cm/pages/ServeBLOB.php/L/IT/IDPagina/1/YY/ 2011/MM/12. Document authored by Libera and Avviso Pubblico, accessed 5 April 2012.
15. http://www.19luglio1992.com/index.php?option=com_content&view =article&id=4331:le-agende-rosse-aderiscono-alla-manifestazione-a-difesa -della-costituzione&catid=42:documenti, accessed 15 March 2012.
16. These two groups are not, however, included in the frame analysis since they are dedicated to news services rather than commentary.
17. http://www.notav.eu/modules.php?name=News&file=article&sid=5514, accessed 28 February 2012.
18. http://occupiamobankitalia.wordpress.com/appello-12-ottobre, accessed 29 March 2012.
19. http://www.italianrevolution.org/italia-indignataalzati-e-cammina, accessed 30 March 2012.
20. See Note 10.
21. http://www.italianrevolution.org/276, accessed 30 March 2012.
22. See www.rifiuticampania.org.
23. http://www.italianrevolution.org/dal-presidio-permanete-al-presidio-diffuso, accessed 30 March 2012.
24. http://actiondiritti.net/index.php?option=com_content&view=article&id= 1898:crisi-finanziaria-e-crisi-della-democrazia-in-europa&catid=97:eventi, accessed 9 March 2012.

25. www.arci.it/dwn.php?trigger=K8KAAA, http://www.arci.it/speciale/iniziative/
    rifondare_leuropa_con_la_democrazia_partecipativa/index.html, accessed 18
    March 2012.
26. http://www.italianrevolution.org/dal-presidio-permanete-al-presidio-diffuso,
    accessed 30 March 2012.
27. See Note 13.

References

della Porta, D. (1995) *Social Movements, Political Violence and the State*. Cambridge:
Cambridge University Press.
della Porta, D. (Ed.) (2007) *The Global Justice Movement in Cross-National and
Transnational Perspective*. Boulder: Paradigm.
della Porta, D. (Ed.) (2009) *Another Europe*. London: Routledge.
della Porta, D. (2011) 'Mobilizing for democracy: Social movements as actors
of democratization', *EUI Review*, pp. 8–9, Accessed online at http://dialnet
.unirioja.es/servlet/revista?codigo=17944.
della Porta, D. (2012) 'Mobilizing against the crisis, mobilizing for "another
democracy": Comparing two global waves of protest', *Interface: A Journal for
and About Social Movements*, 4(1), pp. 274–277.
della Porta, D. (2013) *Can Democracy Be Saved?* Cambridge: Polity Press
della Porta, D., Andretta, M., Mosca, L. and Reiter, H. (2006) *Globalization from
Below*. Minneapolis: University of Minnesota Press.
della Porta, D. and Caiani, M. (2009) *Social Movements and Europe*. Oxford: Oxford
University Press.
della Porta, D. and Giugni, M. (2009) 'Democracy from below: Activists and
institutions', in D. della Porta (Ed.) *Another Europe*. London: Routledge,
pp. 86–198.
della Porta, D. and Reiter, H. (2012) 'Desperately seeking politics: Political attitudes of participants in three demonstrations for workers' rights in Italy',
Mobilization, 17(3), pp. 349–361.
della Porta, D. and Zamponi, L. (2013) 'The policing of protest of
the October 15th demonstration in Italy', *Policing and Society*, 23(1),
pp. 65–80.
Koopmans, R. and Rucht, D. (2002) 'Protest event analysis', in B. Klandermans
and S. Staggenborg (Eds.) *Methods of Social Movement Research*. Minneapolis &
London: University of Minnesota Press, pp. 231–259.
Kriesi, H. (2011) *About cows and PIIGS: Contention and convention in the popular
reactions to the financial and economic crisis in Western Europe*. Paper presented at
the Conference in Honor of Sidney Tarrow, Cornell, June.
Kriesi, H., Grande, E., Lachat, E., Dolezal, M. Bornschier, S. and Timotheos,
F. (2008) *West European Politics in the Age of Globalization*. Cambridge:
Cambridge University press.
Kriesi, H., Koopmans, R., Duyvendak, J.W. and Giugni, M. (1995) *New Social
Movements in Western Europe*. London: UCL Press/University of Minnesota
Press.
McAdam, D. (1982) *Political Process and the Development of Black Insurgency*.
Chicago: University of Chicago Press.

McAdam, D. (1999) 'The decline of the civil rights movement', in J. Freeman and V. Johnson (Eds.) *Waves of Protest*. Oxford: Rowman & Littlefield, pp. 325–348.

Rootes, C. (2003) *Environmental Protest in Western Europe*. Oxford: Oxford University Press.

Tarrow, S. (1989) *Democracy and Disorder. Protest and Politics in Italy 1965–1975*. Oxford: Oxford University Press.

4
The 'Swarm Intelligence' and Occupy: Recent Subterranean Politics in Germany

Anne Nassauer and Helmut K. Anheier[1]

Introduction

Civil society actions take many different forms: people join in political actions for different reasons, with different claims and in different forms of organisations. These forms change over time and new actors and organisations emerge.

In this chapter we analyse protest groups in Germany. Our aim is to understand how actors in Germany have recently organised and mobilised. We hypothesise that these recent actions can be analysed under the concept of subterranean politics, which we will explore throughout this chapter. As in the other country-specific studies of this volume, we aim to develop this concept based on our analysis of protest groups and to explore its analytical value. As a working definition we define subterranean politics as politics outside the formal political sphere, including organised and unorganised political action. By studying the German case, we test whether this concept allows the inclusion of all political activities outside of political parties or governmental organisations, and set a special focus on novel political practices and developments.

We aim to conduct an explorative study on recent protest forms in today's Germany to generate hypotheses and to indicate aspects for future research. Therefore recent protest groups in Germany were mapped to search for commonalities and patterns in recent trends.

Through this mapping and analysis we found several similarities with the research groups in other countries. At the same time we brought a specific angle to the concept of subterranean politics: several recent German protest groups can be described under the concept of 'swarm intelligence'. To date this term has mainly been used in biology, computer sciences and the media. Based on our findings we imported it into social sciences research, to capture the current trend in subterranean politics in Germany.

Examples of swarm intelligence groups discussed here are: Anonymous in Germany, GuttenPlag and Occupy Germany. These groups brought new aspects to the field of subterranean politics in Germany during 2011–2012, but to our knowledge only scant studies on them exist in the social sciences thus far and these groups reveal valuable insights in the field of recent subterranean politics in Germany as a whole.

In this chapter we show how current protest groups in Germany are driven by a general distrust of established political institutions and by deep-seated notions of scepticism and discomfort at the way political decisions are made. Drawing on our analysis, we will discuss the concept of subterranean politics, in acting outside of the formal political sphere, without formulating a formal political agenda and engaging in new ways of organisation. We will show that while we see a high level of political apathy in Germany, these groups do engage in political activities but try to find new ways of organisation: that of the swarm. The German groups aim at more participatory, transparent, basis-democratic and web-based modes of governance, which activists are eager to employ. By studying their aims and practices we aim to contribute to the exploration of the concept of subterranean politics.

Many of the groups discussed in this chapter were able to attract citizens who had never previously participated in political action, and also to mobilise a new generation of activists. While not large in number, those who join the various protests continue to do so over time. The modes of organisation and mobilisation for protest movements have changed, as has the technology available to them. The current Internet technology that allows communication by blogging, sharing, video platforms and others is vital for the protest groups we studied. Most importantly, activists seek to combine theory and practice. They not only discuss societal or political problems, but they also seek new ways of changing the status quo by mobilising the 'swarm'.

Mapping protest groups in Germany led us to capture new actors and emerging trends. After briefly summarising the German context and the methodology used, we give an overview of these subterranean groups and analyse their actors, the topics they discuss and their forms of organisation, in order to discuss the concepts of subterranean politics and swarm intelligence.

The German context

With the European Union (EU) and many of its member states entangled in the current debt crisis, Germany arguably presents a rather exceptional case when it comes to subterranean politics in Europe. Compared, among others, with Greece, Italy or Spain, Germany has recovered rather quickly from the global financial and economic crisis of 2008 (Statistisches Bundesamt 2012; Zeit online 2012a). It is therefore not surprising that Germany has not seen protests on the scale that Greece, Italy or Spain did in 2011 and 2012.

But while the German case may be exceptional in this regard, we argue that it would be wrong to conclude that civil society actions are absent in Germany or less relevant than in other European nations. In fact, protesters address similar topics found in other country-specific reports within this volume. Hence, the German case illustrates that the concept of subterranean politics is not necessarily a phenomenon of socio-economic crisis.

Several aspects are particularly interesting about the German case. First, it is surprising that people in Germany are actually joining the global protests, even if the noticeable impact of the crisis is relatively low. Although Germany is experiencing economic growth, the discomfort among citizens towards the German democracy and in political decision making is drastically high: only 10% of the German public trust in politics to solve their problems (Bertelsmann Stiftung 2011; Schwan 2011).

Second, Germany is an interesting case since recently many people are engaging in protests were not previously politically active in any organisation or party. It is all the more surprising because these people engage in strenuous protest activities, involving considerable risk (e.g. occupying public spaces, which can lead to prosecution), and go to great lengths (e.g. camping, which is more time consuming than other forms of protest).

In this chapter we will analyse and explain these recent protest forms and developments in Germany, explore the concept of subterranean politics and develop the concept of 'swarm intelligence' protests.

Methodology

To map protest groups in Germany we conducted several steps of analysis. We first conducted a media content analysis and Google Trends searches, to filter current protest groups. To investigate public interest in newly emerging groups, we analysed Google Trends search results from 2011. The extent to which a certain claim or protest group was searched on the Google website in Germany reflects its importance in shaping the public political and social discourse. Google is a representative search machine, since in Germany it held a market share of about 85% in 2010 and 2011 (Panagiotis Kolokythas 2011). Nevertheless, Google Trends was used not only to illustrate the public interest in a certain group but also as a criterion to filter groups relevant to the events of recent years.

Second, we conducted open interviews, participant observation and a media content analysis with the selected groups. Both interviews and participant observation aim at exploring the background, resources and modes of organisation and mobilisation as well as the policy objectives, motivations and practices of this generation of activists. Content analysis of recent media reports and statements by the protest groups also complemented our research on the groups' actors, topics and organisational structure.

Since the actors of Anonymous frequently operate in a legal grey zone, it was not possible to find interviewees. We therefore drew on media content analysis for the section on Anonymous, as well as for that on GuttenPlag.

For the main section on Occupy Germany, we analysed media content, interviews and participant observation. Seven 40–60-minute in-depth interviews with Occupy activists from Frankfurt and Berlin were conducted, and the results qualitatively analysed. Participant observation was conducted over five meetings, panel discussion events and protests by Occupy Berlin. Third, a substantial media analysis on Occupy in different German cities was conducted and the audio recording of a group interview by journalists from the German newspaper *Tagesspiegel* with five Occupy Frankfurt activists was analysed.

The swarm intelligence protests

To conduct an exploratory study on the concept of subterranean politics in Germany, our working hypothesis of subterranean politics is: subterranean politics are politics outside the formal political sphere, including organised and unorganised political action. The concept of civil society has been extensively discussed in the literature (for recent examples of a discussion of means and ends in civil society see Anheier 2007; Kaldor 2003; Keane 2003; Munck 2006; Taylor 2004) and frequently associated with normative assumptions. The concept of subterranean politics in contrast could be useful to exclude normative considerations and to include all political activities outside of political parties and governmental structures: civil initiatives, non-governmental organisations (NGOs), associations and loose coalitions of activists. The concept can therefore be especially useful to capture recent trends.

Recent subterranean politics groups focus on the political practices of basis-democratic decision making, strongly rely on the Internet as a platform and issue of protest and tend to influence mainstream politics, as we also see in other chapters of this volume. To narrow the scope of analysis, we decided to focus on protest groups that

- have been studied rarely or not at all;
- have brought some sort of novelty to the field with regard to their organisation, actors and topics;
- are particularly relevant in elucidating the concept of subterranean politics.

Several groups were excluded at the first mapping since they did not comply with these criteria, such as citizens' initiatives, protests for nuclear phasing out, right-wing groups and the Pirate Party. These groups are often affiliated with parties, are long established or no enhanced media interest in them is evident; furthermore, several use established political practices. In contrast to the Hungarian case presented in this volume, the German Pirate Party for example does not qualify as a part of subterranean politics, since it mainly acts within a formal political sphere, primarily engages in established political practice and therefore hardly differs from other German parties (Hefty 2012; Rosenfeld 2012). We can thereby sharpen the concept of subterranean politics by excluding German parties from the concept of subterranean politics as they *do* act within a formal political sphere.

We concluded that two subterranean groups fulfil the above-mentioned criteria and help us to explore the concept of subterranean politics: the Wutbürger ('anger protests')[2] and what we labelled the 'swarm intelligence groups' – Anonymous Germany, GuttenPlag and Occupy Germany. Since several studies have previously analysed the actors, organisation and topics of Wutbürger protests (see inter alia Göttinger Institut für Demokratieforschung 2011a, 2011b; Rucht et al. 2010), and due to the diminishing public attention paid to these protests in the media and Google Trends searches, we focused on the 'swarm intelligence' groups.

The 'swarm intelligence' groups feature new organisational forms and new subterranean actors. To date, they have barely been studied by social science research, and media searches and Google Trends search results showed high media and public interest in these groups over recent years.[3] Even though media interest and the public profile of some of these groups has fallen recently, they form a paramount example for the study of recent protests in Germany, as they accurately capture a current trend that helps us to shape the concept of subterranean politics.

The term 'swarm intelligence' is adopted from biology – usually referring to bees, fish, ant swarms, bacteria or cells, but has recently been used increasingly in regard to electronic engineering and computer science. By actions based on simple rules, groups fulfil tasks that could not have been achieved by the individual alone. Groups organised by swarm intelligence are usually self-organised, adaptive and, when one individual drops out, another individual can take their place. Problems are solved by the group as a whole without hierarchies or leaders. Every member can participate in the solution of a problem just as much as could any other member (for more on crowd judgements and social influences see inter alia Lorenz et al. 2011: 1).

The media have used the term 'swarm intelligence' to describe recent protest groups (Martenstein 2011; Sueddeutsche Zeitung 2011), and activists use the label in interviews and on their blogs. Yet, to our knowledge social sciences have not adapted and comprehensively conceptualised this useful notion.[4] Drawing on our findings, we define 'swarm intelligence' protest groups as protests that are:

- collectively self-organised (everyone can participate in a way that she or he wants to);
- adaptive (every individual can take the place of someone dropping out; the collective decides what happens and this collective depends on its members);
- decentralised and non-hierarchical (no leaders, basis-democratic decision making, ideas are shared, discussed and further developed by the swarm).

In contrast to the concept of crowd sourcing (see inter alia Wexler 2011), where a crowd sourcer gives a task to a crowd and filters the input, swarm intelligence has no organiser. The whole swarm can navigate in a particular direction following the individual's decision to do so.

By studying the protest groups that we filtered for investigation under the 'subterranean politics' concept we found that all exhibit swarm intelligence and are strongly focused on this adaptive, consensus-based decision making. As we will see in more detail below, we found that everyone can participate in these groups and the collective further develops ideas. The groups have no precise demands as the actors are too diverse, but they have common topics with which they are all concerned. These groups are decentralised, transparent and non-hierarchical. The Internet plays a central role in organisational matters, but it is also used as a space for protest.

Anonymous

Anonymous and GuttenPlag (see Boxes 4.1 and 4.2, respectively) are two examples of 'swarm intelligence' groups that are based specifically on the Internet. Beyond this commonality, Anonymous and GuttenPlag are quite distinct. While GuttenPlag was short-lived but had strong political impact, Anonymous is a long-term international protest group.

Anonymity – as the name implies – is fundamental for the Anonymous activists. The actors that gave press interviews in the name of Anonymous in Germany were students, pupils or self-employed people in their 20s and 30s (Horn 2011), but Anonymous claims to be comprised of people of all ages and social backgrounds. It seems that many activists have not been previously active in any political organisation. The Berlin Anonymous group encourages people to visit their protest marches and tells them not to be afraid, stating that many of them have rarely or never been to a protest march prior to joining Anonymous (Anonymous Berlin 2012). Hence, we see that many new actors engage in these protest groups.

While Anonymous Germany is generally open to all participants, some German Anonymous declarations state clearly that they reject being instrumentalised by any parties, especially right-wing parties (Thommes 2011). In German Anonymous videos, activists reject the politics of the conservative Christian Democratic Party (CDU) and call for joining the Occupy Wall Street protests (Anonymous 2011).

In general, because Anonymous specifically rejects acting within the formal political sphere, it is therefore organised as a swarm. Anonymous DDoS attacks are an excellent example of how swarm intelligence can work: over the Internet, people discuss what would be a useful target and why – then they time the attack. The more people that participate, the easier it is to overload the website to make it temporarily unavailable.

Box 4.1   Anonymous Germany: An overview

While Anonymous is an international phenomenon, Anonymous Germany focuses on Scientology and the freedom of information as their main topics. Anonymous groups have a common slogan and a common logo. However, since any individual can take actions in the name of Anonymous, the group's actions are very diverse. Anonymous mostly uses the protest form of cyberattacks with the motivation to protect the freedom of the Internet as a community. These are often distributed denial-of-service (DDoS) attacks that render webpages temporarily unavailable for users. Anonymous groups attacked several institutions and companies they held responsible for limiting the freedom of speech or the freedom of the Internet (Frankfurter Allgemeine Zeitung 2011; Horn 2011; Ondreka 2011; Schmidt 2012), like *Gema* – a state-approved trustee representing copyrights in Germany.

However, Anonymous Germany's protest actions are not merely Internet based. Activists distribute flyers and carry out protest marches. The Berlin Anonymous group Project Chanology regularly protests on the streets against Scientology. Other Anonymous members call for participation in protests against anti-piracy laws and those on intellectual property rights, such as the Stop Online Piracy Act (SOPA), Protect IP Act (PIPA) and the Anti-Counterfeiting Trade Agreement (ACTA). These legal frameworks on intellectual property rights would, in their view, constrain the freedom of information. While the EU itself does not play a major role in discussions about Anonymous Germany, these laws are seen to be representative of the feeling that treaties with drastic consequences for citizens are resolved at the EU level and pushed through without any public debate (Wedekind 2012). At the same time, there is criticism of the fact that important regulations are formulated very vaguely and therefore can be implemented in various ways to restrict freedom of information.

German Anonymous activists state that they are not an organisation, but only the labelling of an idea (Anonymous Berlin 2012). Therefore, as stated by one German interviewee, no one can join Anonymous but everyone can be Anonymous (Starodub 2011). They have no apparent leader or hierarchies. What unites them is a respective topic related

---

Box 4.2   GuttenPlag: An overview

GuttenPlag Wiki is a website anonymously created after the Law Professor, Andreas Fischer-Lescano, stated a suspicion of plagiarism regarding the dissertation of the German minister of defence, Karl-Theodor zu Guttenberg, in February 2011 (Schnabel 2011). The minister then declared this accusation to be absurd. Subsequently, unknown activists started a Google Docs online document to collectively find plagiarisms in the dissertation. Soon GuttenPlag had to use a Wiki platform so that more than 100 users were able to simultaneously work on the document. A spokesperson said that this website had received more than one million visitors within the first 24 hours (Sander 2011). Everyone was invited to participate and the website was accessible to everyone. In a transparent way, activists highlighted the plagiarised parts of the dissertation and the original documents plagiarised by zu Guttenberg.

The GuttenPlag Wiki led to the renouncement of the doctoral degree awarded to zu Guttenberg and his resignation from office and all political mandates in March 2011. Additionally, the federal state of Bavaria, where he wrote his dissertation and acquired his academic title, announced a review of its doctoral regulations (Scherf 2012). The GuttenPlag webpage received the Grimme Online Award in 2011, an award for Internet journalistic quality by the prestigious German Grimme Institute. Several other webpages searching for examples of politicians' plagiarisms followed and subsequently other politicians had to renounce their doctoral degrees and resign (Zeit online 2012b). GuttenPlag is, however, the first and most prominent of these webpages.

---

to the specific common action, for which activists join forces. In a radio interview, a German activist states that the collective decides what happens and what happens in the collective depends on its members (Horn 2011). This is distinctive for all 'swarm intelligence' groups. The communication in the groups is decentralised, non-hierarchical and heterogeneous (Starodub 2011): in one interview a German activist first formulated the answers with other members in a chat (Horn 2011). Just as with other 'swarm intelligence' groups discussed below, Anonymous Germany has no single, clear demand – it is concerned with a variety of issues regarding the freedom of speech. It primarily distinguishes itself from other protest groups in its forms of novel practices, rather than content – a characteristic of several subterranean politics groups, as will be seen in other chapters of this volume. Similar to other 'swarm intelligence' groups, such as Occupy, we find the feeling that politicians do not follow the interests of citizens, but only the goals of their own party (Horn 2011). This is one reason that the organisation as a 'swarm' is so appealing to participants: in a genuine basis-democratic manner every actor can shape actions on socio-political topics with which he or she is concerned.

GuttenPlag

The GuttenPlag webpage is an exceptional example of swarm intelligence in Germany, since it had a very narrow and specific goal and was exclusively Internet based. Although the project was short-lived, it shows the power of the swarm and the ways in which it can work.

Many of the activists engaged in the GuttenPlag Wiki were university or doctoral students. An online survey, conducted when the search for plagiarism had reached its peak, found that 60% of active users of the GuttenPlag Wiki had a university degree and almost 20% held a PhD degree. The average age of the 1034 respondents was 38, of which 82% were male (Lehmann and Valin 2011).

While motives for the volunteer activists might have been diverse, protection of the scientific integrity of dissertations in Germany was certainly one motive for many of them. In general, GuttenPlag was – like Anonymous and some groups of Occupy Germany – concerned with the handling of intellectual property. As in the example of Anonymous, the initiators and actors of GuttenPlag stayed anonymous and acted individually for a collective cause. The GuttenPlag Wiki was organised in a decentralised, non-hierarchical and transparent way. In these aspects it corresponds to the structure of other 'swarm intelligence' groups like Anonymous or Occupy Germany. All 'swarm intelligence' groups are highly non-bureaucratic and basis-democratic – one person initiates an idea and the swarm collectively develops it further. By a collective effort of the swarm a high-ranking German politician, the Minister of Defence, Karl-Theodor zu Guttenberg, had to resign.

Occupy Germany

Even though activities by Occupy Germany (see Box 4.3) have decreased since July 2012, Occupy Germany is a paramount example of subterranean politics as it exemplifies in many ways a recent protest trend in Germany, as well as the concepts of subterranean politics and a 'swarm intelligence' organisation.

Box 4.3   Occupy Germany: An overview

Occupy in Germany is usually used as a label for different individuals and diverse groups including Echte Demokratie Jetzt, Campact, alex11 and acAMPada (acAMPada 2011). From 15 October 2011, different German Occupy groups met on a daily basis over subsequent months to discuss different topics in *asambleas*. In Germany, more than 50 cities participated in the protests, with main marches of about 10,000 protesters in Berlin and 6,000 in Frankfurt. Working groups emerged and camps were established in Berlin, Hamburg and Frankfurt. The protest forms of Occupy in Germany are wide-ranging: classical demonstration marches, spontaneous protest actions, *asambleas* in public places, political education, occupation of public spaces, Internet protests and 'rich people's flash mobs'. Activists organised movie evenings on the financial crisis and panel discussions, while the Frankfurt activists founded European Occupy Central Bank (EOCB) (Occupy Frankfurt 2012a).

To communicate with a large group without the use of amplified equipment, Occupy Germany uses the human microphone technique.[5]

Many German interviewees explain that it is almost too trivial to formulate the global problems with which Occupy is concerned, because these are the same topics with which people have been concerned for decades: environmental destruction, war, limitation of democratic participation, an unjust world order, putting profits before people, disrespect for human rights, and drastic cuts in education and social services, to name the most prominent.

Study of this fairly recent protest group is particularly interesting in regard to recent protests in Germany, in five main aspects. First, as we saw above, the financial crisis has not hit Germany as hard as other countries, but still many people mobilised by Occupy Germany had not previously been active in any political group or initiative. Second, these people not only become active without experiencing the impacts of the crisis, but even engaged in intensive protest activities such as occupying a public space by camping on it. Third, Occupy received large media coverage even though over the winter visible public activities by Occupy groups in Germany dropped considerably. Fourth, Occupy

Germany has scarcely been studied by social scientists due to its new-ness and the difficulty – visible in both media and public discourse – in defining the group. Fifth, the claims and organisational structure of Occupy Germany reflect a trend in recent subterranean politics that is also visible in other chapters of this volume.

This section aims to clarify what Occupy in Germany is and what role it plays in the German arena of subterranean politics. Therefore we first analyse actors and their motivations, showing how Occupy reflects an atmosphere that also motivates activists in the 'swarm intelligence' groups discussed above. Second, we examine the topics addressed by Occupy to discuss whether it faces a fictional consensus and whether it can be defined as a social movement. Third, the organisation of Occupy is analysed to show how the organisation as a 'swarm' has resulted from both actors' claims and their reasons for mobilisation. Last, we investigate Occupy as an exemplary case of subterranean politics in Germany.

Actors

With regard to the actors in Occupy Germany, we first reflect on their demography and second on their motivation for joining the organisation.

The participants in Occupy Germany are diverse. According to inter-views and participant observation, while a small majority of activists are between 25 and 35 years old, in general the age range is 15–60. Regarding gender, Occupy in Germany shows a slight majority of men in several groups. Activists are mostly educated and middle class, ranging among students and self-employees, retirees, employees and unem-ployed people. In the Frankfurt Occupy group, several bank employees and fund managers participated according to respondents. About half of the activists were previously politically active: for peace, against nuclear energy, for a basic income or for global justice, while the other half had been politicised but not politically active before joining Occupy.

With regard to actors' motivations, Occupy Berlin states on its web-page that it consists of many and widely differing people who no longer feel represented by political parties – they see severe democratic shortcomings in the current representative party system (Occupy Berlin 2012a). Activists have different political convictions, but they are united by concern and anger in the light of the current political, financial and societal perspective, as stated by one activist on the homepage of Occupy Frankfurt (Occupy Frankfurt 2012c).

Several people we interviewed had not previously been politically active. They were politically interested, but did not see an effective way to change things until they learned of Occupy. 'Occupy appeals to many people like no established party ever did before', said Ina,[6] an activist from Frankfurt in her 20s, in her interview. YouTube videos from Spanish *asambleas* motivated many German activists to join Occupy in Germany. 'My heart was beating. I couldn't understand a word of what they were saying, but I thought: awesome! They meet at a public square and talk to each other!', one activist told us.

Frank, unemployed and in his 40s and who was not politically active in any way before joining Occupy, explained that he was so thrilled by the concept of the human microphone that he spoke in front of 500 people at the second *asamblea* that he attended, even though he claims to be rather shy. Many activists we interviewed were under the impression that anyone could speak and that everyone was even encouraged to speak. Interviewees saw this in contrast to the established political parties. This openness of Occupy and its way of acting outside of the formal political sphere, and trying to include *everyone* in the decision-making process, appealed to many actors and motivated many to engage in political action for the first time in their lives.

Many interviewees see this collective action in stark relief to the perceived madness of intangible levels of financial speculation and government debt, incalculable numbers of death due to war and famine, or the inestimable amount of environmental destruction. In the *Tagesspiegel* group interview recording, a 26-year-old Frankfurt activist stated: 'All these things are just happening to us. We are sitting here and we feel that we can't do anything about it.' She perceived Occupy as a means towards feeling empowered again. While perceived hierarchies and interests in power had discouraged many activists from participation in other groups or parties, their general discomfort with the way political decisions are made and the perceived existing global injustice drove them to participate in the novel ways of protest organisation under the label of Occupy. Many people were mobilised because they perceived Occupy to be less hierarchical than parties or established social movements, and more transparent. We see that these motivations correspond to the protest groups we analysed above and reflect a current trend in subterranean politics – not only in Germany, as other chapters of this volume show.

These actors' motivations influence both Occupy's topics and its specific organisational structure in Germany.

Topics

In this section, we first identify the problems addressed by Occupy and the role of the EU. Second, we will illustrate the three main pillars of Occupy in Germany: non-violence, transparency and the absence of leaders. Third, we will discuss whether a fictional consensus exists in the Occupy Germany groups. All three aspects will help us understand why Occupy Germany is a paramount example to use in the development of the concepts of subterranean politics, as well as of swarm intelligence.

The global problems with which Occupy activists are concerned (see Box 4.3) touch so many aspects of human life that many activists see no way to address them all at the same time and no possibility of deciding which would be the most important issue to address first. There are so many symptoms that Occupy wants to get to the root of these: in the view of activists, they know that the system is not working in its current state but what they do not know is how it could work in the future. This is why they come together and search for solutions. 'Everyone is invited to join in this search', said Peter, a self-employed activist. At the same time many groups explicitly distance themselves from all discriminating ideologies, such as racism, sexism, islamophobia or homophobia (Occupy Berlin 2012b).

Many interviewees claim that if the group cited one specific aim or demand, all problems in relation to this demand would be swept under the table, a phenomenon associated with agenda making by established parties. The risk activists see is that this demand, once decided upon, would be pushed forward no matter how useful its implementation and how severe the problems it entailed. As a consequence of these considerations, all participants viewed Occupy Germany as highly process driven, with a focus on asking the right questions, rather than always pretending to have answers. Second, as explained by one activist in his 40s, even if demands could be made 'the question remains: articulate demands on whom?'. Hence, not only broad topics are addressed, but participatory possibilities are also questioned as a whole. Therefore the topics focused on by Occupy Germany are less a discussion of the problems discussed above, nor of solutions to them, but more a reflection on how participatory democracy should work.

While freedom of information proposals such as ACTA and other legal frameworks, like the Protect IP Act (PIPA) and SOPA, are discussed by the groups, Europe and the EU are not crucial concerns for Occupy in Germany. Although 100,000 participated in ACTA protests in several German cities on 11 February 2012 (Sander 2012), our participant observation at these protests showed that the EU was not specifically addressed in posters, slogans or calls for the protest.

However, interviewees state that the European Stability Mechanism (ESM) (for more information see European Central Bank 2011) and the Lisbon contracts have been an issue for some working groups and protests. With regard to these issues, a lack of both democratic decision making and transparency are major points of criticism (Occupy Frankfurt 2012b). Hence, aspects of EU policy are addressed that reflect the general frustrations with the lack of transparency, paucity of participatory democracy and the principle of profit over people.

Occupy relies on three pillars: non-violence, transparency and the absence of hierarchies. All three aspects were evident in participant observations and cited by activists in interviews. We identify these pillars as common claims.

First, Occupy Germany is radically peaceful. This includes the goal of non-violent communication in consensus-based decision making. Second, because transparency is a central issue for Occupy Germany, all discussions and meetings are made transparent, mostly via the Internet. Third, the rejection of hierarchies and leaders is crucial for Occupy Germany. Everyone is invited to start a working group on a topic she or he finds interesting, but everyone speaks for herself or himself. Thus some working groups become large due to many interested activists, while others cease to be active since no one is interested in the topic. This organisation as a *swarm* will be discussed in greater detail below.

This vast diversity of topics addressed by Occupy have led the media, some social scientists and even participants of Occupy themselves to assume a strong fictional consensus between activists. However, this fictional consensus is not present, according to our study: on one hand, activists do not believe that they even have a consensus while on the other they state surprisingly similar goals and issues for their motivation.

Many interviewees expressed the fear of a fictional consensus and stated that the motivations of actors were very diverse. Hence, in contrast to other protest groups working on one specific demand and which are potentially affected by a fictional consensus, we claim that Occupy Germany faces no strong fictional consensus, since activists realise the diversity of motivations and claims within their group and therefore do not believe in a specific consensus.

Moreover, all interviewees expressed the same concerns, difficulties and observations in regard to Occupy as stated above. A widespread consensus is acting outside the formal political sphere. The three pillars – non-violence, transparency and non-hierarchical structure – were stressed by all activists and were evident in all participant observations that we conducted. We note that all three claims focus on specific political practices rather than on political content.

The organisation of the swarm

These topics that are at the heart of the Occupy agenda are reflected in the group's organisational structure; we see non-hierarchical structures and loosely connected groups aiming for consensus-oriented and strictly democratic procedures. According to respondents, forms of organisation are very diverse and depend on what the swarm wants to achieve.

In the following, we will therefore analyse Occupy's organisation as a 'swarm', give examples of swarm-based protest actions and discuss the role of the Internet for the swarm. Subsequently, we will examine reasons activists gave for organising in such a way.

Occupy Germany is organised as a 'swarm': This means that everyone is an expert on something and can thereby contribute to the groups' actions, whether it is cooking, web design, public relations or logistics. 'Occupy rejects the concept of a small circle protecting their knowledge', Peter states in his interview. Every idea is shared, discussed and further developed. This is also the way in which Anonymous and GuttenPlag function. Working groups form in a decentralised way on a specific topic for a certain time, or people join spontaneously for a specific limited action and then regroup for other topics. As one female resident of the Frankfurt camp told us, 'everything works based on the division of labour: everyone participated the way they could and wanted to'.

One interviewee, a student in his 20s, gave a practical example of how 'swarm intelligence' can appear: he printed flyers on a specific topic and distributed some of them; then he dropped the idea and engaged in other actions. When he participated in a protest about a month later, someone he did not know handed him an improved version of the same flyer. It looked much more professional and included, for example, a PO box for questions on the topic. The activist was very happy that someone had taken his idea and that it was further developed by the 'swarm'.

While Occupy welcomes party members who participate in a transparent way, just like any other interested individual, they clearly reject being organised as a party or being 'taken over' by any special-interest group or party. They emphasises the retaining of practices beyond the mainstream practices of parties – be it the established German parties or younger parties, such as the Pirate Party. The hierarchical structure of all parties, as well the arena in which they act, is strongly rejected as an organisational form by all three swarm intelligence groups. Even though the non-hierarchical organisation faces difficulties when administrating issues, all interviewees perceived these problems to be part of their process. As Peter stated, 'No form of hierarchy could solve these differences in opinions when different people meet.'

The Internet – especially the networking and interactive culture frequently referred to as web 2.0 – is highly relevant for the organisation of Occupy (for a discussion on the use of the Internet to increase political participation see Emmer and Wolling 2010). Several people who had participated in one meeting, but who could not attend subsequent ones, followed the meetings online via a live stream. They thereby remained informed and affiliated to the movement and went back to join the protest in person shortly after. At the same time, YouTube transports events from protest movements all over the world to all interested activists or onlookers. Occupy discusses topics and plans meetings online. German activists agree that after decades of protesting, the Internet has given protest a new quality. One interviewee in her 20s described her impressions as follows: 'Previous protest groups were looking backwards to learn from the past and forward towards a utopian future. Today, with the help of the Internet, people can look sideways and see what is going on in other places.' Activists thereby see common problems, symbols and claims. These shared experiences and feelings might even help in developing a collective identity: for Occupy, as well as for other 'swarm intelligence' groups discussed above, the Internet can substitute for many aspects usually derived from meetings and direct interaction. At the same time the focus on the Internet also entails difficulties, since its anonymous nature readily leads people to criticise others in a disrespectful or more drastic manner than they would probably dare to in real life, as stated by many respondents. A study on the role of the Internet for these groups can thus be particularly interesting with regard to rituals and emotions for the establishment of the group's collective identity (for a discussion on the collective identity of protest groups, see della Porta and Diani 2006; Eder 2000; Jasper 1999; Polletta and Jasper 2001).

Understanding subterranean politics in Germany: The organisation of the swarm

Based on our findings, we conclude that the concept of subterranean politics – defined as political action outside of the formal political sphere – allows us to identify and analyse recent protest groups in

Germany. As we have seen above, activists specifically focus on acting outside the formal political sphere, as they reject the framing of a formal political agenda, the production of organisational cohesion and leadership structures. All groups reject formal political agendas and the established ways of political activism. Acting on a subterranean level is therefore highly important to them.

Further, we introduced a new angle on this concept of subterranean politics, by conceptualising the recent German protest groups as 'swarm intelligence protest groups'. This explicitly subterranean form of 'swarm intelligence' activism induced some citizens to protest for the first time in their lives; those who had never previously been politically active in any organisation have started to become involved. We showed that the concept of swarm intelligence helps to group, analyse and characterise this current German development, since all three groups examined here are collectively self-organised, adaptive, decentralised and non-hierarchical.

More precisely, all groups reject authorities, leaders and hierarchical structures. They aim to implement democratic decision making in which everyone can participate. At the same time, every individual can be replaced by someone else in the swarm. Every person can be part of Anonymous and can conduct actions in its name; everyone was invited to participate in the GuttenPlag Wiki or in the actions of Occupy; all three groups demonstrated the organisational structure of the swarm.

The process-driven nature of these groups is shaped by their mistrust of political structures in dealing with the above-mentioned problems. Consequentially, they have tried to find a new way. As with subterranean politics groups in other countries discussed in this volume, this new way is related much more to new political practices than to new political content. Instead of formulating specific demands, Occupy for example addresses the system of political decision making per se to create something outside of the known political sphere. We see the same motivations in the other 'swarm intelligence' groups above. Activists do not want to rely on the procedures that are used in politics to shape positions, but aim to reflect the ideal of democracy. No single individual decides what to do, but the group backs the decision and improves on it collectively. The answer to the mistrust in current politics is found in a new way of activism, by the collective work of the swarm in which everyone can participate.

In summary, by analysing different protest groups, we show that a common trend is evident in subterranean politics in Germany, which was also found in reports in this volume from other countries.

First, the groups are concerned with politics and the current state of democracy. Activists do not address specific political contents, but the general process of democratic decision making. They criticise hierarchical structures in politics and the lack of both transparency and inclusion of citizens' interests. Actors in these groups share a common unease with how political decisions are made and they question political elites. We see that actors perceive that politics is no longer working in the interest of citizens. In all groups we find new activists who were never previously active in any social movement organisation or NGO, or who come from social milieux not normally associated with social activism.

Second, the EU is one example of a distant, non-accountable and illegitimate policy-making process perceived as existing by and for special interests. Consequently, the EU is almost invisible in subterranean politics in Germany.

Third, we see that the Internet plays a crucial role in all subterranean political groups in Germany. These three characteristics are also evident in recent protest activities in other countries discussed in this volume.

Discussion

In this chapter we analysed protest groups active in Germany in 2011 and 2012, developed and tested the concept of subterranean politics and developed the concept of 'swarm intelligence' protest groups. Apart from gaining insights into this area and the two concepts, we generated open questions for further research as well as policy implications.

Based on our findings on recent German protest groups, we suggest defining the concept of subterranean politics as political action outside of the formal political sphere. We further showed that subterranean politics groups in Germany can be considered under the concept of swarm intelligence, since they are collectively self-organised, adaptive, decentralised and non-hierarchical.

By analysing the German case, we were able to demonstrate that the broad concept of subterranean politics is helpful in describing the groups involved in German subterranean politics. Acting on the subterranean level and changing things with no outside aid by consensus-based, transparent and non-hierarchical groups is crucial to this new trend.

Our study revealed that these swarm intelligence groups display three characteristics, which we also see in reports from countries in this volume on subterranean politics:

- engagement in a novel form of politics by focusing on basis-democratic decision making and political practices rather than content;
- a strong focus on the Internet as both a tool and a topic for protest;
- the perception of the EU as bureaucratic, non-transparent and hier-archic.

In addition we generated several open questions for further research through this qualitative explorative study.

First, it is surprising that even though by the end of 2012 Germany had still not experienced the economic crisis as deeply as did other European countries, people however show a broad unease with demo-cratic decision making. While many are satisfied with their own situation, they are dissatisfied with politics in general and thus begin to protest. On the other hand, none of the 'swarm intelligence' groups in Germany have succeeded in any mass mobilisations. While we can only speculate on the number of activists, these groups are not mobilising a large number of German citizens. Hence only a few of the large numbers of disenchanted citizens actually protest, but those who do so protest strongly. These two seemingly contradicting insights represent a potential subject of future studies.

Second, the *organisational structure* of the swarm could be a further subject of future studies. Its potential to mobilise actors and influence political decisions over time, while remaining at the subterranean level, should be studied further. In this regard the emergence of a collective identity of the swarm is highly interesting, as is the role of the Internet.

Moreover, a *consensus fiction* of Occupy Germany, which was not supported in our study, deserves further attention. A consensus fiction of different protest groups could, for example, be compared in relation to the solidity of the groups' claims.

The way in which Occupy can actually qualify as a *social movement* is another interesting aspect to examine. Here, the value of the social movement literature – particularly on the organisation, collective identity and success of social movements – in regard to an analysis of Occupy and vice versa can be especially interesting, as well as insights from the social movement literature to analyse 'swarm intelligence' groups. The emergence of a collective identity, with regard to the subframes of these groups (see Rucht and Neidhardt 2001), can be particularly interesting.

Last, the interface of Occupy and Anonymous with the Pirate Party, as well as the connection between the general disaffection of actors shown above and the success of the Pirate Party in Germany might be of interest for future studies on the influence of subterranean politics on party politics.

Our study on the actors, topics and organisation of recent 'swarm intelligence' protest groups in Germany has provided insight into and generated hypotheses on several of these open questions.

Last, we can discuss the policy implications of this recent German trend. A Berlin activist we interviewed stated that political and economic decision makers had not changed anything yet, but they realised that there was something going on – 'some sort of red light, something that is blinking'. Thus, regardless of any further development of these groups,[7] the case of Occupy Germany in particular reflects a current trend in subterranean politics in Germany which also influences mainstream politics. Due to recent developments, several German parties have tried to incorporate more Internet-based and basis-democratic ideas (Rosenfeld 2012). Hence, the swarm intelligence groups reflect a general atmosphere of subterranean politics in Germany, which also favours for example the Pirate Party: a general unease with the way political decisions are made, the lack of participatory potential, threats to the freedom of information, especially on the Internet, and a lack of transparency in political decision making.

Notes

1. We would like to thank Nicolas Legewie for his valuable comments, David Budde for his helpful remarks, Uwe Mayer for his contribution to the media research and Harald Schumann for providing us with the audio recording of a *Tagesspiegel* newspaper interview with five Occupy Frankfurt activists.
2. Words related to the 'Wutbürger' (anger citizens) were chosen as 'Word of the Year' by Gesellschaft für Deutsche Sprache (German Language Society) in 2010 and 2011. Examples of Wutbürger groups are the Stuttgart 21 protests and protests against the airport development in Berlin, which are both concerned with large-scale infrastructural projects. In Germany these infrastructural projects are usually technocratic processes, in which at most juristic considerations interfere. These two projects, however, led to major protests and became politicised. Activists in both groups show a general unease with how decisions are made and with the lack of transparency and integration of citizens' views in the planning process, similar to the swarm intelligence groups discussed in this chapter (for more information see Göttinger Institut für Demokratieforschung 2011a, 2011b; Rucht et al. 2010).
3. Google searches in Germany for the word 'Anonymous' have increased since March 2011, showing peaks in August and November 2011 and in February 2012; searches for the term 'GuttenPlag' show a peak in February 2011, with two minor increases in June and December 2011; searches for the term

'Occupy' show a sudden increase for October 2011, a slow decrease until March 2012, another peak in May 2012 and a decrease since June 2012.
4. Mason (2012: 82) uses the term 'swarm tactics' to describe current networks and their actions against hierarchical structures. He does not conceptualise these swarm tactics in detail, however. Furthermore, he uses a military example to illustrate 'swarm tactics', in which these tactics were characterised by a strongly hierarchical structure rather than an intelligent swarm.
5. The entire group repeats the speaker's words and thereby amplifies what she or he is saying. Hand signs – adapted from sign language – are used to show the listeners' position on what is said. Activists refrain from applause, as this would interrupt the speaker and create too much noise. Other groups had used consensus-based decision making and identical or similar hand signs prior to their adoption by Occupy, such as the Direct Action Network (Polletta 2004) and the Quakers (Howker 2011). However, Occupy introduced this form of consensus-based decision making to a larger public audience.
6. The names of all respondents have been changed. We refrain from giving joint information on gender, exact age, the activist's profession and participation in either Occupy Frankfurt or Berlin, as this information could make interviewees identifiable by the group. Quotes taken from interviews in German were translated into English by the authors.
7. Both the media and German activists frequently discuss which structures would be needed for Occupy to constantly and substantially intervene in political processes. Many doubt that mobilisation will continue if the decentralised, non-hierarchical structure does not change. One German newspaper suggests following the good example of Greenpeace and other environmental organisations in Germany, which have tight structures but operate in loose coalitions. In this respect the path of the Green Party that emerged from the environmental movement in Germany is also frequently suggested (Lüke 2012). Currently, the formation of a party is, as we saw above, strongly rejected by protesters. Activists do not want to bring a topic to the agenda that they perceive to be insufficiently addressed – as was the case with the German Green Party in 1980. They explicitly want to act at a subterranean level.

References

aCAMPada (2011) 'The Story of aCAMPada Berlin', Accessed online 20 February 2012 at http://acampadaberlin.blogspot.com/.

Anheier, H. K. (2007) 'Reflections on the concept and measurement of global civil society', *VOLUNTAS: International Journal of Voluntary and Nonprofit Organizations*, 18(1), pp. 1–15.

Anonymous (2011) 'Anonymous – 15.10.2011 Occupy Frankfurt', Accessed online at http://www.youtube.com/watch?v=bjB8L9IeOzQ.

Anonymous Berlin (2012) 'Wer sind wir?' Accessed online 1 March 2012 at http://berlinonymus.wordpress.com/.

Bertelsmann Stiftung (2011) 'Pressemitteilung – Umfrage: Bürger wollen sich an Politik beteiligen', Accessed online 20 February 2012 at http://www.bertelsmann-stiftung.de/cps/rde/xchg/bst/hs.xsl/nachrichten_105735.htm.

della Porta, D. and Diani, M. (2006) *Social Movements: An Introduction*. Oxford: John Wiley & Sons.

Eder, K. (2000) *Kulturelle Identität zwischen Tradition und Utopie: Soziale Bewegungen als Ort gesellschaftlicher Lernprozesse*. Frankfurt am Main: Campus Verlag.

Emmer, M. and Wolling, J. (2010) 'Online-Kommunikation und politische Öffentlichkeit', in Wolfgang Schweiger and Klaus Beck (Eds.) *Handbuch Online-Kommunikation*. Wiesbaden: VS Verlag für Sozialwissenschaften, pp. 36–58.

European Central Bank (2011) 'The European Stability Mechanism', Accessed online 2 March 2012 at www.ecb.int/pub/pdf/other/art2_mb201107en_pp71 -84en.pdf.

Frankfurter Allgemeine Zeitung (2011) 'Angriff auf Internetseite der Gema', *FAZ.NET*, 22 August, Accessed online 1 March 2012 at http://www.faz.net/ aktuell/gesellschaft/aktivisten-gruppe-anonymous-angriff-auf-internetseite-der-gema-11106904.html.

Göttinger Institut für Demokratieforschung (2011a) 'Die Proteste gegen den Flughafen Berlin Brandenburg', Accessed online 1 March 2012 at http://www. demokratie-goettingen.de/studien/die-proteste-gegen-den-flughafen-berlin -brandenburg.

Göttinger Institut für Demokratieforschung (2011b) 'Neue Dimensionen des Protest? Ergebnisse einer explorativen Studie zu den Protesten gegen Stuttgart 21', Accessed online 3 March 2012 at http://www.demokratie-goettingen.de/ studien/neue-dimensionen-des-protest.

Hefty, G.P. (2012) 'Die Piraten Eine Partei wie die anderen auch', *FAZ.NET*, 3 May, Accessed online 15 August 2012 at http://www.faz.net/aktuell/politik/inland/ die-piraten-eine-partei-wie-die-anderen-auch-11738945.html.

Horn, D. (2011) 'Interview mit einem Aktivisten – Er ist Anonymous', Accessed online 22 February 2012 at http://www.einslive.de/magazin/extras/2011/06/ anonymous.jsp.

Howker, E. (2011) 'Hands up if you want to protest', *The Guardian*, 10 April, Accessed online 3 March 2012 at http://www.guardian.co.uk/world/2011/apr/ 10/hands-up-to-protest.

Jasper, J.M. (1999) *The Art of Moral Protest: Culture, Biography, and Creativity in Social Movements*. Chicago: University of Chicago Press.

Kaldor, M. (2003) *Global Civil Society: An Answer to War*. Malden, MA: Blackwell.

Keane, J. (2003) *Global Civil Society?* Cambridge: Cambridge University Press.

Lehmann, Von A. and Valin, F. (2011) 'GuttenPlag und VroniPlag Wiki: Jäger der verlorenen Zitate', *die tageszeitung*, 20 April, Accessed online 27 February 2012 at http://www.taz.de/!69463/.

Lorenz, J., Rauhut, H., Schweitzer, F. and Helbing, D. (2011) 'How social influence can undermine the wisdom of crowd effect', *Proceedings of the National Academy of Sciences*, Accessed online 3 March 2012 at http://www.pnas.org/ content/early/2011/05/10/1008636108.

Lüke, Von F. (2012) 'Digitale Bürgerrechtsbewegung: Freiwillige Freizeit-Feuerwehr', *die tageszeitung*, 17 February, Accessed online 3 March 2012 at http://taz.de/Digitale-Buergerrechtsbewegung/!87923/.

Martenstein, H. (2011) 'Mainstream: Der Schwarm', *Die Zeit*, 14 November, Accessed online 30 April 2012 at http://www.zeit.de/2011/46/DOS -Mainstream/seite-4.

Mason, P. (2012) *Why It's Kicking off Everywhere: The New Global Revolutions*. London: Verso Books.

Munck, R. (2006) 'Global civil society: Royal road or slippery path?' *VOLUNTAS: International Journal of Voluntary and Nonprofit Organizations*, 17(4), pp. 324–331.

Occupy Berlin (2012a) 'Echte Demokratie', Accessed online 18 February 2012 at http://occupyberlin.de/.

Occupy Berlin (2012b) 'aCAMPada/EchteDemokratieJetzt/Occupy Nazifrei!', Accessed online 20 February 2012 at http://ocuppyberlin.de/.

Occupy Frankfurt (2012a) 'EOCB – European Occupy Central Bank', Accessed online 3 March 2012 at http://forum.occupyfrankfurt.de/viewtopic.php?f=41& t=196.

Occupy Frankfurt (2012b) 'Stoppt den ESM!', Accessed online 20 February 2012 at http://www.occupyfrankfurt.de/projekte/esm/.

Occupy Frankfurt (2012c) 'Unsere Ziele', Accessed online 17 May 2012 at http://www.occupyfrankfurt.de/unsere-ziele/.

Ondreka, Von L. (2011) 'Nazis im Internet: Vom Kollektiv lahmgelegt', *die tageszeitung*, 5 May, Accessed online 1 March 2012 at http://www.taz.de/ !70239/.

Panagiotis Kolokythas (2011) 'Aktuelle Marktanteile – Browser, OS & Google', *PC-WELT Online*, 1 February, Accessed online 1 March 2012 at http://www.pcwelt.de/news/Januar-2011-Aktuelle-Marktanteile-Browser-OS -Google-1457221.html.

Polletta, F. (2004) *Freedom Is an Endless Meeting: Democracy in American Social Movements*. Chicago: University of Chicago Press.

Polletta, F. and Jasper, J. M. (2001) 'Collective identity and social movements', *Annual Review of Sociology*, 27(1), pp. 283–305.

Rosenfeld, D. (2012) 'Liquid feedback: Wenn alle mit allen über alles reden. Immer', *Die Zeit*, 27 April, Accessed online 15 September 2012 at http://www .zeit.de/2012/18/Piratenpartei-Liquid-Feedback.

Rucht, D. and Friedhelm, N. (2001) 'Soziale Bewegungen und kollektive Aktionen', in Hans Joas (Ed.) *Lehrbuch der Soziologie*. Frankfurt am Main: Campus, pp. 627–652.

Rucht, D., Stuppert, W., Baumgarten, B. and Teune, S. (2010) 'Befragung von Demonstranten gegen Stuttgart 21 am 18.10.2010', Accessed online 28 February 2012 at http://www.wzb.eu/de/forschung/beendete forschungs-programme/zivilgesellschaft-und-politische-mobilisierung/ projekte/betragung-zu-st.

Sander, L. (2012) 'Acta in Deutschland: Entscheidend ist das Kleingedruckte', *die tageszeitung*, 12 February, Accessed online 26 February 2012 at http://taz.de/ Acta-in-Deutschland/!87527/.

Sander, R. (2011) ' "GuttenPlag Wiki" prüft Guttenberg-Dissertation: Das Netz jagt Dr. Copy & Paste – Digital', *stern.de*, 18 February, Accessed online 3 March 2012 at http://www.stern.de/1655530.html.

Scherf, M. (2012) 'Plagiatsaffäre: Neue Regeln für Promotionen in Bayern', *sueddeutsche.de*, 1 February, Accessed online 30 April 2012 at http://www .sueddeutsche.de/bildung/neue-regeln-fuer-promotionen-in-bayern-keine -chance-fuer-schummler-1.1273252.

Schmidt, J. (2012) 'Neues Portal Nazi-Leaks: Hacker starten "Blitzkrieg" gegen die rechte Szene', *sueddeutsche.de*, 2 January, Accessed online 3 March 2012 at http://www.sueddeutsche.de/digital/neues-portal-nazi-leaks-hacker-starten -blitzkrieg-gegen-die-rechte-szene-1.1249099.

Schnabel, U. (2011) 'Plagiatsaffäre: "Ich wollte es nicht glauben"', *Die Zeit*, 24 February, Accessed online 30 April 2012 at http://www.zeit.de/2011/09/ Interview-Fischer-Lescano.

Schwan, G. (2011) 'Zerstörerische Macht des Misstrauens', *FAZ.NET*, 20 December, Accessed online 2 March 2012 at http://www.faz.net/aktuell/ feuilleton/merkels-politik-zerstoererische-macht-des-misstrauens-11571755. html.

Starodub, Interview: Alissa (2011) 'Anonymous-Aktivisten gegen Facebook: "Das Internet ist meine Front"', *die tageszeitung*, 4 November, Accessed online 1 March 2012 at http://www.taz.de/!81221/.

Statistisches Bundesamt (2012) 'destatis Arbeitsmarkt', Accessed online 1 March 2012 at http://www.destatis.de/jetspeed/portal/cms/Sites/destatis/Internet/DE/ Content/Statistiken/Zeitreihen/WirtschaftAktuell/Arbeitsmarkt/Content75/ arb210a.psml.

Sueddeutsche Zeitung (2011) 'Plagiatsverdacht: Schwarmintelligenz bringt Guttenberg in Bedrängnis', *sueddeutsche.de*, 17 February, Accessed online 30 April 2012 at http://www.sueddeutsche.de/digital/plagiatsverdacht -internet-schwarmintelligenz-bringt-guttenberg-in-bedraengnis-1.1061459.

Taylor, R. (Ed.) (2004) *Creating a Better World: Interpreting Global Civil Society*. Sterling, VA: Kumarian Press.

Thommes, F. (2011) 'Anonymous: Keine Vereinnahmung von Occupy Germany', *PC Magazin*, 25 October, Accessed online 25 February 2012 at http:// www.pc-magazin.de/news/anonymous-keine-vereinnahmung-von-occupy -germany-1208243.html.

Wedekind, K. (2012) 'ACTA bedroht Netz-Freiheit: Europa verpennt eigenes SOPA', *n-tv.de*, 19 January, Accessed online 3 March 2012 at http://www.n-tv .de/technik/Europa-verpennt-eigenes-SOPA-article5264981.html.

Wexler, M.N. (2011) 'Reconfiguring the sociology of the crowd: Exploring crowd-sourcing'. *International Journal of Sociology and Social Policy*, 31(1/2), pp. 6–20.

Zeit online (2012a) 'Konjunktur: Starkes Wachstum drückt deutsches Defizit', *Die Zeit*, 11 January, Accessed online 1 March 2012 at http://www.zeit.de/ wirtschaft/2012-01/deutschland-wirtschaft-wachstum.

Zeit online (2012b) 'Plagiat: Noch ein FDP-Politiker verliert Doktortitel', *Die Zeit*, 6 March, Accessed online 2 March 2012 at http://www.zeit.de/studium/2012 -03/plagiat-djir-sarai.

5

The 15-M: A Bet for Radical Democracy

Jordi Bonet i Martí

Introduction

This chapter is centred in the irruption of the 15-M in the Spanish political arena as one example of subterranean politics in Southern Europe. In contrast to previous cycles of mobilisation (anti-globalisation or anti-war, for example), the 15-M represented a milestone in relation to the subjects, repertoires and claims of the mobilisation. The novelty represented by these changes connects the 15-M with other experiences of subterranean politics around the world, such as the Arab Spring, Occupy and the Icelandic revolution. In all these episodes we can find some similarities: the rejection of traditional political arrangements, civil society empowerment and its rise as a new political actor, the claims for a deeper democracy and the strategic use of technological devices as information and coordination tools. The main aim of this chapter is to analyse how the impact of the economic crisis in the Spanish social and political context has transformed the shape and the content of social mobilisation through the innovation of repertoires, the coalition actors and the frames of mobilisation.

Methodology

This chapter is based on research into the evolution of the 15-M during its first ten months (May 2011–March 2012). The data was collected from 15 interviews with key participants in Madrid and Barcelona, two focus groups held in those cities and a documentary analysis of the manifestos, news and websites related the movement.

Background

There are two primary contextual factors that favoured the uprising of the 15-M. The first of these was the social discontent caused by the socio-economic crisis; the other was the end of the political cycle that began with the accession of the socialist Partido Socialista Obrero Español (PSOE) to the national government in 2004 and ended with the Conservative victory in the 2011 general elections. Both factors are inter-related, since the recession profoundly influenced the agenda of the second term of Prime Minister José Zapatero's government.

Politics...

From 1995, Spain's economic development model was based on the growth of the real-estate market and the financialisation of the Spanish economy. From 1997 to 2006, the growth rate was one of the highest in the European Union (EU) (3.9% compared with 2.3% across the Eurozone) and by 2006 Spain had become the fifth largest economy in the EU, accounting for 8.5% of the Union's GDP (Plihon and Rey 2011). Yet this growth rate was not all it seemed, as the highly financialised basis of its economy was extremely fragile, its evolution strongly dominated by the fluctuations in the international markets. Thus, the outbreak of the United States' sub-prime mortgage crisis in 2007 and its ensuing evolution into a global financial crisis in 2008 should have raised alarm bells with the Spanish government, given the size of the real-estate bubble accumulated during the previous years. However, Zapatero's government resolved not to introduce regulatory measures in the housing market and the financial sector, but instead focused its efforts on the rescue of the banking sector (which was facing a cash-flow crisis), and to the subsidising of capital infrastructure in an attempt to re-energise the flagging construction sector.

The situation changed drastically in May 2010, when the global crisis resulted in the euro crisis. Stock markets in Ireland, Portugal and Spain plummeted, and the risk premium of these countries rose sharply (Sanz de Miguel 2011). After Greece's first rescue package of €110.000 million was agreed, the threat of rescue hung over Spain and Portugal, and Merkel and Sarkozy urged the Spanish president to begin structural reforms in order to control the public deficit.

From this moment a U-turn took place in Spanish social and economic policies, which went from being strategy oriented towards employment growth and the development of a new productive model to being restricted by austerity. In this context labour reforms were passed which introduced greater flexibility in redundancy packages, public sector wage cuts, increases in the retirement age and the withdrawal of state benefits in order to satisfy market demands. The marked conservative turn of these proposals resulted in the disorientation and demobilisation of the progressive electorate – a fact that would favour the victory of the conservative parties in the various elections held in 2011 (autonomous, local and general). The emergence of the mobilisations of the 15-M has to be analysed within this frame.

In the months leading up to 15 May 2011, there was a rise in tension and disputes between the trade unions and the government: the public sector strikes of June 2010, the general strike of 29 September 2010, and various protests in the public health system and education sector. Although the unions simmered down following the December 2010 agreement between the government, the socialist Unión General de Trabajadores (UGT) and the Comisiones Obreras (CCOO) (the largest trade union in Spain) on the reform of the pension system, this agreement created discontent amongst both progressive activists and the rank-and-file union members themselves, who lost faith in trade unions as agents capable of leading the growing wave of citizen discontent.

At the same time, in the political sphere, the PSOE was dealing with a leadership crisis as a result of Zapatero's decision not to stand for the candidacy, while the political parties further to his left, Izquierda Unida and Equo, were experiencing strong internal turmoil which prevented them from becoming a viable alternative. To this unease, we should add a growing dissatisfaction as a result of the different cases of corruption, linked to illegal funding and extra commissions, which affected the two main parties, PSOE and Partido Popular (PP). Thus, in the May 2011 CIS opinion poll, 22.1% of respondents considered politicians and political parties the main problem in Spain, well above immigration (11%) and terrorism (9.1%) (CIS 2011).

This climate of anxiety, the uncertainty generated by the crisis, the absence of leadership and the lack of cohesion between the institutional left-wing elite, together with the growing fear of a new conservative hegemony, presented a chance for the outbreak of a new-style progressive citizenship response which could channel the latent discontent of Spanish society.

However, the success of the 15-M was a surprise to all, not least to its organisers (see Box 5.1). Although it is true that there were favourable structural conditions for the uprising of a mobilisation cycle, nobody could have foreseen that the demonstrations called on 15 May 2011, in 60 cities of the Spanish state under the slogan 'Occupy the streets!

Box 5.1   The genesis of the 15-M

The roots of the 15-M emerged in discussions that started across social networks during the early part of 2011, with disparate groups converging over a joint concern about the lack of citizen reaction to worsening social conditions and the austerity policies introduced by the government. Unlike other periods of protest that had their origin in the alternative social movements, the genesis of the 15-M emerged from recently established citizen platforms, formed by young people who organised themselves through the social networks (at first Facebook and subsequently Twitter).

The first of these were the blog Estado de Malestar, the bloggers' network No Les Votes (formed against the introduction of the anti-piracy laws) and Juventud Sin Futuro (a group that brings together student societies from the Madrid universities). These groups began to coordinate meet-ups and protests via Facebook, which led to the creation of the digital platform Real Democracy Now (¡Democracia real YA!). This platform then launched the call for a day of demonstration across Spain on 15 May 2011, to mark the election campaign's halfway point. The call to protest was defined from the start as non-partisan. Towns, cities and different collectives (the Association for the Taxation of Financial Transactions and Aid to Citizens (ATTAC), neighbourhood and resident associations, grassroots Christian movements, student societies and more) added to the call, spreading the word mainly via the Internet.

Real Democracy Now! We are not merchandise in hands of politicians and bankers' would become the spark that would start the fire, causing one of the most significant citizens' protests in Spain since the return of democracy.

... and Publics

The success of the initial demonstrations, in number as well as in demonstrators (130,000 demonstrators in 58 cities), was a taste of what was to come. During the following weeks, camps multiplied in a large number of Spanish cities, witnessing the mobilisation of between 0.8 and 1.5 million people by August 2011 (according to a report from

IPSOS Public Affairs). In addition to those actually demonstrating, the 15-M protesters drew strong social support. According to a report from Metroscopia for the newspaper *El País*, published on 26 June 2011, 64% of those polled backed the 15-M and 74% considered that it was a peaceful movement that purported to revitalise democracy (in comparison with just 17% that considered the 15-M a radical, anti-establishment movement).

The success of the 15-M has been its ability to encapsulate social discontent in Spanish society at a time when traditional social agents have been unable to lead. In the same way as the Occupy movement in the USA, it has its roots in a climate of discontent which can account for its initially more reactive than proactive character. The main body of the movement is formed by left-wing voters, primarily from the new middle classes, whose economic security is threatened by the crisis and the fear of downward social mobility, and who express their dissatisfaction with the political decisions of their governments which they see as being in conflict with their own interests.

Although the manifesto of the 15-M declared itself ideologically transversal – 'Some of us consider ourselves progressive, others conservative. Some of us are believers, some not. Some of us have clearly defined ideologies, others are apolitical' – the results from the June 2011 Center of Sociological Research (CIS) opinion poll demonstrate that support for mobilisations varied depending on the political vote of those polled: 80.6% of PSOE voters and 86.6% of Izquierda Unida voters showed their support for the movement, compared with 45.8% of PP voters.

We can therefore deduce that some Spaniards who made the left-wing parties' 2004 13-M victory possible (like those Americans who voted Obama to the presidency in the 2008 elections) are the same individuals who have since supported the occupying of the city squares under the slogan 'They do not represent us' or 'We are the 99%', sharing the space with the activist core of the social movements. Without the presence of these disillusioned people, the 15-M would have never attained the critical mass necessary to continue beyond the initial campaign stage of the first demonstrations and become an asocial mobilisation protest cycle.

Another factor to take into account is the social background of those who participated in the protest. A comparison between different CIS opinion polls shows us that, as of October 2011, the new middle classes, the upper middle classes and, to a lesser extent, the lower skilled workers were those who showed the greatest increase in participation in the demonstrations from the beginning of the protest, and this pattern seems to be reflected in the post-materialist issues of mobilisation, as well as in the strategic and intensive use that the participants have made of emerging technologies. However, if we focus on participants in the camps, the profiles vary slightly: campers were young people between 19 and 30 years old, students, so-called 'digital natives', unemployed and with left-wing views (Calvo et al. 2011).

Thus the mobilisations appear to be the result of a combination of the fear of downward social mobility among the middle classes and the lack of future expectations among young people, due to the damage caused by a crisis that not only stopped, but also reversed social mobility. Hence, unlike other movements which have focused on socio-economic disparities, the 15-M has expanded the battlefield to include disparities in political participation, denouncing the subordination of politics to economic interests and questioning directly those agents that are con-sidered responsible for the crisis for having evaded their responsibilities: the socio-democratic political parties and the trade unions.

Reasons for political detachment among left-wing voters are many, but those frequently mentioned by 15-M participants include: the approval of the so-called Sinde Law (anti-piracy law), which generated a wide mobilisation in the Internet surfer community and which is in the origin of the campaign #nolesvotes; labour reforms; the reform of the pension system; the discontent caused by government aid to a banking sector seen as responsible for the wave of evictions and mortgage exe-cutions; the protests that took place at universities in response to the introduction of the Bologna Plan; and cuts in both the public health system and education (Pedret 2011).

Rejection of political parties is evident in the manifesto itself:

> In Spain most of the political class does not even listen to us. Politi-cians should be bringing our voice to the institutions, facilitating the political participation of citizens through direct channels that pro-vide the greatest benefit to the wider society, not to get rich and prosper at our expense, attending only to the dictatorship of major economic powers and holding them in power through a two-party system headed by the immovable acronym PP & PSOE.
>
> (15-M Manifesto, ¡Democracia real YA!)

In this sense, it is symptomatic that the platform of citizen organisa-tions that supported the 15-M demonstration excluded the possibility of political parties and union trade organisations joining in.

Another dimension that contributed to the success of the 15-M, and one that is no less important, is the cultural one, which has two facets:

the transformation of the cultural habits associated with the irruption of the new technologies (changes in the dissemination and access of information, and in the production and consumption of cultural goods); and the decline of the consensus forged during the transition to democracy, which had marked the cultural and political process of change in the Spain and in which the younger generation do not see themselves reflected (Fernández-Savater 2011).

Aspects of 15-M mobilisation

In this section, I will analyse different aspects of 15-M mobilisation. First, I identify the different coalitions of actors involved in mobilisation. Second, I examine the various frames employed by the 15-M – in particular that of indignation. Next, I describe the repertoire of encampment and the strategic use of media and technological tools in the diffusion of the movement, and link it to the greater resonance of the 15-M with the Spanish public. After analysing the roles played by anonymity and networks in the protests, I then compare the 15-M to previous mobilisations in Spain before finally looking at the multiscalarity of the protests and situating them in the protest climate of 2011. Through the study of these different aspects we can obtain a deeper understanding of the richness and heterogeneity of this movement and links with other experiences of subterranean politics across Europe.

Coalition of actors

Although the 15-M has acquired its own self-organisation, superseding the traditional activist groups and coalitions thanks to the many meetings and committees that emerged during the occupations and their subsequent incarnation into neighbourhood assemblies, its structure has been influenced by the different groups and networks that have organised, supported and collaborated with 15-M in its different gestation phases (see Figure 5.1). According to the data collected in our research, the actors involved can be placed in concentric circles that reflect different degrees of commitment and collaboration, ranging from immersive involvement to sporadic support. However, this categorisation can vary from one local context to another.

Central actors. Those who have focused their actions on creating and promoting the movement: Real Democracy Now (the organising platform of the 15-M demonstration), No Les Votes (a group of bloggers and Internet surfers that emerged as a result of the approval of the

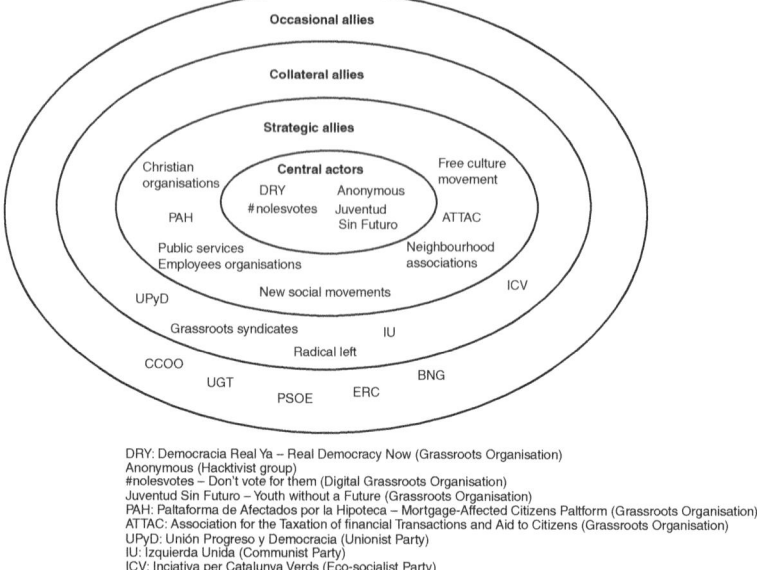

DRY: Democracia Real Ya – Real Democracy Now (Grassroots Organisation)
Anonymous (Hacktivist group)
#nolesvotes – Don't vote for them (Digital Grassroots Organisation)
Juventud Sin Futuro – Youth without a Future (Grassroots Organisation)
PAH: Paltaforma de Afectados por la Hipoteca – Mortgage-Affected Citizens Paltform (Grassroots Organisation)
ATTAC: Association for the Taxation of financial Transactions and Aid to Citizens (Grassroots Organisation)
UPyD: Unión Progreso y Democracia (Unionist Party)
IU: Izquierda Unida (Communist Party)
ICV: Inciativa per Catalunya Verds (Eco-socialist Party)
CCOO: Comisiones Obreras (Trade Union)
UGT: Unión General de Trabajadores (Trade Union)
ICV: Iniciativa per Catalunya Verds (Eco-socialist Party)
IU: Izquierda Unida (Communist Party)
PSOE: Partido Socialista de los Trabajadores (Social Democratic Left Party)
ERC: Esquerra Republicana de Catalunya (Catalan Nationalist Left Party)
BNG: Bloque Nacionalista Galego (Galician Nationalist Left Party)

Figure 5.1   Configuration of actors involved in the 15-M

Sinde Law) and Juventud Sin Futuro (a group of young students from the Madrid universities inspired by the movement Geraçao a Rasca de Portugal). Anonymous (a group of hacktivists who organise themselves via the Internet to defend their neutrality and guarantee the freedom of information) also belong to this group, but they joined after 15 May.

Strategic allies. Those who have committed themselves to the development of the movement, although this is not their main raison d'être. Here we find the Platform of People Affected by Mortgages, ATTAC, public health and education worker collectives, resident associations, associations of the unemployed, grassroots Christian movements, new social movements (feminist, ecologist, squatters, alter-globalisation), the free culture movement, collectives in defence of public universities and so on.

Collateral allies. Those who have supported the movement in different phases of its development: the rank-and-file union movement, political parties and coalitions such as Izquierda Unida (United Left),

Iniciativa per Catalunya-Verds (a Catalan eco-socialist party), Unión Progreso y Democracia (UPyD, a Spanish anti-nationalist party) and alternative left-wing political organisations, including Trotskyist groups and pro-independence organisations from Catalonia, Galicia and the Basque Country.[1]

Occasional allies. Those who have supported the movement at various crucial mobilisations: the trade unions (CCOO and UGT), PSOE representatives and associations, and left-wing nationalist parties such as the Esquerra Republicana de Catalunya and Bloque Nacionalista Galego.

According to the classification suggested by the analysis of our interviews and other data, we can see that the traditional actors with methods which are more institutionalised, bureaucratised and of long standing (trade unions and political parties) are placed at the periphery of the movement, while the more recently created, more informal, reticular structures that organise themselves online are the ones in the centre. This aligns with the notion of subterranean politics as discussed elsewhere in this book. Strategic allies are those groups and movements with low institutionalisation, with network functioning models and with a high degree of thematic specialisation. Collateral allies are political organisations and trade unions, with a strongly defined territorial state or autonomic basis, but which unlike the previous grouping (the occasional allies) are not, or only partially, involved in the consensus reached during the transition.

This analysis differs from that carried out by Carlos Taibo (2011a, 2011b), which supports the existence of two streams in the movement: the social alternative movements and the young 'Indignados' movement. Without denying that these two elements are present, I believe that the groups of actors mobilised by the 15-M are much more complex, and therefore the collaboration dynamics and the alliance between actors that usually occurs amongst groups in the closest spheres becomes increasingly more controversial between groups in those spheres farthest apart.

The 15-M frames

In order to analyse the genesis of the mobilisation cycle I will use frame analysis methodology (Gamson 1992; Ibarra and Tejerina 1998). According to this methodology these frames are general, standardised and predefined structures that allow knowledge and guide action. For Gamson (1992), the collective action frames have three components: *injustice*, which in the case of the 15-M is reflected in indignation at the political and socio-economic disparities worsened by the crisis; *agency*, that is to say, the awareness that it is possible to change this situation through collective action and which is represented by the occupation of city squares; and *identity*, the dichotomy between 'us' and 'them' which is reflected in the slogans 'We are not merchandise in the hands of politicians and bankers', 'We are the 99%' and 'they don't represent us'.

At the same time we can distinguish between a *diagnosis frame*, centred on the definition of the problem and the conferring of responsibilities; a *prognosis frame*, referring to those solutions which could reverse the situation; and a *motivational frame*, which is a call to action. In the case of the 15-M, the diagnosis frame can be defined by the effects of the crisis and the inability of traditional political actors to provide any response – it is a frame of *disappointment*. The solutions presented in the prognosis frame are based on a proposal of deepening democracy which would cover different levels: political, economic and social – the prognosis frame is thus a frame of *radical democracy*. And the motivational frame can be seen in the call to action to change the present situation through the occupation of the city squares – it is a frame of *indignation*.

Table 5.1 illustrates these frames linked to those topics to which they refer and their translation into the different slogans which have become popular in the demonstrations and social networks.

The indignation frame

The 15-M can be seen as one of social protest that started as a consequence of the gap between what is and what should be; one that generates a grievance situation which transforms a shared feeling of disappointment into an indignation frame onto which social mobilisation takes place. However, in order to understand the success of the indignation frame as a mobilisation frame, it is necessary to observe its construction, for it did not occupy a central position at the beginning of the movement. Although the manifesto included two references to 'indignation' – one in the introduction: 'but we are all concerned and angry about the political, economic, and social outlook which we see around us: corruption among politicians, businessmen, bankers, leaving us helpless, without a voice', and another in the final call to action: 'For all of the above, I am outraged. I think I can change it. I think I can help. I know that together we can' – the word *Indignado* had no relevant position in the 15-M demonstrations.

The success of the word *Indignado* is actually the result of a symbiosis between the label used by the press with which the movement was identified; the popularity of French author Stéphane Hessel's

Table 5.1   15-M frames

	Diagnosis frame	Prognosis frame	Mobilisation frame
	Disappointment	Radical democracy	Indignation
Topics	Consequences of the crisis in family economies Decline of the transition Burst of the real-estate bubble Attribution of responsibility of the traditional political agents for their inability to find solutions for the crisis	Democratic control of the economic power and financial sector Demanding of measures to stop corruption in political institutions Acknowledgement of new ways of democratic participation Overcoming the two-party system through a reform in the Electoral Law	Novel relevant role of civil society Occupation of public spaces Internationalisation will of the protest
Slogans	We are not merchandise in the hands of politicians and bankers They don't represent us #nolesvotes We won't pay for the crisis It isn't a crisis, it's a swindle It isn't the crisis, it's the system We aren't anti-establishment, the system is anti-us Violence is a 600 euro salary	Real Democracy Now! They call it democracy and it isn't Restarting the system Democracy 2.0 Apolitical? Superpolitical Democracy isn't dead	Take to the street #spanishrevolution #europeanrevolution #globalrevolution We aren't afraid A Cairo in each neighbourhood I'm Icelandic, Icelandic, Icelandic Yes, it can We are slow, cause we are going far SOLution Square

book, *Indignez-vous!*, exalted by the press as the *Indignados'* intellectual manifesto; and the subsequent appropriation of this label as an emblem by some of the demonstrators once they had occupied the city squares. A substantivisation of the word *Indignado* took place, from a qualifying adjective, 'I'm *Indignado* (outraged)', to a noun, 'I am an *Indignado*', 'movement of the *Indignados*'.

'Indignation' became the mobilisation frame which best expressed the discontent of the new middle classes in the face of the loss of their purchasing power, the collapse of their social promotion expectations, the uncertainty over the state of modern capitalism brought about by the financialisation of family economies and, especially, the public's perception of the incapacity of both the government and trade union representatives to provide a satisfying response to this situation.

Resonance, repertoire innovation and diffusion

We must also point out the resonance element of the frames present in the 15-M: that is to say, according to Gamson (1992), the natural advantage that certain frames achieve in relation to others because their ideas and language sound familiar within the broader popular culture. In the 15-M this resonance would be represented by the reappropriation of icons from film; the strategic use of elements from digital culture as symbolic elements of the movement; and the connection that the demonstrators and media have made with the recent revolts in the Arab countries, in Iceland and in Greece.

It should be noted that resonance has been an effect that the movement looked for, differing from the interpretative repertoire commonly associated with social movements. Examples of this usage of elements taken from popular culture can be found in viral marketing strategies using videos which adapted existing movies, such as *V for Vendetta*, *The Downfall* and *The Great Dictator*; the popularisation of the Guy Fawkes mask used by the anti-hero in *V for Vendetta* and the graphic novel of the same name; the naming of sections of occupied city squares after 'Tahrir' and 'Iceland'; the proliferation of Icelandic, Egyptian and Greek flags[2] in the demonstrations; and the reproduction of the language and hashtags of social networks in the slogans that appeared on placards.

One of the immediate results of the appearance of the 15-M was its ability to have a profound effect on the media's pre-election agenda. Part of this was due to the organisers' strategic vision, and their decision to situate the protests at the election campaign midway point (Taibo 2011a), as well as to the media amplification the movement received as the result of occupying city squares.

These occupations did not respond to any previous strategy, but rather emerged spontaneously, as a result of the unilateral decisions taken by dozens of people of camping at the Plaza del Sol to protest about the police charges and arrests that occurred after the 15-M demonstrations in Madrid (Requena et al. 2011). Due to the indignation that followed the eviction of those who camped on 16 May, what might have been a merely symbolic protest spread virally across the most important Spanish cities, becoming a movement expressing latent discontent. This was aided significantly not only by the dissemination of information via social networks (as discussed below), but also by coverage from the left-leaning media (*El País*, *Cadena Ser*, *Público*, *la Sexta*, Radio Nacional) who saw in the 15-M the possibility of breaking the spiral of silence and demobilisation of progressive voters, and by the instant criminalising response of the right-wing media (*La Razón*, Libertad Digital, TeleMadrid, Intereconomía, *la Gaceta*), who perceived in the 15-M an element that could affect the results of the Conservative Party at the next general election.

This polarisation raised the profile of the 15-M to the category of an event before which the different parties and social agents had to position themselves. The protests changed the media agenda by bringing to the front page topics previously ignored in the election programmes, such as the requirement of 'payment in kind' to cancel mortgage debt; control of the financial transactions; reform of the Electoral Law; and the defence of Internet neutrality against attempts to control the downloading of files. This situation gave 15-M a central role at the end of the election campaign, displacing the political acts from prime time.

One external factor that led to the spread of the protest was the decision by the Provincial Electoral Board in Madrid – then endorsed and extended across all of Spain by the Central Electoral Board – to prohibit the camps during the reflection day (21 May) and the day of the elections (22 May). However, these attempts backfired because no camp was actually dismantled; instead, they also served to increase further the popularity of, and participation in, the protests (Taibo 2011a, 2011b).

However, the movement would not have passed the campaign phase if it had limited itself to only the demonstrations called for by the 15-M. It was after the idea of occupation began to take hold that the mobilisation cycle started to take shape. So the camp protest of a hundred people at Plaza del Sol was widely disseminated by the social networks, which encouraged others to repeat the experience in Barcelona, Valencia, Seville, Palma, Bilbao and other cities. An attempt to evict the Plaça Catalunya (Barcelona) on 27 May using a disproportionate display of police brutality only added, yet again, to the popularity of the movement, whose repertoire of non-violence contributed throughout to popularise its demands and increase the wave of sympathisers towards it. Over subsequent days, other large Spanish cities began to join in and the flow of people participating grew massive. These encampments were linked symbolically to the occupation of Tahrir Square in Cairo, itself a symbol of the Arab Spring, and served to increase the sense that these were not individual protests but the representation of an almost universal sentiment.

However, the crucial innovation of the 15-M repertoire was not the encampments, nor the fact of congregating in a city square or the organisation of meetings,[3] but the combination of these three components: gathering in a city square indefinitely to transform it into a permanent space for dialogue and enunciation. The occupation repertoire of the city squares therefore worked under the logic of swarming as conceived by Arquilla and Ronfeldt (2001), and was defined by the convergence of many demonstrators towards the same place to show their public force (see also Chapter 4). This repertoire would achieve a profound symbolic force, returning to the cities' central areas their function as a space to meet and express oneself and eliminating the logic of consumer fever. One of the more commonly held interpretations of the participants interviewed is that the occupation of the city squares created a time apart from that of production and reproduction linked to the work–consume logic. The occupied squares became a 24-hour citizen agora where the exchange of ideas and their expression was possible.

The importance of technology

Among the elements that contributed to the growth and diffusion of participation in the protests were the speed of transmission of information and the ability to synchronise the actions via social networks – particularly via Twitter, which allowed for mass communication in real time. This led to the facility to reproduce the same action repertoire in numerous places.

In relation to the use of the new technologies Taibo (2011b) affirms: 'The general use of the Internet and cell phones has allowed the forging of a movement that is the product of numerous inter-connections and that has benefited, thanks to these instruments, of remote participation and increased intervention possibilities, as well as the spreading of information.' The role played by the expert knowledge held by the dynamising groups has turned the Information and Communication Technologies (ICT) into the central platform for the development of the movement. They incorporated strategies derived from marketing 2.0[4] to ensure that their actions and proclamations become trending topics on Twitter, and at the same time developed an alternative social network (n-1) where the groups could coordinate themselves, share information and develop their action strategies. However, although the answer is beyond the scope of this chapter, we should ask ourselves whether this technification has not generated exclusions and segmentations in the protests as a result of the digital gap, especially relevant in the dimensions of age, origin and socio-economic status.

The power of anonymity and networks

One of the most innovative traits of the 15-M, and one that differentiates it from other social movements, is its renunciation of a clearly defined movement identity, and hence the borders between 'in' and 'out' become blurry. Our interviews suggest that it is possible to feel part of the 15-M through participating in a commission, collaborating on a project or simply going to the occupation of a city square. Belonging likewise can come from physically participating in the demonstrations, by reproducing content related to the 15-M across social networks – or simply just by agreeing with their demands. This laxity of outlines, which in previous mobilisations might be seen as a weakness, has become one of the main strengths of the 15-M, since the subjective cost of being a member is very low while the expectations are high.

Another element of anonymity has been the explicit renunciation by the assemblies of the need to have an official spokesperson, and the refusal of the organisations and groups that have supported the 15-M to be seen as such – with the exception of its central actors (DRY, Nolesvotes, Anonymous and Juventud Sin Futuro), who, however, have always taken precautions not to speak in the name of the movement. Therefore, we can declare that the 15-M has built its own identity based on de-identification. Although within the assemblies, camps and demonstrations there were a significant number of activists from left-wing parties, unions and the newer social movements (feminist groups, anti-war activists, squatters and so on), nobody went simply on the basis of these previous memberships, and traditional militancy symbols (flags, symbols, etc.) were hidden. In fact, there was a consensus in the public assemblies to avoid the display of any partisan or ideological banner.

This innovative way of organising contentious politics leads us to review previous theories about social movements in relation to the field of identity (Melucci 1996) and communication resources (McAdam et al.

1999). The 15-M has not only used new technologies such as microblogging and instant messaging as dissemination and coordination tools, but it has also imitated their functioning; as in social networks, the ability to position a message on the Internet depends not so much on the prestige of the broadcasting source as on its capacity for replication, the speed of its transmission and its ability to coordinate the flows of action flows. In fact, decisions taken across the social networks have typically achieved more weight than those taken in face-to-face assemblies, which on occasion has become a cause of conflict among off-line participants and Internet activists.

We can conclude that the 15-M is an open network which connects nodes of actors and action and in which information travels in numerous directions and platforms (from social networks to instant messages, in posters, in assemblies and so on) and where the decisions de-virtualise/embody into specific actions from the Internet to the material world and vice versa.

The 15-M and previous movements

There have been other mobilisations in Spain in recent years that bear a resemblance to the 15-M. The Nunca Mais movement originated in 2002 as a result of the sinking of the oil tanker *Prestige*, and employed the innovation of communication frames that transcended the traditional slogans and banners, while the mobilisations against the Iraq war in 2003 saw massive demonstrations. V de Vivienda (H for Housing), a movement that began in 2006, used elements of pop culture to support its demands for the right to decent housing, and the 2009 university mobilisations against the introduction of the Bologna Process for the standardisation of European Higher Education Area were supported by student assemblies rather than students' unions. However, none of these saw the extent of citizen mobilisation witnessed with the 15-M. The only comparable mobilisations in terms of numbers were the protests following the outbreak of the Iraq war, but these differed substantially in terms of the innovation of the repertoire (the anti-war movement reduced their forms of expression to a massive demonstration) and the actors involved (those central in previous movements were the traditional actors of left-leaning parties, trade unions and so on). While previous mobilisations followed a standardised shape in terms of participation, time and forms of expression, the 15-M opened up a new space of politicisation. Although some analysts (Vivas and Antentas 2011) have compared the 15-M to the cycle of alter-globalisation mobilisation, as shown in Table 5.2, there are important differences between them.

Table 5.2 Comparing the alter-globalisation and the 15-M

	Alter-globalisation movement	15-M
Territorialisation	Focuses actions on economic summits	Decentralised and multi-scalar movement
Goal	Focuses actions on criticism of neo-liberalism	Focuses action on lack of democracy and the subordination of politics to economic interest
Organisational methods	Social forums	Assemblies in city squares and social networks
Mobilisation subjects	Greater importance of networks and organisations	Greater importance of informal groups

While the actors involved in the anti-globalisation movement focused their interventions around the major economic summits (Seattle, Prague and Genoa) of transnational organisations such as the IMF and the G-8, the participants of 15-M have focused on occupying city squares and generating their own pace of mobilisation. Neither the aims, the organisational methods nor the actors are the same. While the alter-globalisation groups have as their goal the denunciation of neo-liberalism and the North–South gap, and organise primarily through social forums and transnational meetings where networks and groups participate, exchange diagnosis and design mobilisation agendas, the goal of those behind the 15-M is the denunciation of the lack of democracy – as demonstrated by the 'Real Democracy, Now' slogans, banners and documents – and they organise through local assemblies and the Internet, giving more importance to informal and diffuse groups.

The multi-scalarity of the protest

Another distinguishing characteristic of the 15-M has been its capacity to navigate, without distinction, from the global to the local sphere. We can identify different territorial scales where the 15-M operates: the global scale, which connects the 15-M to Occupy in the USA and to similar *Indignados* protests in Israel, Italy, Chile and beyond; the state scale, which has as its epicentre the Plaza del Sol as symbol and motor of the protest; the regional scale, at which different expressions of the 15-M adopt their own dynamism (especially in Catalunya); and the local scale, initially through the replication of protests in city squares across Spain and subsequently via the spread of neighbourhood assemblies.

The combination of these scales has marked the peculiar geography of the movement, creating its battlefield, which is coordinated through the social networks. One of the characteristics of this multi-scalarity has been the relocation/translation of the protest agenda to its respective contexts. For example, the demand for reform of electoral law has had a major impact in Madrid due to the symbolic weight that the two-party system has in that territory, whereas in Catalunya, where there is a greater plurality of parties, its impact has been much lower; instead, the movement has focused more on the rejection of the cuts and the austerity policy imposed by the conservative government of the region.

Another important element has been the development of an infra-local scale, after the decision made by the public assemblies to dismantle the camps in the summer of 2011 and instead to promote the creation of neighbourhood assemblies. This decision to de-locate the protest has taken away its media visibility; however, it has allowed continuity of the movement and made it sustainable over time, given the difficulty of sustaining a central occupation in each city.

In this game of the scales, the internationalisation of the protest has also played a central role in garnering public support and resonance. To the hashtag #spanishrevolution, through the use of which the protest originally became popular on social networks, #europeanrevolution was added shortly after in an attempt to reproduce the city square occupations in other European countries. At first, this did not achieve the impact wished for – the response was limited to the modest occupations of a dozen Italian cities and a few failed attempts at occupation in France. French *Indignados* tried camping at the Bastille but were harshly put down by the French police.

However, a greater element of internationalisation was forged during summer 2011. Popular 'indignation' marches set off from different points around Spain, convening in Madrid on 23 July where the first 15-M Social Forum was held. From there, on 26 July, a group of marchers decided to continue up to Brussels via France. Arriving on 8 October, they stayed until 15 October, to coincide with a demonstration by 10,000 people on the day of global protests (de la Rubia 2011).

The organisation of this event had been discussed prior to 15 May, in order to enable face-to-face coordination between activists already connected transnationally via the social networks. On 15 September, the Hub Meeting was held in Barcelona. It was organised by different collectives from Spain, Italy, Slovenia and the United Kingdom in order to prepare for global protests on 15 October. As a result of this meeting, the manifesto 'Nothing to lose, everything to win!' was published, denouncing the austerity policies and calling for the democratisation of the economic system and of European governance, Internet neutrality, the rights of the immigrants and for substantive participatory democracy at all levels.

At roughly the same period, on 17 September 2011, following an international call from the Canadian anti-consumerist magazine *Adbusters*, the Occupy Wall Street movement occupied Zucotti Park in New York City, protesting against economic disparity and the power of the corporations over the political sphere. Along with Occupy Wall Street and the Spanish *Indignados*, al Coordinamento 15 ottobre (Italy), student groups in Chile (Chile *Indignado*), Occupy LSX (see Chapter 7) and other groups in 981 cities and 82 countries[5] protested on 15 October, making this day one of the most important milestones of transnational activism.

However, when analysing the multi-scalarity of the 15-M it is important to point out the scant presence of the European scale, represented only by the popular indignation march to Brussels (described above) and the publishing of the book *Crisis y Revolución en Europa* (Observatorio Metropolitano 2011). Most of 15-M's demands (for payment in kind, reform of electoral law, and in opposition to the law against Internet downloads and political corruption, and so forth) addressed the national government. Only those demands that called for control of finance – those demanding a tax on financial transactions, the control of tax havens and a citizens' debt audit – included a transnational dimension that was implicitly European.

The almost complete absence of this dimension, according to the results of our focus groups, is due to three factors: the absence of prior reflection amongst core actors in Spanish social movements about the need to regard Europe as a political action space; the lack of clearly defined policies and spaces of political decision emanating from the European institutions; and the discrediting of the European project as a result of the progressive abandonment of the creation of a 'social Europe', and instead the subordination of this to neo-liberal policies.

Final remarks

The strength of the 15-M resides in its capacity to generate a response to the decline of a public democratic sphere increasingly conditioned by the power of the financial and economic elites, with its growing tendency towards post-democracy (Crouch 2004). In this sense, the movement would represent a bet for the reconstruction of a democratic moment where

> The enthusiasm of political participation is more widespread; there are many different groups and organisations of ordinary people who share the task of trying to build a political agenda, the powerful interests which dominate non-democratic societies are in an unfavourable situation and on the defensive and the political system has not yet been capable of discovering how to manage and manipulate the new demands.
>
> (ibid.: 15)

The establishment of the 15-M has contributed to widening the gap between conventional political action methods and those innovating examples which have transformed collective action practices. However, in spite of the wide dissemination of these practices and of some of their proposals, the impact on the conventional political system has been unequal.

In this sense, the main strengths of the 15-M are:

- The incorporation of new topics in the public agenda, such as the requirement of payment in kind, the reform of electoral law, or the fight against corruption. These have resonated strongly with the public agenda, although their incorporation in the political agenda has been more modest. Other topics such as Internet neutrality and the control of financial transactions and tax havens have had a lesser impact.
- The re-categorisation of political concepts such as politics, democracy, participation and transparency, which have acquired a new meaning though mobilisation. Following the appearance of the 15-M, politics are no longer understood as an election fight between parties, but as active participation of society in the definition of the problems and the finding of solutions; and democracy is no longer identified only by its formal meaning as a way of government, but also as a right of citizen participation.
- The emergence of a new actor, critical civil society, alongside traditional political actors such as political parties, trade unions and even social movements, who have now lost their exclusive political action monopoly in the face of the emergence of new proposals and participation methods. In this sense, the novelty of the 15-M is not so much what – its pragmatic proposals – but how, where how is the bid to construct a new democratic sphere in which the equality principle

and politics are understood as a citizen's right and not as a merely technical business.

However, two questions arise. The first is to what extent this mobilising capacity will have an impact on political decision spaces beyond agenda setting, and thereby generate structural change. And the second is whether this mobilisation cycle can lead to the construction of a new political articulation, not necessarily in the way of a party, that is able to sustain the demands expressed over time. However, it is possible that this impact may not occur in a direct and immediate way, but through a change in the political culture which could still take some years to be absorbed.

Notes

1. Note that in some cities, notably Barcelona and Madrid, the alternative left-wing assumed a more central role as strategic allies.
2. In this sense it is significant to point out how these elements ended in replacing the traditional iconography of the social protest movements in the Spanish state (anarchist, republicans, pro-independence supporters, Cuban, Palestinian or communist flags) whose presence in the different protest calls was peripheral.
3. Other protest movements had already camped to demand their goals, for example the camps that took place to demand that the state assigned 0.7% of GDP to international development aid. Likewise, assemblies are commonplace in students', residents' and workers' movements, as well as the mass meetings in the most important squares of developed cities, to address demands of a civic nature.
4. It is possible to establish a link between the 15-M's strategic use of social networks and the technological profiles of the members of the dynamising groups (bloggers, community managers, digital designers and so on).
5. Analysis of the 15-O mobilisations shows that they have considerable relevance in the countries where they were able to connect to pre-existing protest movements (USA and the incipient movement Occupy Wall Street; Italy and the movement against the government policies of Berlusconi, who was to resign a month later; and Chile with the movement against the privatisation of education), whereas in those countries in which this was not the case the impact of the protest was fairly limited.

References

Arquilla, J. and Ronfeldt, D. (2001) *Networks and Netwars: The Future of Terror, Crime, and Militancy*. Santa Monica, CA: RAND Corporation.

Calvo, K., Gómez-Pastrana, T. & Mena, L. (2011) 'Movimiento 15M: ¿quiénes son y qué reivindican?', Zoom Político, Especial 15-M, (2011/04), 4–17. Madrid: Fundación Alternativas.

CIS (2011) *Barómetro Mayo 2011*. Madrid: Centro de Investigaciones Sociológicas.

Crouch, C. (2004) *Posdemocracia*. Madrid: Taurus.

¡Democracia real YA! (2011) 'Manifesto', http://www.democraciarealya.es/

Fernández-Savater, A. (2011) *La cultura de la transición y el 15-M*. Publicado en el blog Fuera de Lugar el 31 de Agosto de 2011, Accessed online at http://blogs.publico.es/fueradelugar/879/la-cultura-de-la-transicion-y-el-15-m

Gamson (1992) *Talking Politics*. Cambridge: Cambridge University Press.

Ibarra, P. and Tejerina, B. (1998) *Los nuevos movimientos sociales*. Madrid: Editorial Trotta.

McAdam, D., McCarthy, J. D. and Zald, M. N. (1999) *Movimientos sociales. Perspectivas comparadas*. Madrid: Istmo.

Melucci, A. (1996) *Challenging Codes: Collective Action in the Information Age*. Cambridge: Cambridge University Press.

Observatorio Metropolitano (2011) *Crisis y Revolución en Europa*. Madrid: Traficantes de Sueños.

Pedret, F. (2011) *Quan succeix l'inesperat. El 15-M i l'esquerra*. Barcelona: Edicions els llums.

Plihon, D. and Rey, N. (2011) 'L'Espagne, douze années d'aveuglement', Report for the Economistes atterrés, December 2011. Paris: Université Paris-Nord.

de la Rubia, R. (ed) (2011) *Hacia una revolución mundial no-violenta: del 15M al 15O*. Madrid: Editorial Manuscritos.

Sanz de Miguel, P. (2011) 'Spain: Annual Review 2010', European Observatory of Working Life, EurWORK. Accessed online at http://eurofound.europa.eu/observatories/eurwork/comparative-information/national-contributions/spain/spain-annual-review-2010

Taibo, C. (2011a) *Nada será como antes. Sobre el movimiento 15-M*. Madrid: Ediciones la Catarata.

Taibo, C. (2011b) *El 15-M en sesenta preguntas*. Madrid: Los libros de la catarata.

Vivas, E. and Antentas, J. M. (2011) 'Rebellion of the indignant: Notes from Barcelona's Tahrir Square', *International Viewpoint*, Friday 20 May 2011. Accessed online at http://internationalviewpoint.org/spip.php?article2154

6
Hungary at the Vanguard of Europe's Rearguard? Emerging Subterranean Politics and Civil Dissent

Jody Jensen[1]

Introduction

Hungary had a rich tradition of peaceful street protest, from the pro-democracy demonstrations of the late 1980s to the Democratic Charta's anti-fascist, anti-extreme right protests in 1991 and 1992. This peaceful tradition ended in 2006 with what many perceive *post festum* as the breaking of the social contract between Hungarian citizens and their government. A secret speech by Prime Minister Gyurcsány was leaked and broadcast to the public, in which he admitted lying to the country for years about the economy to win the recent election. Repeated, spontaneous demonstrations after the leak turned violent under suspicious circumstances that are still under investigation.

Around the 50th anniversary of the 1956 October Revolution in 2006, many Hungarians identified themselves with the revolutionaries, feeling that their freedom and democracy was under direct threat from what some termed 'a parliamentary dictatorship'. An unspecified anger burst out after people took to the streets to peacefully celebrate the anniversary of 1956, and they were met with sanctioned police violence. There was little to no response from the European Union (EU) or other European countries, or international human rights institutions, in regard to the uncontrolled police violence and obvious manipulation of events by the authorities. The explosion of emotions, frustration and anger surprised everyone. Subterranean politics suddenly revealed itself.

Another example of the resilience and tenacity of protestors and an important series of online and offline actions began in 2010 against the arrest, imprisonment and maltreatment of Ágnes Geréb, a doctor and midwife who attended home births, which are still illegal in Hungary today. This protest was framed in terms of human rights and addressed democratic deficiencies in the country. The protest confronted the lack of choice in weak and fragile (no-choice) democracies that silence voices who speak out against monopolies of power, such as the medical establishment in Hungary. This protest provoked widespread regional and international coverage and support.[2]

Subterranean politics in Hungary encompasses a wide and multi-level range of anti-government and anti-corruption discourses already present before the global financial crisis. Tent cities established outside the parliament after the street battles in 2006 can be seen as forerunners to present day global revolts in terms of format, modus operandi and message. This was also the first time that nationalist, right-wing, anti-government groups took advantage of social unrest and began articulating their message in an organised and structured way.

More protests emerged in 2011–2012 in opposition to the criminalisation of the homeless with actions around the country by groups like A Város Mindenkié (The City Belongs to Everyone). A sudden upheaval of subterranean activity then arose in response to the government's introduction of controversial measures related to constitutional changes, the media laws, retirement age of judges and overseeing of the national bank. A recurring *leitmotif*, sometimes in the background of protests, sometimes in the foreground, was protests against racism, anti-Semitism, anti-Roma and the perceived support by the government of right-wing policies.[3]

Our research concentrated on the period 2011–2012, a time of many pro- and anti-government actions and street protests in response to a variety of triggers, some mentioned above. The research team conducted online searches of groups and their activities in order to map the landscape of protests and the main actors. We conducted both online and face-to-face interviews with protestors, sometimes live during street demonstrations. The main aims of the research were to map the terrains of activity, the issues around which new groups had emerged and organised, and to create a timeline of protests for the period covered by the research to judge their frequency and persistence.

In many ways what we discovered is similar to the emergence of subterranean politics in other parts of Europe and the rest of the world, and events in Hungary mirror the global timeline of activism. There is no question that the global momentum provided impetus and support for an otherwise somewhat lethargic population to take to the streets in protests about the direction in which their country was heading.

There is certainly an effervescent quality to emerging subterranean politics in Hungary today. Protests are generally organised around specific issues and, to a lesser extent, exhibit a broader approach – for example, addressing rampant global capitalism and social injustice, like the *Éhségmenet* (Hunger march).[4] There is also less connection to global movements, although regional and even European-level collaboration can be found on Facebook pages and blogs in English about Occupy! Hungary. Generally, protest is nationally organised and coordinated, with Budapest and a few larger cities, like Szeged and Pécs, as focal points of activity.

The concept of subterranean politics fits particularly well with the current Hungarian situation, first of all because of the interconnectedness of the Hungarian political and economic crisis and the EU and global political, economic and financial crisis; and second because it is too early to talk about a 'social movement' or movements, or actualisation of an emergent aspiration of solidarity which underpins a notion of a democratic civil society. To date, actions in the national context have been too fragmented and idiosyncratic to form an emergent whole in terms of civil society self-mobilisation with a clear civic ethos. That is why adaptation of the new framework of 'subterranean politics' has advantages and resonance, since it helps to constructively package the multifarious and novel manifestations of political dissatisfaction and civil dissent in a new discourse without the restraints and intellectual baggage of notions like civil society and social movement theory. There is something new going on in the way people are communicating, organising and taking action. Some of this has to do with the effect and adaptation of new technologies, which both influence and inform new notions of civic activism, but it is not enough to explain the emphasis on 'process'. This was present in Hungary in discussions of who should participate, and how, in demonstrations, even if this emphasis was less pronounced than perhaps in other countries.

Sharing characteristics with other protest movements in Europe, many groups were unified around a profound disillusionment with politics as such, both at the national and European level. There was also a latent anger and frustration left over from the previous regime of Prime Minister Gyurcsány, which resurfaced in new forms of protest against the present regime of Prime Minister Orbán. Blame and responsibility for the current existential uncertainties and financial hardships, however, were placed in different quarters by different groups – either at the national level with the present government or at the EU level. For anti-government protestors, the overwhelming 2/3 Fiatal Demokraták Szövetsége (FIDESZ, Alliance of Young Democrats) majority in the parliament signified a return to a more authoritarian political style and threatened to undermine democratic principles and practices. It also brought to mind allegations against the former government of 'parliamentary dictatorship', which threaten democratic processes.

On the other hand, a large majority supported the government's stance against attacks and 'Hungary-bashing' from the IMF, the EU and the liberal international media. Many protestors carried signs with slogans that Hungary would not be a colony of the EU, and the additional irritation of austerity measures and sanctions, which directly affected large parts of the population, increased anti-EU sentiments in Hungary as in many other post-communist societies. What may distinguish Hungary, then, from other protests in Europe may be the visibility and centrality of Europe and the discourse about Europe, both positive and negative, in the protests.

The protests in 2011 against constitutional changes and media law are diverse, but they clearly fit the pattern of earlier demonstrations, as in 2010 in support of Ágnes Geréb, that framed protest in the context of European values and practices. This is an important element in the articulation of Hungarian democracy that actively takes on European value sets and sees them as a necessary prerequisite for a functioning civil society. At the same time, Hungarians felt victimised by the criticism levelled at their country and many protestors saw, and still see, a double standard of evaluation imposed and even hypocrisy evident in older EU member states that are also experiencing a crisis of democracy at the national level. This feeling is shared by other new member states that expressed at least sympathy, if not support, for Hungary at European Parliament debates. So even if Hungarians, generally or in particular cases, strongly disapprove of the actions of Prime Minister Orbán's government, many still feel unjustly persecuted by the EU.[5]

The Hungarian context

The trust that Hungarians have in their politicians has not been enhanced with the change of government in 2010. Compared with the rest of the EU, Hungary rates among the lowest in terms of political trust. In a recent survey of 3,000 people, over 80% expressed little or no trust at all in politicians. The researcher who compiled the survey, Ferenc Peterfi, remarked that low public trust is a major problem and has continued to deteriorate since surveys began in 2005. He said that unless this trend changes, low institutional trust will develop into lack of trust between individuals and their (politicians) actions. This would further exacerbate social and economic problems.[6] According to the Public Trust

Research Survey 2010, it is increasingly difficult to call for common action in the civic sphere. As one analyst put it:

> Being a protester in Hungary [is a thankless job]. The waves of far-right protests during the previous government made the role [shameful]...There is a political culture in Hungary where who you are with is more important than what you are for. This is one of the reasons why democracy has been dismantled in this country to the extent it has today.[7]

This may be changing and signal a shift from previous periods because there is a growing frequency of street events, although the number of protestors involved in actions is still comparatively low. In support of the view that attitudes may be changing, a participant interviewed at a recent protest by independent media sources said: 'There are not that many of us here, but I believe that the frequency of events shows a shift in peoples' attitudes. It shows that the younger generation is ready to cope with the shadows of the past, and raise their voice for their rights.' Another interviewee said 'that although the impact of the protests was uncertain, it was important to make sure that these measures [i.e. constitutional changes] go into the history books with the note "citizens protested against it"'.[8]

Many of these trends are based on a historically complex and problematic relationship between citizens and the state. The thesis that has developed is that the nexus between the citizen and the state is flawed or controversial in Hungary, partly because there has been a lack of independent Hungarian statehood continuity over many centuries,[9] partly because of the overwhelming paternalistic attitude of stakeholders in public affairs, and partly because 'transition' to democracy and a market economy was coupled with polarisation, impoverishment and fear about the future. Identification between citizens and state became difficult and the state is viewed as alien or extraneous most of the time, so not to cooperate with it is seen as a heroic struggle. When an independent Hungarian state was finally born after World War I, it had difficulty maintaining the social contract with citizens (i.e. it could not protect them from, among other things, wartime occupation and captivity, deportation, internment, evacuation or emigration). After the systemic change this situation has changed somewhat but, in the perception of citizens, the state itself has remained alien and threatening.[10]

This has consequences today. Hungary, for example, is rated in 18th position (out of 19 surveyed European countries in 2006) in the Active

Citizenship Composite Indicator for 'Protest and Social Change Index'.[11] Even though the subdivision of 'Protest' was relatively high in all countries, the low position of Hungary was driven by a low value in 'working in organisations' (only 3% in Hungary compared with 30% in the top performing Scandinavian countries). Hungary was also placed 18th in the Representative Democracy Index. Although Hungary performs well in democratic values and voting (75% in national elections, 38% in European parliament elections), it scores low in participation in politics. It is exactly this criterion that separates those countries that perform well from those that don't. In the composite ranking for active citizenship, Hungary is bottom in 19th position.

The disillusionment with democracy can be traced back in Hungary, and in other Central and Eastern European countries, to the failure of the transition to involve people in transitional processes. The kind of political unrest in Central Europe which can be viewed as regressive, although very different in content in the various national contexts, can be explained by the fact that people in the region have not overcome their feelings of disempowerment and frustration at the time of the systemic change. In this respect, the demonstrations in 2006 were more like the Occupy movements in their spontaneity and lack of formal leadership, organisers and agenda.

There is a tendency to demonise adversaries in the Hungarian political landscape. This exacerbates the polarisation of political interests, undermines dialogue and constructive consensus building and provides little space for civil initiatives, which are either co-opted or corrupted for political purposes. One common feature of present and past demonstrations is mistrust and fear of civil society on the part of politicians, political parties and institutions. From the beginning of transition, governments have been reticent to include NGOs or civic groups in any policy discussions of social and economic issues.[12] At first, this was argued in terms of slowing down economic transition with social dialogue; later under the socialists, in response to the 23 October 2006 repercussions, it was declared that politics should be confined to the parliament and not taken on to the streets. In older, more developed and consolidated democracies, it is normal that when political institutions are unable to function – or even directly threaten the public good – citizens take to the streets to express their frustration and concern. This is not always understood or accepted by the political elite in Hungary. But a counter to street violence, a new kind of political culture, has been seen to emerge in Hungary since 2006 and which can be termed 'subterranean politics', and has only begun to become part of the socio-political culture and landscape in the recent past. The continuing and growing gap between the people and politicians is only perhaps now being breached by new grassroots-based groups and parties that provide alternative political options such as Jobbik, Milla, LMP and 4K! There is a blurring between the grassroots and politics taking place, a widening grey area in which 'politics' tries to control, manipulate and co-opt with great vehemence and speed.

Taking 'Europe' to the street: subterranean politics surfaces in Hungary

A tale of two protests: anti-government protest (2 January 2012) and pro-government peace march (21 January 2012)

In looking at and for subterranean politics in Hungary, and searching for the relationship between subterranean politics and Europe, we decided to focus on two marches held in early 2012, one in which the presence of the European question was less visible, the other in which it played an important role. In fact, the second demonstration was organised in response to the first and the two are connected. The field researchers attended both marches and spoke with some of the participants in order to find out more about their motivation, aims and orientation. It became clear through interviews and observation, and subsequent analysis of the press coverage of the events, that there is an increasing, yet fragile, solidarity expressed in the demonstrations, which is new.

New dangers are also apparent, like the co-optation of civil initiatives by oppositional political parties who try to piggy-back on the courage of the social activists to increase their political leverage. This issue became part of the public discussion before, during and after the anti-government demonstrations on 2 January 2012 outside the Hungarian Opera House, where the government was celebrating the inauguration of the new constitution. The contrast with the October 1989 declaration of Hungary's new constitution is striking and clearly stuck in the back of people's minds. In 1989, Hungary's new constitution was declared from the window of the Hungarian parliament in an open space where an enormous crowd assembled to celebrate the founding of the Third Hungarian Republic. In stark contrast, the present government's announcement of the new constitution was declared in the confined space of the small Hungarian Opera House and was not an open public event even for the press, but strictly 'by invitation only'. Because of the seriousness of the opposition protests outside the Opera House, it was reported that the secret service had developed a plan to evacuate politicians via a system of underground tunnels if necessary. Prime Minister Orbán 'escaped' after the ceremony through a side door to avoid confrontation with the public outside. This was unprecedented, especially considering his electoral popularity.

The core dilemma of the protest that was organised outside was whether it should be a 'civil' or 'political' protest. This is a real problem, probably more striking in Hungary than elsewhere. As reported in the blog Contrarian Hungarian, if a leader emerged from a political protest, serious political capital could be gained for the political interests they represented. But the stakes were admittedly high for the new, emerging opposition movement: they could alienate demonstrators who did not want to be affiliated with the leadership or organisation of a particular political group. This situation had never been confronted before because, prior to the election in 2010 and the large majority in parliament, protest initiatives had only been organised by civil society organisations. Opposition parties in the parliament had not participated in street demonstrations before 23 December 2011, when Hungary's Green-Liberal Party LMP (Politics can be different) announced a new approach they called 'New Resistance' and resorted to civil disobedience. Rarely have political parties wanted to become involved in street protests to express support and solidarity with demonstrators.[13]

A consensus was achieved prior to the 2 January 2012 demonstration to organise a 'civilian' demonstration. Eight different permit applications for the demonstration, some submitted by oppositional parties, were withdrawn and instead two private individuals representing civil organisations (Solidarity and 'Habitat instead of Jail', a group active in protesting Hungary's criminalisation of homelessness) submitted a joint permit for a collective protest. Political parties were permitted to attend, but no speeches were allowed from party representatives. When this programme for protest was made public, a dissenting view immediately emerged that targeted 'the populism of anti-politics' and advocated the need for professional politicians to remain in the forefront of opposition and political action. This dissenting argument, that political parties should not take a back seat to civilian groups in Hungarian politics, was voiced by the former Hungarian prime minister, Ferenc Gyurcsány, one of the most divisive political figures in recent Hungarian political history. His argument, that if the public turns against the political system and the political elite democracy is jeopardised, gained little support or public acceptance among protestors. It did, however, provide a clearer distinction between the motivations of citizens and politicians in the Hungarian opposition. On the one hand, unity was proposed to protest the changes to the Hungarian 2012 Constitution with civil society groups taking leading roles. On the other hand, political opposition wanted to showcase different political views taking advantage of civil protests to garner political party support. In the conflicting public space, a fragile civil solidarity emerged under the banner of 'supporters of the Republic'.[14]

The second demonstration, the pro-government peace march organised for 21 January 2012, was promoted by pro-government journalists and media owners. Widely varying reports of numbers ranged from 100,000–400,000 to 2 million demonstrators, depending on whether the 'official' media were reporting or alternative sources, but the actual number was probably about 100,000. This was the largest demonstration to date. People carried placards with slogans such as 'we will not be a colony', 'democracy forever', 'Hungarian sovereignty' and '1956 + 1956 = 2012'.[15]

A wide variety of opinions was voiced at this demonstration, and some of the most direct references to the EU and Hungary were made. Some demonstrators did not, in fact, support the FIDESZ government, but came 'on behalf of Hungarians in general'. 'We are not here for FIDESZ, but for the sovereignty of the Hungarian nation', said one of the demonstrators who was interviewed.[16] Others were motivated to attend by the attacks against Hungary in the foreign press, where many people felt that misinformation was being communicated.

Framed as a peace march, a recurring theme was that Hungarians need to make peace with themselves, as reported by one of our researchers. Alternative media sources reported that the absence of an underlying and cohesive message, attractive to both the Eurosceptics and Euro-supporters, led to a very 'silent' demonstration, with few speeches. On the other hand, the official national, pro-government media reported that the march was more dignified than the rowdy protests of opposition actions.

The impact and role of the press in subterranean politics in Hungary

Complaints were lodged against both the pro-government national press coverage and the international coverage of protests and events in Hungary. Locally, protests were downplayed in the national press by pro-government media sources. A typical response was to criticise street actions as lacking a coherent platform of ideas.

> Liberal and conservative pundits wonder if the anti-government NGOs and the opposition parties have a program which could constitute a real alternative to the Orbán government. The commentators suggest the anti-government groups have no clear ideas about what they want to do after ousting Orbán. If successful, such politics would only perpetuate populist rhetoric, they argue.[17]

The danger of street protests, then, according to some journalists is that they would lead to increased populist, that is, right-wing responses.

Reporting on the protest outside the Opera House is a good example of local, pro-government coverage. The background shots taken by Hungarian state television suggested that there were more police on the scene than anti-government demonstrators. The next day they officially apologised for this misrepresentation, but reported that it was due to the closing off of streets in the vicinity of the Opera House and their inability to reach the demonstrators. Typically, the numbers of protestors at events was downplayed to 'a couple of hundred', whereas when the pro-government peace march took place estimates ranged wildly up towards 1 million.

The general evaluation of Occupy-type protests was termed 'tepid' by a Hungarian Brussels correspondent, who described Hungary's joining the international protest chain as consisting of 'a single, marginal group, which could only mobilise a few hundred demonstrators'. This he attributes to the limited public interest in the government's economic policies: 'In Budapest the government is actually implementing the program of the demonstrators.'[18] This is in clear contradiction to the wide range of protests, organised over a sustained period and directed at not just governmental economic policies (e.g. 'F in Math' demonstration, hunger strike by journalists, Blister Circus), but against constitutional changes, media law and information protection issues.

Emerging new public spaces and the European discourse

A new public discourse and new public space may be emerging in Hungary as a result of multiple crises. The concept of 'space' is very important in the Hungarian context. The idea of taking back the civic 'space' for citizens as an arena to interact and to develop ideas is being experimented with and evolving. One only needs to think of the vibrant European Café cultural space that existed for centuries in Hungary. Cafés became focal points for the political opposition before the systemic change where dissidents met and organised. Retaking and occupying public space is a real battleground in Hungary. In March 2012, the FIDESZ government forestalled any opposition demonstrations in Budapest on the national holiday on 15 March marking the 1848 Revolution by reserving the entire downtown area for the day, and the Administration and Justice Ministry and Budapest City Council were granted permits to occupy public areas for the entire week surrounding the national holiday. These permits were also valid for 2013 and 2014. The group Milla (One Million for Press Freedom in Hungary) had announced plans for a major rally on 15 March, but did not receive permission from the police for the demonstration. Milla countered, however, by reserving prime demonstration space for 100 years from 2014. They were instead granted permission for a demonstration organised on 10 March 2012.[19]

With the overwhelming parliamentary majority of FIDESZ and lack of a viable political opposition, conflict has been removed at that level. Confrontation is taking more creative and alternative routes in the form of street demonstrations which may appear, at first sight, as contradictory – one week anti-government, pro-European, the next week pro-government, anti-EU – but there is a clear attempt to reorganise the debate around common issues of public concern. What is important is that in a country that has experienced crisis in one form or another for more than two decades, the reaction is not just to austerity measures, but to the remaking of the political, social and economic landscapes and the retaking of public space. This includes a rearticulation of the public good at the national and EU levels. Even though Hungarian protests lack common and articulated goals, they do share surprisingly many understandings about the way democracy should work and what their role and that of government should be. One basis of understanding is the corrosive influence of money on politics and the desire to have a voice in democratic policy making at all levels. Calls for austerity measures (more taxation, spending cuts on social programmes) are decoupled from discussions of shared European values, but governance is beginning to be understood by people as what they can do together to provide the basic building blocks for the future. This shared understanding is emerging in a diverse milieu – from different economic sectors and social sectors to groups with different political perspectives. One important factor may be not the number of protestors that take to the streets for a time, but the extent to which they are able to sustain their efforts and networks over the long term.

Current protests, not just in Hungary, are asking on whose side the EU stands in the current power constellation – on the side of citizens demonstrating for greater economic justice, transparency and account-ability, or on the side of global capital and finance. Some find strength in the community offered by the EU while others argue for more inde-pendence from global financial markets and retreat into nation state rhetoric. This plurality of approaches is reflected in the Hungarian situation.

At least two particular attitudes can be observed in the current demonstrations:

• those who are against the new government measures pertaining to the media law and new constitution and aim only to change the government and have a local focus on local issues, disconnected from more global movements;
• there are groups that share understanding with other groups globally in their critique of the IMF, global financial institutions and the wider critique of the political elite.

It is interesting to highlight the divisions within certain groups over this issue – for example, Jobbik members were present at both anti- and pro-government demonstrations, though pushed out by the more liberal crowd. Jobbik's relations to the EU and rest of the world were summarised in a report of the party gathering as perpetuating friendly relations with the EU, so that Hungary could reassert 'classical European values', but at the same time conducting a foreign policy of its own and looking towards the east – particularly to Russia and Turkey.[20] In the reality of everyday politics (e.g. burning EU flags in the streets), however, they are clearly anti-EU.

A generational change, even gap, can be seen in the current protests. Older demonstrators followed more of the attitudes towards chang-ing the government, while younger demonstrators connected more with European-wide and global actions. There is evident innovation in the repertoire of these new subterranean groups. Blogs, Facebook, Interfacebook, the election of an 'alternative president of Hungary' on the Internet (which hopes to spread throughout Europe to other countries), the Clean Hands Movement, the Solidarity Movement, the Two-Tailed Dog party, 4K! and Milla are increasingly working in coordinated and collaborative ways with varying degrees of success.[21] We are beginning to see generationally mixed groups in civil groups initiated by young people. It may be that the youth are socialising parents into activism. This is new in Hungary, a country that cannot boast strong cohesion or collaboration even on shared issues. In terms of demonstration styles with speakers on platforms and crowds in the street, Hungary is more traditional and patriarchal on the surface, but there are new dynamics that can be detected at the subterranean level as manifested in the recent student demonstrations and the vivid and innovative blogosphere and social media.

In line with a more traditional approach, a new 'Democratic Opposition Round Table' was created by political party elites. This construction reminded people of the systemic change and 'negotiated reform' of the system by elites in Hungary. The new 'Democratic Opposition Round Table' formulated a basic agenda without the inclusion of people outside of political parties and again reflects a rather elitist, anti-civil society approach to protest.

There are obvious efforts on the government's side to utilise the grand opportunities of the new media. A more innovative approach, and perhaps as a reaction to criticism towards the government for the lack of civic/public participation in the decision-making processes, there is a new online potential for the inclusion and channelling of citizens' views on government practices and state functions: www.joallam.kormany .hu (www.goodstate.government.hu). Here citizens have the opportunity to recommend changes to functions and processes of current decision-making procedures. It appears, therefore, that the protests have already achieved a step towards a more direct way to influence governance and policy-making. E-democracy could provide some relief to the democratic deficit currently felt by many individuals. It could be a useful tool both to channel opinions and reduce unrest, especially since most demonstrators are young. Some events have been organised on online spaces and web2 communities, mostly related to LMP and Jobbik, the new parties in the parliament that frequently use these technologies to mobilise people.

In many ways, because of its unfortunate experience of national leadership and unstable and shaky democracy, Hungary was a forerunner of contemporary protests in 2010–2011; on the other hand, because of the fragmentation and deep political, ideological, 'bipolar' dividedness of society, social interests and a political culture of demonisation, Hungary has further to go than other countries to construct strong social cohesion connecting with others – with similar global and national movements. As in the case of many burgeoning social movements, the momentum may change. What has begun may fall apart, it may cohere, it could morph into something totally different or it could grow and become more cohesive, reaching out to other like-minded movements. The salience of movement tenacity and perseverance has been surprisingly strong, with a variety of innovative and sustained actions.

The timeline in Box 6.1 provides highlights of innovative street actions and illustrates the richness of dissent fermenting on the streets of Hungary today.

Some civil society groups in Hungary are calling on Brussels to restrain what their national government is doing in specific areas such as media law, constitutional changes and information protection; at the same time, large public demonstrations were organised in support of the Hungarian government in opposition to edicts from Brussels over austerity measures. The changes being wrought in Hungary today do not reflect the values of many in Hungarian society and a majority of the population support the EU. Many take the view that the government is experimenting with 'opportunistic nationalism' or with new forms of 'leader democracy'. In the name of security the government is practising fear-mongering, with the EU depicted as an imperialist power. This conflict between the public's primarily positive view of the EU and the government's recalcitrance towards the EU also increases public distrust in the institutions of democracy.

Europe is more than the EU and comprises many other institutionalised and non-institutionalised civil forms of communication, cooperation and collaboration. This is clearly evident in the number of coordinated events throughout Europe which make up part of this study on subterranean politics, and surely includes Hungary in terms of acts of civil organisation, disobedience and protest. The emergence of polarising and populist movements in a significant number of European countries poses alarming challenges for a future, hopefully more unified Europe. It is clear from the present confrontation of populist-nationalists in Hungary and the EU that without proper and obviously new communication channels, solutions will not be found. This may provide a new opportunity and space for civil movements, for subterranean politics – joined to other, similar forces throughout Europe – to fill the vacuum. It is evident that the vanguard/rearguard actions of the current Hungarian government have struck a particular chord both nationally and at the European level, provoking a variety of responses, positive and negative, and moving the discourse on Europe in new directions.

Box 6.1   Timeline of dissent

15 October 2011: **Occupy Wall Street.** About 500, mostly young, demonstrators took part in a candlelight procession in Budapest in sympathy with the global day of action 'Occupy Wall Street' (World Revolution) movement. Rallies were also held in Pécs. The main message of the demonstrations was to support a humane, socially and environmentally sustainable global society. The demonstration ended with a concert in the city's financial district. One organiser commented: 'We are connecting with "Occupy" protests elsewhere in the world today... There are people here from both the right and the left of Hungarian politics. There are humanists, philosophers, artists, painters, engineers, people from all walks of life.' He added, 'We want to live in a world which doesn't revolve around money, greed, consumption.' The demonstrators had wanted to spend the night in tents on the square but were not given a permit by city authorities.

23 October 2011: **'Don't Like the System? – Protest!'** Organised by the Hungarian Facebook group, Milla (One Million for the Freedom of Press in Hungary), the action attracted tens of thousands to different venues in the city. A song was sung called 'I Don't Like This System', with the instructions to sing the refrain loud enough to be heard in Brussels. Prominent representatives from several civil organisations spoke, including the Hungarian Civil Liberties Union, 4K!, Roma groups, the Network of University Students and The City Belongs to All initiative. More innovative approaches included the acceptance of nominations for an 'alternative president of the republic'; 50,000 'press IDs' were randomly distributed to promote citizen reporting, to encourage greater public transparency and accountability.

11 November 2011: **Real Democracy Now and People's Assemblies.** The methodology of the Real Democracy Now movement was imported from the Spanish Indignados movement. The establishment of the People's Assemblies is to promote democratic discussions at all levels about what kind of society people want. The working principles of the Assemblies are intentionally adapted to Hungarian conditions with the use of online and off-line

Box 6.1   (Continued)

mobilisation techniques. The main topics for the discussions at the assemblies were:

- real democracy and direct participation;
- the role of the state;
- how to evaluate fundamental human, social and other rights;
- reform of economic and social conditions;
- sustainability.

1 December 2011: **Night of Solidarity.** This event was organised to protest against the criminalisation of homelessness in Hungarian legislation. Events took place in 16 locations (10 in Budapest, 4 in other cities and 2 abroad), and activists spent the night in the open air on the streets with the homeless.

3 December 2011: **'F in Math Campaign'.** A number of grassroots organisations joined forces to demand the dismissal of György Matolcsy, the minister in charge of economic and fiscal policy after the downgrading of Hungarian bonds to junk status. Protestors included the independent trade unions, One Million for Press Freedom, the Hungarian Solidarity Movement, student organisations and homeless activists.

5 December 2011: **St. Nicholas Actions.** In protest against the appointment of a far-right actor and playwright to the New Hungarian Theater, St. Nicholas delivered special gifts to Budapest mayor, István Tarlós. A group called Az nem lehet, hogy (It's not possible that…), which was formed almost immediately after the mayoral appointments, delivered a tri-colour booklet (in the colours of the Hungarian flag) to the city hall. On red pages 10,395 signatures were collected against the appointment; white pages were printed with a critically annotated version of the actor's application materials, and green pages featured a selection of the international comments related to the appointees and their supporters. A performance by a group called Blister Circus accompanied the delivery of the gifts in front of the city hall. Included with the booklet were tickets to performances of Hungarian playwrights for each day in the month of December, because the mayor had stated that not enough Hungarian plays were being produced in Hungarian theatres.

17 December 2011: **Protests and flashmobs at 29 locations simultaneously throughout the country.** The Hungarian Solidarity Movement is a decentralised organisational network that reaches into the most diverse strata of Hungarian society. Only two of the 29 locations were in the country's capital, and all 19 Hungarian counties took part. They produced a poster reminiscent of the famous campaign poster for the first free elections in Hungary in 1990, but this time with the image of Viktor Orbán and the slogan 'Comrades, it's over!' Unfortunately, when the printer realised the political content of the posters, he refused to deliver them in time for the demonstration, so people simply drew them on placards themselves.

19 December 2011: **The Network for the Freedom of Education (*HAT: Hálózat a Tanszabadságért*), a civilian group of educators held its last 'office hour'.** This was organised to protest against the controversial bill on the Hungarian educational system to be voted into law by parliament. The teachers and education experts in HAT held 'office hours' outside of the parliament on days on which the bill was under discussion. These educational experts tried to go beyond simply expressing their disagreement with the bill, and made themselves available for consultation especially to members of parliament. The bill passed without incorporation of any of their suggestions on 20 December 2012.

28 December 2011: **'Music is Not Torture' protest in solidarity with hunger-striking journalists.** Days before Christmas Eve, high-power reflectors and loudspeakers were lowered from above to the 'designated hunger-strike area'. The speakers repeatedly blasted three extremely irritating Christmas songs at the hunger-strikers. On 27 December, two of the group were fired from their jobs which also meant that they lost access to the building and were literally left out in the cold. The demonstration was organised by the Hungarian Solidarity Movement and relied on famous Hungarian jazz players to bring quality music to the hunger-strikers.

11 February 2012: **Stop ACTA (Anti-Counterfeiting Trade Agreement) protest in Budapest.** The protest, of over 1,000 young people, was organised by the Hungarian Anonymous Group and Occupy Budapest. Protestors took to the streets of

---

Box 6.1 **(Continued)**

Budapest outside the Hungarian parliament and finished at the Hungarian Intellectual Property Office to demonstrate against the ACTA signed by Hungary and 22 other EU countries in January. This was simultaneously coordinated with anti-ACTA demonstrations in London, Paris, Madrid, Lisbon, Prague, Sofia, Bucharest and 60 cities in Germany. Demonstrators shouted slogans such as 'Internet freedom!' and 'Copy right, Copy left!', and held posters proclaiming 'Broadband or Death!' and 'Stop ACTA!'.

3 March 2012: **Rhythms of Resistance (RoR) Samba Action.** This group was founded in October 2010 as a member of the international RoR network and comprises drum crew that plays batucada as a political action. In solidarity with the Italian NO TAV struggle against the development of a high-speed railway, a protest was staged outside the Italian Embassy in Budapest.

4 March 2012: **Anonymous hacktivists break into Constitutional Court website and change the New Hungarian Constitution.** Among the creative changes made to the text included one arguing that those in the IT sector should retire at age 32 with a pension representing 150% of their salary; another change stated that 'the people have the right to eliminate tyranny or rebel against it'; 5 November was made Guy Fawkes Day and gave Anonymous the power to fight against the country's internal and external enemies.

It will take time before real and effective solidarity emerges among the various groups in Hungary and with Hungary and others, but there is certainly an inclination and gathering momentum. This is dominated by new social networks and social media, networked resistance and savvy young activists who have no lack of innovative techniques and approaches to addressing contemporary political, economic and social problems. It no longer matters so much where you are in time and space, since these networks, supported by technology, can provide for a more equal playing field for civil actors. Perhaps the first, real post-1989 generation is finally emerging to reinvent politics, democracy, governance and activism in response to the failures of the past 20 years.

Table 6.1 Mapping major Hungarian grassroots/activist organisations

Organisation and description	Date of founding	Target	Number of supporters*	Political orientation	Tactics	Position on Europe, if any
Milla (Egymillióan a magyar sajtószabadságért; 1 million for Press Freedom)∗∗ Community, grassroots organisation, possibly the largest anti-FIDESZ (government) organisation	December 2010 with the installation of FIDESZ with a 2/3 majority in parliament, and as soon as the first draft of the New Media Law was published	Followers are primarily young activists and 'Budapest intelligentsia'. Demonstrators include poets and writers who presented anti-Media Law speeches to protestors. It has expanded to include people across the age range. Milla maintains that it is a non-political body although they have strong ties to the new party, 4K! (The 4K! leader was a speaker at their March 2011 demonstration)	Facebook support has reached 99,089. Estimates of their last protest ranged between 60,000 and 100,000	On their website they say that their two main goals are to (1) show politicians that citizens and civil society hold an important and active role in politics with the ability to challenge unpopular politics or politicians; and (2) create a platform for alternative civil, grassroots and political groups to be heard	Public demonstrations in the streets with speakers; Facebook activism to draw attention to the un-democratic and anti-human rights actions of FIDESZ, primarily against the new media Law and new constitution Election online of an alternative Hungarian president∗∗∗	More pro-EU and in favour of harsh measures being imposed on the Hungarian government; have subsequently become disillusioned with the EU in not taking a firmer stand

Table 6.1 (Continued)

Organisation and description	Date of founding	Target	Number of supporters*	Political orientation	Tactics	Position on Europe, if any
Szolidaritás (The Hungarian Solidarity Movement) Anti-FIDESZ (government) community organisation	October 2011	Szolidaritás has drawn a more middle-aged crowd. Some say this is due to their stronger links with MSZP and SZDSZ (weak opposition parties) and others say its base is more in the old workers' union organisations This is an organisation of former political elites said to consist of MSZP, The Hungarian Communist Party, SZDSZ and LMP	Facebook supporters estimated at 10,159. This is a loose coalition of old socialists. It is difficult to say how many individuals comprise the group or how many the round table or 'workshops' will incorporate	So-called 'left-liberal'	Their main aim/activity was to organise the *BAKA 'Left Round Table for Change'* in February 2012 BAKA developed recently to unite five different liberal-left parties/organisations that would like to have a round table (similar to those in 1989) Although this group might not be incorporated directly into what we consider 'Subterranean Politics', they do have some interesting similarities with grassroots activism such as the fact that their first meetings were in cafés and kept secret from politics at large. They are perhaps taking on the subterranean activist tactics in trying to re-establish new techniques in the political arena The BAKA group was created in order to hold round table discussions and workshops around the country to draft action plans on how to fix the socio-economic woes of Hungary. The first major plenary session was scheduled to take place 28 February 2012	More nationalist orientated and less pro-EU

Occupy Budapest/ Világ Forradalom + Valódi Demokráciát Most!(World Revolution + Real Democracy Now)/ Occupy Hungary Online communities	After October 2011	Mostly young people and university students	On Facebook the numbers are, respectively, 882, 732 and 1,136	Anti-neo-liberal economics	They forge links with the larger anti-neo-liberal movement globally, so it is important mainly for that reason though it is a weak movement in Budapest. There are many YouTube videos showing their main event in October 2011; they also use the 'Guy Fawkes' mask logo so there is a visual symbolism for anti-capitalism that was originally developed in the film *V for Vendetta*	Most posts critique the global financial structure and want more equal distribution of wealth; not per se anti-EU, but anti-EU economic policies. Many posts on Világ foradalom (World Revolution) are anti-Union
Anonymous Online community of hacktivists	Became active in Hungary in 2011	Probably, as in other countries, young people and other hacktivists	Nearly 4,500 Facebook members	Anti-FIDESZ, anti-authority	They hacked into the Constitutional Court website and changed the wording of the new constitution. They hacked into the Ministry of Education website and wrote the lyrics of Pink Floyd's song, 'We Don't Need No Education' all over it. They also hacked IKSZ's website and put Guy Fawkes faces on it. Images documenting their hacking can be seen on their Facebook images	They do not specifically address the EU, but are clearly anti-hierarchical and anti-neo-liberal capitalism

Table 6.1 (Continued)

Organisation and description	Date of founding	Target	Number of supporters*	Political orientation	Tactics	Position on Europe, if any
Előlánc (Living Chain) Online community as well as a self-proclaimed civil movement, but few know it is actually registered as a political party	Founded already in 2005, it describes itself as a civil movement. Registered as a political party	This is a small group who wants to promote local production and consumption and a green economy	169 Facebook members	It is a kind of alternative community with green aims; it describes itself as eco-political	They have participated in demonstrations organised by others	Do not want interference in the sovereignty of Hungary
4K! 'Fourth Republic' A civil movement initially designed with specifically non-political ends. It is a youth movement aimed at reclaiming space for young people	Founded as a civil movement in autumn 2007 Established as an official political party in October 2011	Largely a youth-based movement/party. Most of the members are aged between 18 and 30, according to members	On Facebook they have 8,930 followers	As a political party, 4K! is an alter-political activist party developing into what they define as the 'patriotic left'. They have been active in helping organise and participate in Milla demonstrations	Organising activities that would bring young people into the streets to feel they had space within society They arranged a national pillow fight day, capture the flag across Budapest, and iPod follow the leader to mock consumerist capitalist culture	Pro-European in terms of culture and values and anti-EU neo-liberal economic policies. More global than other groups in their perspective because many have spent time abroad

Jobbik Magyarországért Mozgalom (Movement for a Better Hungary)	Founded as a political party in October 2003 but really began attracting support only after the 2006 riots against the MSZP government. Gained electoral support in the 2009 European parliamentary elections and 2010 national elections	The group was originally a youth group that turned into a political party. Jobbik is known for having a very strong youth base. Recent research on Facebook has shown that they attract mostly young, male, educated supporters (in common with many strong populist-nationalist parties)	It is hard to determine the exact number of supporters they have, but there are currently 40,215 supporters on Facebook	The party is a populist nationalist party also considered radical right. Their aim is to create a stronger 'Hungary for Hungarians'. which is a popular slogan and rhetorically 'Hungarians' do not include those of Jewish or Roma descent. Last year they moved away from overt anti-Semitic and anti-Roma rhetoric. They have now moved towards overtly anti-EU, anti-globalisation and anti-democratic language in the last year and specifically in the last 6 months of 2012	Participation in and organisation of street demonstrations and symbolic acts of defiance against the EU	They have burned EU flags at rallies or symbolically cut out the stars from the EU flag (reminiscent of 1956). They are Hungarian right-wing nationalists and want to turn instead to Russia and Turkey
64 County Youth Movement (HVIM) This is a youth movement	The youth movement was established after the 2006 riots	Similar to Jobbik, HVIM supporters are mainly young males. They also tend to be more rural based though not exclusively	On Facebook they have 666 followers, although they draw larger crowds at the events they organise such as at their festival which draws a few thousand people annually	They are an irredentist nationalist group that works closely alongside Jobbik and Jobbik's youth group, though they do not have official political ties with them. HVIM has the greater goal of supporting movements that might win back the lost territory of Transylvania, as well as supporting the strengthening of Hungary as a nation	They have a very successful national rock festival that they stage annually called Magyar Sziget (to counteract the 'European' and 'corrupt' Sziget Fest that takes place in Budapest)	The group is openly anti-EU and anti-globalisation; linked with an international network of right-wing groups

Table 6.1 (Continued)

Organisation and description	Date of founding	Target	Number of supporters*	Political orientation	Tactics	Position on Europe, if any
Magyar Kétfarkú Kutya Párt (Two-Tailed Dog Party, TTDP) A mock political party which employs satire and humour	Founded in 2006 by 'István Nagy'. This is a joke because this name is the most common Hungarian name, symbolising everyone	TTDP supporters are mainly younger, liberal people, but also some FIDESZ supporters speak well of the party, meaning that they can cross political boundaries by mocking the entire political system rather than attacking one side or the other like many of the other grassroots groups that can more easily be labelled on a political spectrum	On Facebook TTDP has a quite large number of followers (currently 70,992) considering that it is a mock party group	This is a satirical, mock political party that crosses political boundaries	The party is a satirical party aiming to point out the false rhetorical content of mainstream politics and the corruption and bad politics by means of humour. Example: they promised eternal life, the one-day working week and free beer to those that support them	This is not an issue on which they take a position

* We recognise that counting the number of Facebook supporters and/or 'likes' on Facebook does not accurately represent a group's popularity or intensity of activities. It is very difficult, however, to measure these groups and their networks.
** Milla has recently been the subject of an investigation by the National Tax and Customs Administration in Hungary. This is viewed as a clear case of government harassment against their activities.
*** Unfortunately, this initiative has fallen flat because of manipulation of results of election of the Alternative President of Hungary. Milla has since apologised, but their reputation has been tarnished as a result.

Notes

1. With research contributions from Erin Saltman and Hajnalka Szarvas.
2. See: http://www.facebook.com/pages/Free-Gereb-Agnes, http://www.face book.com/pages/Podpora-pro-Ágnes-Geréb-Support-for-Ágnes-Geréb.
3. Clashes occurred, for example, between about 50 supporters of the far-right party Jobbik and anti-fascist demonstrators after the appointment of a right-wing director to the New Theater in Budapest. Even after enormous international pressure, including an open letter in *The Guardian* newspaper signed by internationally known artistic directors, actors, directors and playwrights, among others, the mayor responded non-committally. This has been the approach of the government to accusations of supporting the right wing and giving no clear signals or messages condemning or condoning the actions of Jobbik.
4. In February 2013, hunger marches from ten towns were organised from northern Hungary to Budapest (200 kilometres) to demonstrate against poverty and the new, controversial work schemes for the unemployed planned by the government. This initiative was supported by the Socialist Party, who hosted their representatives in Brussels in March 2013.
5. With regard to the debt ceiling provision in the new constitution, on the same day that the European Commission criticised Hungary, they called on other member states to decrease state debt – even with constitutional measures if needed. This was reported in Info Rádio's Arena programme on 3 February 2012. Many in Hungary felt that the EU elite from older member states did not approve of innovations coming from new member states – for example, taxing the banks, which was subsequently adopted by other EU member states.
6. MIT, *Survey shows Hungarians still distrust politicians.* 22 February 2011 (accessed 6 March 2012). http://www.politics.hu/20110222/survey-shows -hungarians-still-distrust-politicians.
7. The Contrarian Hungarian, *Civil Sphere and Grassroots Protests in Hungary: December, 2011.* 2 January 2012 (accessed 5 March 2012). https:// thecontrarianhungarian.wordpress.com/2012/01/02/civil-sphere-and -grassroots-protests-in-hungary-december-2011/.
8. Ibid.
9. Csepelli (2000).
10. Közösségfejlesztõk [Community Developers] (2010) *Public Trust 2010 Research* (accessed 23 April 2011). http://reszvetelhete.wordpress.com/.
11. See: Massimiliano Mascherini and Brony Hoskins, Building a Composite Indicator to Measure Active Citizenship in Europe. http://www. csdiworkshop.org/pdf/3mc2008_proceedings/session_15/ Mascherini.pdf.
12. For more on this topic see, Jensen and Miszlivetz (2006) 'The Second Renaissance of Civil Society in East Central Europe – and in the European Union', in Peter Wagner (Ed.) *The Languages of Civil Society,* New York, Oxford: Berghahn Book, pp. 131–158.
13. The Contrarian Hungarian, *To The Margins of An Early January Protest in Hungary,* 8 January 2012 (accessed 2 March 2012). The political parties included LMP, the Hungarian Socialist Party, the Democratic

Coalition as well as 4K! and the Fourth Republic Movement. https://thecontrarianhungarian.wordpress.com/2012/01/08/to-the-margins-of-an-early-january-protest-in-hungary/.

14. The new constitution replaces the word 'republic' from Hungary's official by the common term 'country'.

15. In Hungary the distant past is ever present in the current subterranean dialogue as a reference point. This is expressed by the symbolic use of the past in slogans, signs and images. One of the reasons for the relatively small number of demonstrators is that people's current political attitudes and behaviours are very much affected by the strong presence of past traumatic events circumscribed in a rather 'cautious collective memory'.

16. Reported in The Contrarian Hungarian, *Pro-Government Rally in Hungary, Jan. 21, 2012*. 23 January 2012 (accessed 2 March 2012). https://thecontrarian hungarian.wordpress.com/2012/01/23/pro-government-rally-in-hungary-jan -21-2012/.

17. *Anti-government platform lacks coherent program*. 7 January 2012 (accessed 3 March 2012). http://budapost.eu/2012/01/anti-government-platform-lacks-coherent-program/

18. *Tepid Occupy Wall Street – Saturday in Budapest*. 18 October 2011 (accessed 3 March 2012). http://budapost.eu/2011/10/tepid-occupy-wall -street-saturday-in-budapest.

19. Hungary Around the Clock, *Government said aiming to block all opposition protests in downtown Budapest on March 15 national holiday*. 19 January 2012 (accessed 6 March 2012). http://www.politics.hu/20120119/government-to -block-all-opposition-protests-in-capital-on-march-15-national-holiday/.

20. Before the anti-government rally outside the Opera House, they announced the formation and introduction of a New Hungarian Guard, a paramilitary organisation which was illegal until 27 January 2012. The far right called their parallel protest 'Let's Clean the Dirt from the Streets', and was in part organised as revenge against former MSZP government politicians from the Socialist Party who were held responsible for attacks on citizens with rubber bullets and truncheons in October 2006. Because of ineffective police oversight, groups of right-wing and opposition protestors clashed on several occasions at the demonstration in January, which resulted in injuries. About 150 Jobbik activists were reported as having taken part. The Contrarian Hungarian, *Hungarian Guards Judicial Victory, Jobbik Chairman Considers Armed Conflict Unavoidable*. 29 January 2012 (accessed 6 March 2012).

21. Milla, for example, has been co-opted and integrated into the new political party Together 2014 led by Gordon Bajnai, the last prime minister before the fall of the socialist government.

Bibliography

Blanch, D. (2005) *Revisiting Youth Political Participation. Challenges for Research and Democratic Practice in Europe*. Strasbourg: Council of Europe.
Budapesti Corvinus Egyetem (2010) *Magyarország 2025 Research*. Budapest: Timp Kiadó.

Csepeli, G. (2010) *Társadalmi szolidaritás — Összetartó társadalom*, Accessed online at http://www.kka.hu/_Kozossegi_Adattar/PAROLAAR.NSF/274d6703 6bb315838525670c008147c9/e134d884d2d08cb5c12577c00043cf1f? OpenDocument.

Hoskins, B. (October 2010) *Social Context: Differences and Similarities in the Field of Active Citizen Attitudes in Europe*. Research presented at the Europe of Active Citizens conference organised by Active Citizenship Foundation, Hungary & Democracy and Human Rights Education in Adult Learning, Budapest.

Hunyadi, B. (October 2010) *Assessment, Policy Responses and Recommendations on Active Citizenship Education*. Summary of the Europe of Active Citizens conference organised by Active Citizenship Foundation, Hungary & Democracy and Human Rights Education in Adult Learning, Budapest.

Jensen, J. (2006) 'The Social Costs of a Lumpen Political Class', *Találjuk-ki Közepeuropa* (Reinventing Central Europe), Accessed online at www.talaljuk-ki .hu.

Jensen, J. and Miszlivetz, F. (2006) 'The Second Renaissance of Civil Society in East Central Europe – and in the European Union', in Peter Wagner (Ed.) *The Languages of Civil Society*, New York, Oxford: Berghahn Books, pp. 131–158.

Lane, J. E. and Ersson, S. (2005) *Culture and Politics: A Comparative Approach*. Aldershot: Ashgate Publishing Company.

Mascherini, M. and Hoskins, B. (2005) *Building a Composite Indicator to Measure Active Citizenship in Europe*, Accessed online at http://www.csdiworkshop.org/ pdf/3mc2008_proceedings/session_15/Mascherini.pdf.

Miszlivetz, F. (2007) *Mi lett veled, Magyarország?* (What Happened to You, Hungary?). Szombathely, Kőszeg: Társadalomtudományok és Európa Tanulmányok Intézete.

Ross, A. (2008) *A European Education. Citizenship, Identities and Young People*. Stoke on Trent: Trentham Books.

TÁRKI (2009) *Értékek-World Value Survey*, Accessed online at http://www.tarki.hu/ hu/research/gazdkult/kutatas.html.

7
Political Blockage and the Absence of Europe: Subterranean Politics in London

Sean Deel and Tamsin Murray-Leach[1]

Introduction

London does not represent the United Kingdom as a whole: it is a 'global city', a place where 'an immense array of cultures from around the world...are reterritorialized' and whose links to that new territory are 'far less likely to be intermediated by the national state or "national culture"' (Sassen 2000: 88–90). As a global city, London is understood as a point of convergence for local, national and transnational identities, as well as a wide range of overlapping political formations organised around anything from community or diaspora concerns through to national issues and on to global justice. Studying subterranean politics through the views and strategies of its diverse informal political actors, then, brought an interesting dimension to the overall project. It required that we engage with these overlapping identities, which, we hoped, might help reveal the nature of the relationship of subterranean political actors to Europe beyond the national context.

Subterranean politics in London 'bubbled up' in very visible forms in 2010 and 2011 in a quickly changing economic and political landscape, with new movements and actors providing a fertile ground for research. In order to focus in from the broad remit of the concept of 'subterranean politics', we decided to concentrate primarily on newly emergent non-institutional political actors, particularly those who offered either systemic critiques or who used single issues to illuminate a broader political failing. Particularly important to the London investigation of these actors was the concept of scale: on what (political, geographic) levels were participants active? At what levels were they formulating political critiques and seeking solutions? What, in their view, constitutes political membership? Implicit in these questions was an attempt to uncover the role of 'Europe', a scale of political belonging not often explicitly invoked. Did the apparent 'invisibility' of Europe suggest its irrelevance, its suffusion as a political and social fact – or something else?

This chapter focuses on the motivations of participants in four non-institutional political groups or movements: Occupy LSX, UK Uncut, London Citizens and student protestors challenging changes in educational funding. Through semi-structured interviews, we explore their diagnosis of what is considered to be a blocked institutional politics and their views towards established or long-standing contentious political actors, like trade unions and the World or European Social Forums. We also analyse how their experiments with democratic forms and practices, modes of contention and conceptions of politics not based solely around the nation state relate to these views. Following on from this, we investigate participants' various conceptions of 'Europe' and the possibility that a shared set of cultural and social experience provides a sense of political membership at this level.

We proceed with an overview of the social and political context in which the groups emerged, before moving onto a discussion of how both this context and the parameters of 'subterranean politics' influenced our methodology and research design. Two substantial sections follow, supported by qualitative interview data, and a conclusion then reflects on what significance the narratives of London's subterranean political actors have for a fractured Europe.

London as a global city and the context of the protests in 2010–2012

Demographically, London, the most populous municipality in the European Union (EU) (Eurostat 2011), clearly fits its designation as a 'global city' (Sassen ibid.). Three hundred languages are spoken by its more than eight million residents. One third of Londoners were born outside the UK (Office of National Statistics ONS 2011), and nearly one tenth of the city's population are citizens of other EU countries (ONS 2012b), a much higher proportion than in the national population. According to Sassen, global cities, by dint of being major hubs of flows of capital and labour from all over the world, are sites of politics and identity formation on multiple scales. National politics and contestation play out through public sector strikes and protests over austerity measures imposed by lawmakers; community organisation groups articulate political programmes on behalf of diaspora communities; new conflicts arise between strata of an international labour force; and new, transterritorial political formations begin to emerge that are not linked solely to national membership.

All of these levels overlap and interact in the same geography; to dub a city 'global' does not mean that other scales of politics are not at play. At an institutional level, London's central role in global finance shapes the national economy, which in turn affects both the city's and the nation's relationship to the EU. Likewise, while London cannot be treated as a distillation of the country at large, national issues and policy reforms[2] did contribute to the 'bubbling up' of subterranean politics in the city – which, after all, is home to 12.5% of the British population (ONS 2012b). Furthermore, the way in which these domestic policies were articulated in the press and by politicians shaped debates on the future of Europe and the UK's uneasy place within it.

Despite its position as a core EU member state, the UK remains outside of the monetary union. British politicians have asserted this distance throughout the European debt crisis, perhaps most strikingly when, in December 2011, Prime Minister David Cameron vetoed proposed EU treaty changes that would have made the country's financial services industry subject to EU regulation. The Fiscal Compact has gone ahead without ratification by the UK, which also exempts it from other diktats governing, among other things, structural deficit levels, which the UK maintains at a high level. Government response in relation to Europe's debt crisis has reflected the tension between, on the one hand, the Euroscepticism of some Conservative MPs and, on the other, the recognition that the UK's membership in the single market affords it good trading relations with eurozone countries.

Meanwhile, British public opinion has always been cautious in regard to European integration, and even a casual analysis of public opinion polls would suggest that this has intensified since the start of the crisis. Survey data from May 2011 show that among UK respondents the national government was considered the most effective institution in dealing with the effects of financial and economic crisis, contrasting with responses from 17 EU member states, which put the EU at the top of the list (Eurobarometer 2011a: 12). A more recent survey goes further, claiming that most British citizens 'want national control of almost all policy-areas' and a looser relationship to the EU (YouGov 2012). A growing body of work in European studies finds that identification with

Europe is heavily influenced by social class and that national affiliation is still central, in part because narratives of European integration are constructed by reference to national frames (Díez Medrano 2003, 2011; Fligstein 2008; Duchesne 2012). British respondents in qualitative studies on European identity often feel 'out of Europe' (Duchesne 2012). How this perspective plays out in the 'global city' of London, where almost 10% of the population are citizens of other European nations, is a question that the survey data do not answer, and to which we shall return in our analysis.

Domestically, while the UK's fidelity to its sovereign currency exempts it from the strictures of EU policy encroachment and pressures from the European debt crisis, it has nevertheless been subject to the strains of the wider economic crisis. Unemployment rose to its highest level since 1994 by the end of 2011 (ONS 2011), GDP has only been growing slowly since the 2008–2009 contraction (ONS 2012a) and household disposable income has dropped considerably (Kollewe 2012). And in London, unemployment in the period just prior to the beginning of our research, from November 2011 to January 2012, had risen to 10.3%, higher than the national level (ONS 2012a). Even without the pressure of the single currency, the UK government responded to the crisis by instituting a programme of cuts to social spending, as is the case elsewhere in Europe. Recent public sector reforms have included several hundred thousand public sector job cuts, pension reforms, pay freezes, proposals for a major overhaul of the National Health Service, an increase in the annual university tuition fee cap from just over £3,000 to £9,000, and cuts to housing, education, employment and other social benefits.

Accompanying the cuts has been the shift, in the general election of May 2010, from a Labour government to a Conservative–Liberal Democratic coalition. In this chapter and elsewhere in this book, we discuss the idea that subterranean politics emerges as a response to a 'political blockage' – a sense that democratic representative institutions no longer represent the interests of their constituents. While the Conservative Party's reputation for favouring business over public interests is, as suggested in our interviews, a contributing factor to this sense of 'blockage', the relative success (in terms of share of votes) and crucial role of the Liberal Democrats in that election, in which no party achieved an absolute majority, should also be taken into account. If their higher poll numbers on election day reflected discontent with the Labour and Conservative parties and an enthusiasm, especially amongst younger voters, for a party that advocated banking and tax reform and environmental policies, their later policy reversal on key issues – most notably on university tuition fee increases – and their decision to form a coalition with their ostensible ideological opponents, would have contributed to a feeling that the political class, regardless of party affiliation, is insular and unaccountable.

Against this national backdrop, and in the wider context of political uprisings and large public protests throughout the world, including in North Africa and the Middle East, the United States, and other countries in Europe, London has been an epicentre for contentious political action. Even before dissent against austerity began to resonate across a wider public, the 2009 G-20 Summit on Financial Markets and the World Economy, hosted in London, was a precursor of protests to come. The summit became a point of convergence for a wide range of formal and informal protest groups demonstrating on a broad range of related issues including climate change and environmental issues, tax justice and financial transactions, and the ongoing wars and conflicts throughout the world.[3]

Late the next year (2010), a series of student protests, including university occupations, followed the new government's university tuition fee hikes and cuts to educational allowances. The first of the large anti-austerity actions, the 'March for the Alternative' was held on 26 March 2011. Although primarily organised by the Trades Union Congress (TUC), it was accompanied by actions from a number of emerging groups such as UK Uncut (see Box 7.2). In August 2011, major riots in several boroughs of London, and later other cities in England, broke out after police shot and killed local resident Mark Duggan in Tottenham. This was followed by much public debate as to whether this wave of destruction could be considered a political act of revolt alongside the Greek riots, the Arab Spring and the takeover of public squares in Spain. Then, on the Global Day of Action on 15 October 2011, following a burgeoning number of anti-austerity protests taking place across the UK, a group of activists established what would become a long-term occupation of space in the financial centre of London, near the London Stock Exchange, emulating the occupation of Wall Street in New York that had begun just a month earlier and generating a sympathetic response from not only large numbers of the public, but venerable British institutions such as the Church of England (*The Guardian* 2011).

Politics in London, whether institutional, informal or contentious, reflects the many overlapping scales and sites of politics that belong to the city. London is a centre of global finance, a major European metropolis, a national capital and a major immigration hub. How these imbrications expressed themselves in the narratives of subterranean political actors, and in particular where Europe was situated within them, are the questions that drove our research.

Research design: from concept to case studies

Concepts

In shedding the conceptual, normative and methodological baggage of concepts such as 'civil society' and 'social movements', the conceptual frame of 'subterranean politics' required an act of interpretation before it could be operationalised. The research in this chapter therefore aims to explore the potential of this concept, and the design of our two-pronged approach to data collection in the UK has been, primarily, to work with the various hypotheses and questions proposed during the initial two meetings of the Subterranean Politics research teams and remain reflexive to the data collected, in order to generate more grounded hypotheses and point out interesting/fruitful areas for future research.

Since the frame could potentially capture a wide range of actions, groups and individuals, our effort began in part with choosing our cases. Distinguishing between expressions of 'subterranean politics' and more traditional contentious politics (and, additionally, uncovering expressions of subterranean politics *within* traditional contentious politics) was a conceptual challenge, made easier by taking the definition of 'subterranean politics' as *emergent*, or as *being in the state of emergence* as a given, and thus hypothesising that both traditional and/or more formal forms of contentious politics and newer, more informal forms of grassroots politics could fit the 'subterranean politics' frame, so long as the fact of emergence, or 'bubbling up', was brought to the fore.

We recognised early on, however, that 'subterranean politics' was not merely a label for novelty. Even where a 'new' group was concerned, like Occupy LSX, we found that actors, practices, tactics and resources were mobilised quickly by building on a legacy of recent political action. Conversely, we also decided that if actors within existing groups had changed their tactics, or the frames that justified their action, this could also constitute 'subterranean politics'. That is, finding what was 'new' also involved searching for what was 'new' within what was 'old' – or rather, finding the point at which existing practices and forms 'bubbled up' from the subterranean realm and resonated in mainstream discourse and practice.

The second conceptual consideration was that of 'Europe'. We deliberately decided to leave this category open, in order that interviewees would bring to bear their own definitions and priorities into our conversation – whether to them Europe meant the governance of the EU, a geographical area, a shared historical/contemporary culture or something else. Our hypothesis was that even if 'Europe' (in any of these guises) did initially appear absent from the agenda of subterranean actors in London – which appeared to be the case both from our observations of the seemingly national nature of the protests across Europe and, more specifically, from the prevailing public discourse of British insularity from the EU – the *impact* of the EU as an actually existing entity may yet be suffused in the current wave of subterranean action. Including both British- and foreign-born residents of this global city in our research meant that the outcomes could potentially point in two very different directions. Should Europe, in any guise, appear on the agenda of foreign-born (particularly European-born) London residents active in subterranean politics, but not on that of British Londoners, our work would support poll data and sociological claims of British insularity with regard to Europe (Fligstein 2008: 24, 136). However, if Europe failed to appear in the discourses of either, despite the fact that it is the existence of the EU that permits the presence of the European-born activists in London, this would point to something rather different – it would support, at least on the surface, the apparent lack of perceived relevance of Europe to 'subterranean politics' at this moment in time, in addition to raising further intriguing questions about the role of identity in politics.

Research design

Mapping subterranean politics

Employing this criteria of 'bubbling up', then, along with our desire to unpack and uncover 'Europe', we took a two-pronged approach to gathering our data. The initial step was a survey of both groups who might fit the 'subterranean politics' concept, and EU-related initiatives (supporting either more or less UK integration with Europe) currently active in the UK. As mentioned above, we originally hoped to carry out qualitative research throughout the UK, and decided that while a lack of time and resources prevented this for the second stage of the work, our mapping exercise would consider the entire country. The intention behind this exercise was twofold.

First, we needed a method of selecting suitable case studies. We took an iterative approach, first plotting major protest events that occurred during late 2010 to early 2012 using newspaper coverage as the initial starting point for selection. In many cases, the media had already organised relevant articles by protest, occupation and, in some cases, by specific organisations.[4] Organisations, actors and initiatives involved in these events were then mapped; online research into their activities, and recommendations from activists and groups already selected, led to further organisations, actors and initiatives. Actors were deemed suitable for initial inclusion as part of the mapping exercise if they fit one or more of the following criteria: they had demonstrably affected UK policymaking; they had achieved consistent coverage in the UK's mainstream newspapers; they had been central to organising nationwide or large, London-based direct actions and protests; and/or they had produced informative, online content that was visibly and widely shared on social media platforms. Although the 'subterranean' landscape shifts constantly as new groups and coalitions form and thus it is impossible to be exhaustive, what we attempted to do was create a snapshot of activity in the UK. The exercise resulted in a map that plotted events geographically and extensive cross-referenced lists of events, organisations and initiatives, categorised by form and content, using an adaptation of the coding system used in the claims analysis by della Porta and Caiani (2009) in their book *Social Movements and Europeanization.*[5]

The second reason for the mapping exercise was to investigate our hypothesis that there was very little crossover between the protests and events investigated and those initiatives focused on the future of the EU. We will return to this in the section on Europe, below; suffice it to say here that this was found to be the case sufficiently as to inform the design of our research questions in the second phase of the research.

Case studies

It should come as no surprise to even casual observers of protest events in the UK during 2010–2012 that our mapping exercise highlighted three groups whose actions were covered heavily by the media. Occupy the London Stock Exchange (Occupy LSX; see Box 7.1, pp. 176–7) is a 'new' group of actors, which, in as much as it has concrete 'aims', calls for systemic change at the global level and is part of a loose transnational network. However, at least in 2011, Occupy did not make specific claims on Europe or the EU. By contrast to the global focus of Occupy, UK Uncut (see Box 7.2, pp. 178–9), another 'new' group, focuses on national policies. While this group had a single-issue focus and target – the non-payment of tax by UK corporations – it remained to be seen whether the group's actions were part of a systemic argument against austerity and how they engaged with other groups working on similar issues in Europe. The third 'group' were participants in the student protests

Box 7.1 Occupy London

The occupation of the forecourt of St Paul's Cathedral began on 15 October 2011 as part of an international day of action for global change, coinciding with the five-month anniversary of the first Spanish 15-M Movement protests, and almost one month after the start of Occupy Wall Street. The encampment, in a high-profile site in the City of London, a major national and global financial centre, was intended for neighbouring Paternoster Square, outside the London Stock Exchange (LSX), but police blocked public access to that site. At its peak, the occupation at St Paul's was sustained by hundreds of campers and attracted support from public intellectuals, politicians and policymakers, artists and academics. The occupation hosted frequent speaking events, included a 'Tent City University' and organised working groups that met regularly to discuss social, political, environmental and economic issue areas. These groups fed into a general assembly, where (radical) alternatives in these issue areas were proposed, discussed and debated. The group put strong emphasis on radical democratic processes developed over the previous decade within the global justice movement, including horizontality (as opposed to hierarchy) and procedural innovations such as the use of hand gestures to indicate levels of support or disagreement within discussion forums.

According to our respondents, the idea of Occupy London was raised at an impromptu general assembly on Westminster Bridge during a UK Uncut demonstration. Following coordination over social media, the group mobilised existing resources from other activist groups, in particular from activists related to WikiLeaks. Environmental activists, including many involved in 2009's Climate Camp, provided much of the infrastructure and expertise to set up the encampment. Although heterogeneous beliefs were welcomed, a broad consensus formed around the control of financial institutions, social justice and on radical democratic process and the strengthening of substantive democracy through consensus-based decision making.

The camp's presence outside a prominent Church of England (CoE) institution caused controversy within the church. Though the St Paul's Institute had already been established to work on issues of corporate and financial responsibility from a Christian perspective, the presence of the Occupy camp on its steps forced confrontation. Two high-ranking CoE officiates and a chaplain resigned over positions taken by the Church during the occupation. Occupy LSX became an anchor for the national media to take up discussions around social justice, financial regulation, economic inequality, the banking system, redistribution and present government policy. However, activists disagreed on whether Occupy should directly engage with mainstream media and politicians; while the *Financial Times* opened a 'Capitalism in Crisis' series and published an article written by members of Occupy's Economics Working Group, other activists considered this a violation of the group's values and procedures, as it had been arranged outside of the general assembly structure.

Occupiers were evicted from St Paul's by bailiffs in February 2012, after a High Court ruling found in favour of the City of London Corporation over land use. Several other sites in London were occupied between October 2011 and June 2012, including the last to go, in Finsbury Square. Occupy London continues to organise and publicise events related their concerns and hold working groups and general assemblies; however, the post-occupation stage has seen some fragmentation. *The Occupied Times of London*, formed during the occupation at St Pauls, has renounced its affiliation with Occupy London, citing 'a number of decisions and stances taken by the latter which are completely opposed to the ethos of the publication'.

http://occupylondon.org.uk
http://theoccupiedtimes.org

against the rise in university tuition fees initiated in 2010. While not a 'novel' group in a broader social movement sense, this fit the subterranean politics frame both in that it 'bubbled up' dramatically, emerging into the public consciousness, and that actors within this group – many of them first-time activists – brought different tactics and frames than had been previously used by student groups, to the extent that elements of the movement attempted to distance themselves from existing actors and practices. In this case, the movement was making claims on a national target – the UK government – but, like Occupy LSX, included many non-British-born actors within its ranks. Our final case study did not feature largely in the protests, but has been gaining increasing

Box 7.2   UK Uncut

UK Uncut is an activist network that aims to call public attention to economic injustices in UK government policy. Specifically, the group aims to counter narratives justifying austerity measures and cuts in public services by calling attention to policies favouring corporate and financial institutions.

The main assertion of UK Uncut is that the government's justifications for imposing deep cuts in social spending are spurious, and that government initiatives to counter tax evasion and tax avoidance by wealthy individuals and large corporations would more than make up for budget shortfalls while leaving social programmes intact. Instead, ideologically driven austerity policies have disproportionately harmed poor and vulnerable people, widening the gap between rich and poor in society and revealing collusion between the political class and corporate interests.

The group's actions are aimed towards raising public awareness rather than at lobbying the government directly. The group grew into a nationwide activist network following an initial sit-in in October 2010 by 70 protestors at Vodafone's flagship store on Oxford Street. That action effectively shut down the store, calling attention to its history of tax avoidance and the UK government's leniency in pursuing the company's unpaid tax bill. Using online tools like Twitter and, later, a UK Uncut website where activists can plan and advertise direct action, activists coordinate similar events on high streets throughout the UK to bring public attention to tax justice.

The group's tactics eschew traditional forms of protest like marches in favour of attention-grabbing forms of direct action and civil disobedience. Aside from Vodafone, UK Uncut actions have targeted other large corporations known to avoid tax, including the Arcadia Group (which owns the fashion giant Topshop), Boots and Fortnum & Mason. In December 2011, the group took legal action against HM Revenue and Customs, claiming that the UK's tax authority had failed to give reasonable justification for not collecting billions of pounds in tax revenue – from a list of companies that included Goldman Sachs.

As with Occupy London, UK Uncut is a horizontal network of activists without official organisational leaders. Likewise, UK Uncut's direct actions facilitated a public discussion in the media of alternatives to austerity and in particular corporate tax avoidance and tax justice more generally. While UK Uncut is generally regarded as having been successful in raising awareness about the tax delinquency of its targets, actions have dwindled since 2012 and online activity is now primarily focused around lending support to other groups' actions.

http://www.ukuncut.org.uk

attention for its citywide campaigns, notably during the last London mayoral election of 2012. London Citizens is a community organising group influenced by the Chicago tradition of community organising; part of a broader national (and international) network formed in 1996, its campaigns on such issues as the Living Wage have significant resonance, and many of its community organising practices can be seen echoed in the more novel movements (Lundquist et al. 2012). Additionally, a large number of its members are also active in groups that work on the politics of their diaspora; we were curious to examine their relationship to Europe as a political space.

Interviews

The second phase of the research took an ethnographic approach. Our mandate was both to grasp the subterranean nature of the groups that we chose to examine, and to explore the motivations and identities of actors within those groups in order to unearth ideas of Europe. Although existing data from a number of questionnaires that have sought to explore either public perceptions of the current political and economic situation and the EU, or the motivations, aims and networks of protesters that fit the 'subterranean' frame,[6] were helpful for the overall Subterranean Politics project in terms of context, we felt that such survey-based investigations do not allow for in-depth discussions about identity, conceptions of Europe and how these interact to inform the activism of subterranean political actors. Hence our decision to employ semi-structured interviews, which would allow us to both grasp the broader context of these actors and actions and to probe beyond the one-dimensional answers that a more rigid questionnaire or interview demands. Both before and during the research period we attended meetings, marches, campaign drives and working groups, which afforded greater understanding of the background, context, organisation and forms of the groups studied.[7]

Box 7.3   UK student protest movement

In many ways the harbinger of the protest activity in the UK in 2011, the student protests of late 2010 took place in several cities and with the participation of tens of thousands of students and activists, in response to cuts to education allowances and a threefold rise in tuition fees proposed by the Conservative–Liberal Democratic Coalition Government. Despite the fact that these reforms were suggested by a review commissioned by the Labour government – the Browne Review into higher education funding – the protestors viewed the recently elected Coalition government, with their move to act on the review's recommendations, as their target.

The Liberal Democrats in particular were seen to be capitulating to their coalition partners in accepting the reforms, some of which directly countered the party's pre-election manifesto pledges. Many media commentators appeared to view these protests as the inevitable consequence of a Conservative victory. As one journalist put it, 'Right on cue, exactly six months into David Cameron's premiership, the ancient British roar of "Tory scum" echoed across central London again' (White 2010).

The first protest took place in central London on 10 November 2010 during a planned demonstration organised by the National Union of Students (NUS) and the University and College Union. The demonstration route passed the Conservative Party headquarters in Millbank Tower, where a group of protesters broke in and occupied the offices while others burnt placards outside. Riot police were brought in to control the crowd. This event set the tone for subsequent demonstrations that were held on 24 November, when mounted police charged at protestors, and on 30 November, when the protest was largely hampered by a heavy pre-emptive police presence.

On 9 December, when the vote on education reform was taken, protests saw further vandalism of government buildings in Whitehall, police violence and the 'kettling' of protestors (including minors) in Parliament Square. Characteristics of the student protests would reappear in 2011, including sporadic violence (initially attributed to 'black bloc' anarchists, police agent provocateurs and/or apolitical youth gangs, though this has been contested); heavy police presence; the use of 'kettling' tactics by the police; the marginalisation of more traditional civil society groups (in particular, the NUS, which denounced the Millbank violence); and the occupation of various university buildings in universities across England and Wales.

The student protests and the issues that provoked them are seen as having been responsible for radicalising young student-activists resident in the UK (including those from other European countries), many of whom had not been politically active prior to the student protests, and some of whom went on to participate in Occupy and other movements in subsequent years. While the immediate issue being contested was educational funding – including cuts to the Educational Maintenance Allowance for students from poorer families – this was seen as representative of the government's ideologically driven cuts to social programmes which left profligate corporate and financial organisations relatively unreformed.

We began the interview process with a small focus group in which the researchers participated. This helped us to reflect upon our guiding questions, respond to unexpected themes that emerged, and refine the topics to explore with subsequent interviewees. Our topic guide was divided into three sections: participants' views on the organisational structure and forms of their group; participants' views on the core issues they sought to address; and the spatial, institutional and subjective (in terms of identity) levels participants felt were relevant in diagnosing and addressing those issues. The order in which we attempted to arrive at these topics within each interview was designed so that there was space for participants to bring Europe into their responses much earlier on in the interview than the point at which the specific questions on Europe were asked.

Political blockage

Trying to discover what mix of conditions converged to stimulate the emergence of subterranean politics in Europe at a particular time and in a particular way can only be approached piecemeal and, as this project recognises, can only be done by investigating the differences in that emergence in different contexts. Approaching the question through interviews with subterranean political actors in London, we hoped to

Box 7.4   London Citizens

Citizens UK is a nationwide community organising group that identifies political priorities through community outreach, organises local or national campaigns around particular issues and lobbies politicians to add them to the political agenda.

London Citizens, which has in recent years subdivided into more locally based groups, brings together civil society groups throughout the city to direct issues of relevance at political figures, including the mayor. These issues are determined by working with community leaders – many centred around religious institutions and schools – to determine issues of importance to citizens, including diaspora groups. The group, founded in 1996, forms the core of the now nationally based Citizens UK alliance. As the group has grown, it has established itself as a relevant political forum outside of state-organised processes. During the UK general election in 2010, Citizens UK hosted a forum in which the candidates from each of the three major political parties addressed its members.

The group positions itself as an important civil society mediator on a variety of social issues ranging from housing, crime and employment wages. The Living Wage campaign, for example, tries to combat working poverty by independently determining a base wage higher than the national minimum wage and offers accreditation through the Living Wage Foundation for employers who have committed to paying their employees accordingly. Its Diaspora Caucus addresses issues of multiculturalism and migration in the UK by providing a forum from which migrant communities can discuss and organise around aspects of life and integration in the UK.

Unlike UK Uncut and Occupy, Citizens UK was established before the financial crisis and is modelled on US-based community organising networks dating from the 1940s. It trains community leaders in its model of community organising to bring about practical reforms, and while it addresses formal political structures to push for those reforms, it does not rely on legislation to carry them out, as the Living Wage Foundation demonstrates.

http://www.citizensuk.org/

discover a partial answer obliquely by discussing activists' motives for becoming politically involved. While the results of the media analysis in our mapping exercise led us to expect that most involvement was in reaction to the wide-ranging austerity policies introduced since May 2010 by the Coalition government, with most events (65%) and most organisations (83%) primarily focused on alternative ideas to austerity, subsequent interviews revealed a surprisingly consistent and systemic critique of the condition of contemporary politics.

One of the most consistent parts of this critique was a frustration with the state of formal politics and fatigue with past forms of contestation. The idea that people feel disenfranchised by formal electoral democracy, especially in established Western democracies, is not new and has been of interest to political scientists for many years (see for example Pharr and Putnam 2000). Nevertheless, the language of a 'political blockage' – an insular or insincere political class not representing public interests, politics as entertainment or public relations exercise, the decline of a substantive left-wing political agenda – emerged in the course of our interviews. This political blockage extended into frustrations with forms of resistance: respondents recognised that past forms of contestation had reached their limits or were too easily co-opted. This explicit critique suggests some explanation not only for the emergence of new democratic experiments and protest tactics, but also the particular forms and processes that were adopted.

Political blockage

There's a lot to be said about frustrations with political processes. After working in media, you see things, hear things that lead you to conclude that this is a screwed up system in terms of allowing people to have a say, policies for the common good, informed debate [and] critical media coverage.

(German activist, Occupy LSX)

Activists from Occupy London, the student movement and UK Uncut often identified failures in representative democracy as practised in the UK as part of a systemic critique that contributed to their activism. The critique included several issues: failures of the notionally centre-left political parties to articulate a meaningful political programme to which activists could subscribe; the perception that politicians were relatively homogenous in terms of social background and (by consequence) the interests they represented; and that blatant reversal of policy agendas was so commonplace that people felt disenfranchised regardless of electoral participation and access to other formal political channels. These frustrations were not restricted to particular political parties. While the recent election of a Conservative-led coalition government and the imposition of austerity measures in the UK were seen as an important factor in stimulating the recent waves of mobilisation, most respondents extended the crisis of representation across the political spectrum:

> I don't want to just pick on the Conservative and Liberal parties implementing the cuts, because probably Labour would have done the same.
>
> (German activist, student movement/Occupy LSX)

> Even the political Left (like New Labour, Third Way) doesn't have a lot of solutions and doesn't articulate the things I want to see articulated and a lot of other people want to see articulated. Questioning the workings of parliamentary politics is not an anti-conservative argument, not an anti-liberal argument. It's a systemic argument.
>
> (German activist, Occupy LSX)

To reinforce the critique by counter-example, one Norwegian respondent explained that Norway had not experienced a wave of protests in part because they are 'comfortable', but also because Norwegians are 'much closer to the politicians': the Norwegian parliament includes younger MPs, and even high-level representatives are obliged to meet with citizens (Norwegian activist, Occupy LSX).

These concerns chime with some sociological accounts of the declining democratic situation in Western democracies, which focus on the effects of large socio-economic changes such as the mobility of capital relative to national regulation (economic globalisation), the changing nature of labour and the changing composition of the labour force and the political parties and organisations created to represent its interests (Crouch 2004). These changes will be particularly pronounced in sites like global cities where they are concentrated. These accounts also suggest that the political class is occupied by a narrow class of specialists that mainly concerns itself with facilitating the relationship between government and business lobbies rather than articulating the priorities of an electorate, a notion that accords with some of our respondents' diagnoses.

The blockage at the level of representative institutions through political parties was coupled with a fatigue with forms of contentious politics. When respondents mentioned familiar mobilising blocs like the 'traditional Left', it was mostly in relation to forms and processes within these organisations that were compromised or co-opted: a bureaucratic form of decision making and a vanguardism which fixed an ideological agenda that could not be renegotiated. Forms of contestation typical of past political movements, such as protests and marches, were described as obsolete or ineffective. One respondent described protest marches as a 'modern-day carnival' where participants 'come out for a day and wave placards, then go back home', and several respondents pointed to the failure of the 2003 global protests to stop the invasion of Iraq as a clear sign that past forms of protest were 'dead' (English activist, UK Uncut; German activist, student movement/Occupy LSX). Against this background of political blockage at the institutional level and at the level of 'bottom-up' mobilisations, activists asserted the potential in novel forms of direct action and in horizontal organisation structures and consensus-based forms of decision-making.

Novel forms and autonomous politics as claim-making

> Occupy is a symptom that there is no real Left anymore... Leftist politics and advanced, late capitalism are not really compatible. So, the political system we've got now is entwined with huge business and things that are at odds with Leftism.
>
> (English activist, Occupy LSX)

In response to a lack of representation by both politicians and traditional activists, subterranean political actors experiment with new forms of direct action ranging from long-term occupations of public space to short-term tactics designed to generate media publicity. UK Uncut activists suggested that their experiments with 'attention-generating tactics', like short-term staged occupations and sit-ins in high-street shops, along with a framing of the issue of tax avoidance as 'a simple injustice', managed to strike a chord with the public because, whereas the 'traditional Left often managed not to talk with people', UK Uncut 'seeks to engage humorously with the public and speak in everyday language rather than delivering a lecture about an issue' (Scottish activist, UK Uncut). The Occupy camp at St Paul's cathedral generated public attention by its persistent presence, though it was also conceptualised by some participants as a comment on the relationship between the global and the local. The physical occupation – which one respondent asserted was a metaphor for a political occupation (English activist, UK Uncut) – grounds the 'global' in concrete localities:

> [Occupy is about] creating roots in the locality. [There is a] long last- ing tension between the local and the global. [They are] [t]argeting the City of London because it embodies the relationship between the local and the global.
>
> (English activist, UK Uncut)

> Occupy is a critique of the global by saying, 'it's not just a neat global sphere' through its quite specific, concrete occupations.
>
> (English activist, Occupy LSX)

If part of the implicit frustration with formal political institutions is that their hierarchical structures allow a narrow group of specialists to capture the political process and marginalise citizen participation, then the adoption of 'radical democracy' (della Porta and Rucht 2013, and especially Haug and Rucht: 179–213), horizontal and leaderless organisational forms, consensus-based decision making and procedural innovation – like the use of non-verbal hand signals during meetings and assemblies – form the response. The most radical form of this response is practising autonomous politics – the creation of a separate space of political practice which avoids co-optation by established polit- ical, media or business agendas by enacting a parallel agenda rather than responding to the terms and priorities set by existing institutions. Within that space, prefigurative politics (see Chapter 8) is practised in order to not defer the political ideal to a future moment, but to 'create other worlds' through 'do-it-yourself politics' (English activist, Occupy LSX). Again, this is most clearly manifested in Occupy London's 'tent city':

> The presence of the camp: the physical, the material and the symbolic has been so important – you can't ignore it; the bankers that pass by can't ignore it, it is already creating an alternative to the main system and demonstrating the alternative.
>
> (Norwegian activist, Occupy LSX)

Amongst the groups we investigated, the importance of process also formed a central concern. Notably, Occupy is premised on a leader- less structure which allows for full participation and the possibility of debating a wide range of issues, while London Citizens aim to be effec- tive by keeping participants' energies from being dispersed by engaging community leaders who foster one-to-one relationships and reducing broader issues into 'winnable' policy items. Both groups, nevertheless, aim at reducing the bottlenecks of the political process by broadening participation in decision-making processes:

> We've realised through other work that we've done, that where you have these chairpersons, it doesn't really work – that person immediately becomes a bottleneck... nothing can get done without that person there to okay it, so what we're trying to do is to have project managers... a group of people within the organisation to lead, if you like, but not control.
>
> (Zimbabwean organiser, London Citizens)

> The death of all political movements is someone becoming the boss and deciding what is to be done. The principles of horizontal organisation may be more painstaking, but they're the key thing that must be preserved.
>
> (Scottish activist, UK Uncut)

Despite their similar aims, there was disagreement between these two forms of organising, and criticism of horizontal and autonomous forms arose from within the groups we investigated. While not hemmed in by legacies of institutional priorities or processes, it comes under criticism for therefore having a tendency to become self-referential and not engaging with existing political institutions, or for placing too much emphasis on 'horizontality' to the exclusion of other models of organisation. A respondent from London Citizens criticised autonomous politics as a form of disengagement: 'the Occupy ethos [...] is anti-hierarchical, anti-structure, considers the system to be broken. Therefore, [they'd] rather opt out and create [their] own little words of change' (English organiser, London Citizens). The respondent also suggested that there was no reason to think that non-hierarchical network structures are more accountable than hierarchical structures: both are open to abuses of power. Even some Occupy activists were wary about tendencies for this type of politics to become insular and self-referential – as well as being implicitly hierarchical. While formally there are no leaders, several respondents pointed out that the amount of time individuals devoted to organisational efforts established an informal system of authority amongst participants that was implicitly exclusionary:

> Anyone that pretends Occupy is a completely leaderless movement is just denying reality. There's a core group of maybe 20 people, maybe 30 people that are basically coordinating the work that's

happening: facilitating amongst working groups outside of the open forum processes – background work. The non-hierarchical focus creates a certain mindset that anyone who tries to exploit the ability to do things on personal initiative is very quickly reminded of the limits.

(German activist, Occupy LSX)

Most participants recognised the utility of leaders but nevertheless stressed the idea of horizontality as an important ideal which, even if in practice could not be achieved, shaped a political culture that was inclusive, non-bureaucratic and placed limits on the ability of individuals to use implicit authority to dominate others or determine the group's priorities. Some respondents suggest that these innovative processes are already clashing with the practices of activist forums that have been around for ten or 15 years, suggesting that subterranean politics as process finds further emergence in asserting its legitimacy in existing forums, like the World Social Forum (WSF) and European Social Forum (ESF), who attempt to tackle similar issues:

> ... at the [European Network Academy for Social Movements], [there were] some very good speakers on a panel, high up in the hierarchy of ATTAC,[8] about the ESF, and then those watching said that we had to discuss too, [and] so applied the Occupy – or Indignados – model of speech: an open mic, we all have the right to talk, and enforced an open mic in this conference ... you could see some tension between old structures of activism and new structures – or between different structures of activism, however you want to call it.
>
> (German activist, student movement/Occupy LSX)

> [The] traditional left is involved in the WSF, which may explain the clash in process between the WSF and Occupy. WSF hasn't really taken on the assembly structures of Occupy; decisions [are] still made bureaucratically and behind closed doors.
>
> (English activist, Occupy LSX)

This focus on process by subterranean political actors, then, may reflect the notion that the form of the action reflects the content of the claim being made. Political blockage expresses itself as both a negative response – a rejection of traditional forms of mediation and organising – and a positive response – experimentation with a new repertoire of contestation and organisation that aims to re-engage with democratic processes on radically different terms.

Europe: absent yet everywhere?

In attempting to uncover how ideas about 'Europe' were situated in the emerging political currents of 2010 and 2011, London – as a global city – presented a particularly intriguing field of study. Judging by impressions of the public discourse – as evidenced not only in the British press and in political and intellectual debate, but also in the slogans, official statements and websites of those groups involved in the protests – one could hypothesise that subterranean actors within London, if concerned with Europe at all, were most likely to take an anti-European stance, particularly if 'Europe' was defined as the EU. And yet this discourse fails to acknowledge a salient fact of life in the UK, and particularly in London, at the present time. In London, the global city, one in three Londoners is overseas born, and over 10% are non-British nationals of the EU (ONS 2012b). This diversity is true not just in the upper echelons of the 'cosmopolitan' community of international elites, or in the (poorly paid) transnational labour force often occupying low-skilled jobs (cf. Sassen ibid.), but across most of London's social strata, not least in the influx of international students and young, often (relatively) well-paid workers in the creative, IT and service sectors from EU member states and beyond. With considerable crossover between those groups and the activists that were the subject of our case studies, we were curious to discover whether Europe really was as absent in subterranean politics as it first appeared.

Our initial mapping exercise and claims analysis of events and organisations supported the public discourse of British 'exceptionalism' from continental Europe, bringing to the fore two key points. First, that there are very few Europe-related initiatives within the UK (including those which support more or less UK integration into Europe), and those that do exist tend to be located within think tanks that have a specific focus on European policy. Only 12 major initiatives were documented,[9] with two stridently anti-Europe and the majority emphasising EU reform and a rethink of the UK's political and economic influence. Second, there was almost no crossover between the emergent political movements and these initiatives.[10] Those protesting against the national – or global – status quo in 2010 and 2011 rarely evidenced any stance on Europe at all, let alone a pro-European stance. While 83% of the organisations mapped proposed alternative ideas to austerity, and the same number campaigned around issues of social justice (there was considerable crossover across these groups), almost none addressed these issues beyond the UK border.[11]

Initially, too, the interviews seemed to point away from Europe. As noted above in the methodology, while 'Europe' was not brought into the conversation explicitly by interviewers until the third and final section of each interview, the topic list was arranged in such a way as to allow interviewees to discuss this level of political activity unprompted almost from the start, had it been prominent in their thinking – for example in response to questions on whether the group was connected to a wider network of activists, or in relation to the group's broader systemic critiques. Yet during the first section of the interviews, which focused on organisational structure, forms and practices, not one interviewee brought up the subject of Europe, or the EU, or European institutions. Nor did anyone mention the crisis in the eurozone or note the fact that fluid borders allowed both for transnational activism and transnational activists, despite fairly leading questions such as, 'Do you think that there is a more diverse range of participants, and if so why?'; and, 'Why do you think this group/movement has emerged now?' Austerity measures were occasionally mentioned at this stage as a prompt to action or a unifying force (particularly by UK-born participants), along with the negative effects of neo-liberalism (in a very general way) and some interpretation of the global economic/social crisis, but not nearly to the extent of problems with democracy and political blockage, as discussed above.

The second stage of each interview was intended to present even more opportunities for respondents to bring up Europe as a political space, should they deem it relevant. This stage focused on different scales of political belonging in which they acted and in which they saw the loci of the issues on which they campaigned. Again, even when an interviewer mentioned Europe as an option – for example, 'What I'm thinking about in terms of spaces are the differences between action on a community/local level, at the national level, and the regional level – such as Europe – and at the global level', respondents did not take the opportunity to praise or lambast Europe, while local, national and global levels were all cited. A number of interviewees did, at this stage, mention the European crisis as one of a number of causal issues (along with problems with democracy, political blockage, the Arab Spring and neo-liberalism). It is notable that these respondents were European-born residents and not UK citizens, which, even with this small sample size, supports the perception of British insularity. However, not all of the overseas-born respondents mentioned Europe, and there was still no mention at all of European institutions as targets of action, nor of Europe as an arena for civil society action – whether in terms of solidarity and mobilisation or as a political formation that creates opportunities for political transformation. Thus the most striking impression from the first two stages of the interviews was the conspicuous absence of Europe, even more so than predicted: without prompting, it simply didn't appear.

It was only when the interview proceeded explicitly onto questions about Europe that the topic began to emerge – and even here it initially seemed like an unwelcome intrusion. While a question such as, 'do you think that the European level is a relevant one, in terms of addressing your issue?' was designed to be a natural progression from questions of space and scale, most respondents hesitated. 'The EU never occurred to me as a target,' said one German Occupy LSX activist when asked whether Europe seemed a relevant level for campaigning action – and this rather neatly sums up the bulk of the responses. Yet although Europe emerged so reluctantly, and although many interviewees professed both little interest and little knowledge on the topic – 'I think Occupy is thoroughly confused when it comes to Europe, and that's not very surprising given how little people know or care about Europe as an entity' (German activist, Occupy LSX) – the remainder of the interviews suggests that, at least for our interviewees, this was not quite the case. Rather, almost all respondents, whether British-born or not, immediately took 'Europe' to mean the EU, although the interviewers were careful in their questioning to leave 'Europe' as an open category. Once this Europe emerged in the interviews, most (though not all) respondents were quick to criticise this Europe-as-EU as an agent of neo-liberalism. 'What is the EU anymore? What's it supposed to be doing? It just seems like a big function for the markets at the moment,' (English activist, Occupy LSX) was a typical comment. Interviewees also bemoaned the democratic deficit created between the EU and national polities and the tendency of politicians to deflect responsibility back and forth – 'it's like ping pong'. They also frequently cited the purportedly technocratic nature of policymaking in Brussels as a negative. For all our respondents bar one (see below), beyond its alleged facilitating function for neo-liberalism, Europe as a transnational body of governance 'simply didn't work'.

Yet despite this perceived failure, there was appreciation for the *idea* of a post-war unified Europe, even from activists young enough to have been born into the common market: 'The EU used to be a buffer against Thatcherism when it was a social Europe. Now it's a market Europe – a neoliberal project' (Scottish activist, UK Uncut). This thread of contradiction and ambivalence amplified as the interviews progressed, particularly after interviewees had a chance to consider the more personal questions, such as 'What do you mean when you talk about Europe?' and, finally, 'Do you see yourself as a European?' Many explicitly then qualified their initial rejection of Europe/the EU: the lack of functioning was the problem, not necessarily the idea of some form of supra-national regional coordination. Indeed, even those respondents more in favour of national or local governance still saw some transnational governance necessary in certain contexts, to the point of welcoming more integration on issues such as the environment, crime and the free movement of labour:

> An EU that looks different could be a very good model towards providing alternative views for the global organisation of participation, trade, social policy, monetary spending, fiscal solidarity. The EU could be a very, very good model, but it would have to look very different.
>
> (German activist, Occupy LSX)

Interestingly, the one respondent in our study who did perceive the existing EU as a 'good model' of governance was the one who explicitly saw the effects of an EU that 'worked' in comparison with other political systems that did not. However, it is important to note that the relevance of Europe as a political space did not emerge until very late in the interview, when asked if he personally felt European. A non-European citizen, resident in London for 20 years and an active campaigner on behalf of his country of birth and citizenship, Zimbabwe, he replied in the affirmative, explaining that it was because 'wherever we've [the Zimbabwean community] had problems...the European Court of Human Rights has come to our aid'. Furthermore, he added, due to colonial history and long-established trading links between Zimbabwe and Europe, 'the European level is closer to us, and is more influential' than either emerging countries like China or the nations of African Union ('we tried that and it hasn't worked'), and that Europe – and specifically, the support of European diplomats – therefore seemed like a more effective 'platform' from which the diaspora could engage with the Zimbabwean government.[12]

This non-European citizen thus tied both his European identity and the relevance of European institutions to having directly benefitted from these institutions. And, in fact, although the other respondents criticised the institutions themselves, as each interview moved into biographical topics they too made connections between their sense of

European identity and the role that the integration of Europe facilitated by these institutions – particularly the part played by the 'open
border... easyJet culture' (English activist, UK Uncut) in shaping these
identities. While the overseas-born Londoners were somewhat more
likely to immediately identify themselves as European when asked, and
the British-born Londoners were more hesitant, all eventually resolved
themselves to a layering of identities that included several scales of political and cultural belonging, with the majority positive about identifying
with Europe:

> I do [feel Nigerian] in some ways... but in a lot of ways I feel straight-
> forwardly British... and also I've grown up in a period of increased
> European integration so I feel a kind of European citizenship as well.
> (Nigerian-born British citizen, student)

This was true even for those altogether resistant to labels marking
political boundaries. Furthermore, this European identity was not only
a cultural one, but involved a degree of political responsibility and
legitimacy – even if the respondent remained ambivalent in their
European-ness:

> I wouldn't say I feel European; I was brought up to feel affiliated with
> people not with nationalities. But yes I feel more affinity with people
> from Europe, I comprehend politics from a European perspective.
> (Norwegian activist, Occupy LSX)

This sentiment first surfaced at the end of the initial focus group, when
participants were asked *why* they identified as European. A Finnish
member of Occupy LSX reasoned that perhaps it was because she
felt both *legitimate* campaigning across Europe in a way that she did
not when outside the continent and also *responsible* for the actions
of institutions that she saw either as European or as influenced by a
political-economic system in which European governance and markets
were complicit. This reasoning was met with recognition and agreement
by other members of the group, and so was explored further during
the individual interviews through questions like, 'why campaign here
rather than in your home country?' and 'would you feel comfortable
campaigning outside of the UK?'

'I came back to Europe because [...] I can't really speak [in Tanzania]
the way I can speak as a European in the EU,' replied a German Occupy
LSX activist, echoing the sentiments of many of our interviewees; 'there

can be solidarity, but I have to ask, where do I have the capacity to fight the strongest?' This sense was present even when there was ambivalence regarding whether activism should move beyond the prefigurative – '*if* I felt a responsibility/right to change people's ideas about how to live, to push my opinions, I would feel comfortable doing that here, not in South America or Africa' (Scottish activist, UK Uncut). Variations on the same theme appeared repeatedly: a sense of responsibility, legitimacy and effectiveness at the European level, separate from feelings of solidarity at the global level, but alongside convictions, across all respondents, that the problems addressed by their activism are global ones, requiring global solutions. However, it is important to note that, at least in our interviews, these sentiments emerged as ones of identity and not of political action. A number of European Occupy LSX activists did, once asked directly about European solidarity, bemoan the lack of involvement of UK activists with other European Occupy groups and with more established European groups such as ATTAC (*Association pour la Taxation des Transactions financière et l'Aide aux Citoyens*/Association for the Taxation of financial Transactions and Aid to Citizens), offering some evidence to support the assertion that the British are somewhat more insular with regard to European issues than mainland Europeans. But these respondents were no more likely without prompting to raise the subject of Europe as a viable political space, nor express interest in European political reforms.

Unpacking identity is a hugely complex, multidisciplinary endeavour and beyond the scope of this project. Nevertheless, a growing literature on the evolution of European identity/ies accords with our findings. In *The Evolution of European Identities: Biographical Approaches* (Miller 2012), the authors studied groups with a predicted transnational experience of Europe (such as migrants and those who regularly worked across the continent) and observed that, 'attitudes to Europe are quite vague and fuzzy, utterly absent or even denied... [but often] expressed indirectly or symptomatically' (p. 256). They also pointed out that many interviewees had a 'life trajectory [that] had developed within the context of advantageous EU regulations' (p. 183), meaning that 'European realities structured autobiographical accounts indirectly, even if direct references to Europe were completely absent' (p. 198).

The authors of that study proposed the existence of a 'European mental space' (EMS), noting that 'although less than the imagined community of a nation, the European mental space of reference changes the former primordial character of the nation as a resource for [...] political agency' (p. 276), and, furthermore, that this EMS 'is idealistically or critically dealt with and overshadowed – in a distorted and distracting way – by a conspicuously public "big issues" discourse practiced mainly by politicians, journalists and intellectuals' (ibid.). This is something that we recognise in our data: both a suggestion of an EMS itself and the idea that it is intertwined with personal identity and obscured by the 'big issues' of public discourse. Yet one might reasonably ask whether 'Europe' as a political or cultural imaginary was in fact what these activists had in common, or, given their concerns with legitimacy and responsibility, whether it was more broadly a shared experience of democracy.[13] This is where the European story meets the concerns with political blockage described above, which we shall turn to in our conclusion.

Conclusion

In our research, we hoped to discover whether and how the city's position as a major European metropolis, a centre of global capitalism and a national capital with a diverse population was reflected in the repertoires and narratives of its contentious political actors and others working for political change at the 'subterranean' level. Through our interviews, we attempted to determine how they articulated the relationship between these various scales of politics and, specifically, find out whether 'Europe', in its period of crisis, was present as an object of critique, a space of solidarity or political opportunity, or a target of reform.

While one 'Europe' did emerge as an object of critique through our interviews, it was the set of institutions perceived as regulating the integrated economic and political space, and this target did not appear high on the agenda of any of the activists to whom we spoke. Crucially, it was not evident from our interviews that the European economic and political crisis has stimulated specific reflection on the reform and future development of EU institutions' priorities and practices.[14] Members of Occupy LSX offered systemic critiques that did apply to the EU but were more likely to be addressed to national parliaments and the global capitalist system, suggesting that the principal concern was a prior political question and not in reforming existing institutions. London Citizens operate by articulating community concerns to local politicians rather than seeking solutions at more remote levels of political belonging, and while some participants in UK Uncut were broadly concerned with issues of social justice and anti-austerity (issues taken up by protest groups across Europe), most attention was focused at the national level. The same was true for student campaigners.

Neither was Europe considered in terms of political opportunity – but then this is consistent with the claims made by the groups that we interviewed, all of whom were concerned, in their own ways, with participatory or prefigurative democracy. Each offered a diagnosis of political problems centring around an inability to affect politics either through the formal channels of representative democracy or through well-worn repertoires of contestation. This diagnosis extended across political party lines and beyond specific national contexts; it was applied also to the failure of the EU to offer any positive alternatives to blocked national systems and the destructive effects of global capitalism. If subterranean politics is, as we argue, at least in part an expression of political blockage, then the absence of Europe amongst activists' meaningful levels of action is also symptomatic of this broader crisis of democracy in and across the European context. Failing to create horizons for democratic participation or a shared sense of political identity, and understood mainly as a facilitator for markets, Europe remains irrelevant or invisible for the majority of subterranean political actors in London, whether those actors are British or from other European nations.

Yet what did come to light through the interviews was another, more positive conception of Europe, beyond the idea of Europe as a set of bureaucratic political institutions. Our interviews, and other chapters in this book, suggest that, despite the best attempts of a minority of activists, Europe may not yet be a space of 'solidarity' in the sense of explicit ties between organisations. Certainly, in London, despite the presence of non-British European citizens acting at the subterranean level, there appears to be very little in the way of a coordinated trans-European space of contentious politics. However, for both British and non-British residents alike, Europe does exist as a social and cultural space whose political and economic integration have allowed a generation of Europeans to take for granted their own European identity. The importance of the latter for subterranean political actors, we have argued, is present in an implicit sense of expanded political membership as indicated in respondents' notions of their own legitimacy and responsibility in European contexts. According to our findings, the Europe that is reported to be in 'crisis' is not the Europe that underlies the actions of its contentious political actors. We would argue that if any form of regional union is to be preserved and developed, European leaders need to look beyond the strained institutions to the social and political activity in civil society, while subterranean actors would do well to direct more attention to the reshaping of those institutions that underpin their lives as Europeans.

Notes

1. With acknowledgement and thanks to Maro Pantazidou, who was key to the research design and interview phase of the project; see Deel and Murray-Leach (2012).
2. Or at least issues and policies *perceived* as national; for an example on the debate on the national vs. global in austerity politics, see Titley (2012).
3. Although at the time perhaps considered a continuation of the global justice movement(s) that had emerged over the previous decade and described by Pleyers, Pianta and Gerbaudo elsewhere in this volume (see Chapter 2), these protest tactics and institutional response became typical of later protests.
4. *The Guardian*'s website was especially useful as a starting point.
5. As this chapter is focused on the case studies that we selected following this exercise, we have not included the full data here; the results are available to view online at www.subterraneanpolitics.eu.
6. In particular, we studied the Eurobarometer (notably Eurobarometer 75, Spring 2011, 'Europeans, the European Union and the crisis' and Eurobarometer 76, December 2011, 'Public Opinion in the European Union'); the latest phase of the European World Values survey; the 'questionnaire for interviews to representatives of social movement organizations' created by the DEMOS Project (Democracy in Europe and the Mobilization of the Society), coordinated by Donatella della Porta and the protest survey currently being carried out by seven European universities (Bert Klandermans, Stefaan Walgrave, Jacquelien Van Stekelenburg, Joris Verhulst, Jeroen Van Laer, Ruud Wouters, Dunya Van Troost and Anouk Van Leeuwen; Protest Survey 2010).
7. It should be noted that all the researchers involved have a degree of interest in and sympathy with the agendas of the groups under observation, although none are involved at a level beyond normative affinity and occasional actions of solidarity.
8. Association pour la Taxation des Transactions Financière et l'Aide aux Citoyen (Association for the Taxation of Financial Transactions and Aid to Citizens).
9. See Appendix A, Kaldor and Selchow (2012).
10. It is interesting to note that our research did unearth many inactive 'Eurosceptic' initiatives, not included in the results due to their lack of activity, and that these have generally presented themselves as grassroots organisations of 'the people'; many appeared to have been run by a very small group of people, gaining some media attention during periods of public debate on the UK's role in Europe and then lapsing into inactivity. The pro-European initiatives, however, made no such grassroots claims, but rather were explicitly linked to think tanks or business lobbying groups.
11. The exception to this is the Coalition of Resistance (Against Cuts and Privatisation) (www.coalitionofresistance.org.uk), who maintain the website 'Europe Against Austerity' (www.europeagainstausterity.org). Although primarily concerned with cuts and privatisation across the UK, the Coalition nevertheless lists 'liais[on] ... with similar opposition movements in other countries and ... a call for international resistance to austerity measures' as one of the group's ten action points (Coalition of Resistance 2012). It staged

a national speaking tour across the UK in Spring 2012 entitled: 'Cuts in the Eurozone, Cuts in the UK', and has been key in transnational efforts such as the Alter Summit (see Chapter 2). However, Coalition remains primarily focused on issues perceived as local and national, such as the future of the NHS and the unions, and when it does talk about Europe, it does so using the language of what Beck would term 'methodological nationalism' (Beck 1992), using the frame of 'solidarity' with other nations.

12. The example that he cited was that in approaching the UNSC (United Nations Security Council) to support a resolution against Mugabe, it had been most important for the diaspora communities to gain the support of European diplomats.

13. This point was first raised by Erin Saltman at one of the Subterranean Politics project meetings.

14. As of 2012.

References

Beck, U. (1992) *Risk Society: Towards a New Modernity*. London: Sage.

Coalition of Resistance (2012) May 2012, Accessed online at http://www.coalitionofresistance.org.uk/.

Crouch, C. (2004) *Post-Democracy*. Cambridge: Polity Press.

della Porta, D. and Caiani, M. (2009) *Social Movements and Europeanization*. New York: Oxford University Press.

della Porta, D. and Rucht, D. (Eds.) (2013) *Meeting Democracy: Power and Deliberation in Global Justice Movements*. Cambridge: Cambridge University Press.

Díez Medrano, J. (2003) *Framing Europe: Attitudes to European Integration in Germany, Spain, and the United Kingdom*. New Jersey: Princeton University Press.

Díez Medrano, J. (2011) 'Social Class and Identity', in A. Favell and V. Guiraudon, (Eds.) *Sociology of the European Union*. Basingstoke: Palgrave Macmillan.

Duchesne, S. (2012) 'National identification, social belonging and questions on European identity', in Thiel, M. and Friedman R. (Eds.) *European Identity and Culture: Narratives of Transnational Belonging*. Farnham: Ashgate, pp. 53–74.

Eurobarometer (2011a) 'Eurobarometer 75, Spring 2011: Europeans, the European Union and the crisis', Brussels: European Commission, Accessed online at http://ec.europa.eu/public_opinion/archives/eb/eb75/eb75_cri_en.pdf.

Eurobarometer (2011b) 'Eurobarometer 76, December 2011', *Public Opinion in the European Union*. Brussels: European Commission, Accessed online at http://ec.europa.eu/public_opinion/archives/eb/eb76/eb76_first_en.pdf.

Eurostat (2011) *Demography Report 2010*. Luxembourg: Publications Office of the European Union.

Fligstein, N. (2008) *Euroclash: The EU, European Identity, and the Future of Europe*. Oxford: Oxford University Press.

Haug, C. and Rucht, D. (2013) 'Structurelessness: An evil or an asset? A case study', in della Porta, D. and Rucht, D. (Eds.) *Meeting Democracy: Power and Deliberation in Global Justice Movements*. Cambridge: Cambridge University Press, pp. 179–213.

Kaldor, M. and Selchow, S. (2012) 'The "Bubbling Up" of Subterranean Politics in Europe', Report, London School of Economics and Political Science, Accessed online at www.subterraneanpolitics.eu.

Kollewe, J. (2012) 'Incomes Likely to Dip Again', *The Guardian*, Accessed online at http://www.guardian.co.uk/money/2012/mar/12/family-income-dip-again.

Lundquist, L. Tulpule, G., Vang, P. and Pi, C.(2012) 'Community Organizing Models: Assessing Unique Social Action Approaches Throughout History to Determine Their Ongoing Influence and to Assess New or Adapted Models Emerging Today', University of Minnesota Center for Integrative Leadership, 18 October 2013 pdf, Accessed online at http://www.incommons.org/sites/www.incommons.org/files/changemakers_resource/community_organizing_models_march2012_0.pdf.

Miller, R. (Ed.) (2012) *The Evolution of European Identities: Biographical Approaches*. Basingstoke: Palgrave Macmillan.

Office for National Statistics (ONS) (2011) 'Summary of Labour Market Statistics', published on 12 October 2011, Accessed online at http://www.ons.gov.uk/ons/rel/lms/labour-market-statistics/october-2011/statistical-bulletin.html#tab-Summary-of-labour-market-statistics-published-on-12-October-2011.

Office for National Statistics (ONS) (2012a) 'Second Estimate of GDP; Q4 2011: Economic background', Accessed online at http://www.ons.gov.uk/ons/rel/naa2/second-estimate-of-gdp/q4-2011/stb- - -second-estimate-of-gdp-q4-2011.html#tab-Economic-background

Office for National Statistics (ONS) (2012b) 'Population by Country of Birth and Nationality July 2010 to June 2011', in the Migration Statistics Quarterly Report, February 2012, Accessed online at http://www.ons.gov.uk/ons/publications/re-reference-tables.html?edition=tcm%3A77-256033.

Pharr, S. J. and Putnam, R. D. (Eds.) (2000) *Disaffected Democracies: What's Troubling the Trilateral Countries?* Princeton, NJ: Princeton University Press.

Protest Survey (2010) 'Manual for Data Collection on Protest Demonstrations', Caught in the Act of Protest: Contextualizing Contestation (CCC-Project), Accessed online at http://www.protestsurvey.eu.

Sassen, S. (2000) 'The global city: Strategic site/new frontier', in *American Studies*, 41(2/3), pp. 88–90.

The Guardian (2011) 'St Paul's protests: Faith in the City', *The Guardian*, editorial, Tuesday 1 November 2011, Accessed online at http://www.theguardian.com/commentisfree/2011/nov/01/occupy-london-london.

Titley, G. (2012) 'Turning TINA: Budgetjam and the Political-Economic Crisis in Ireland', in Kaldor, M., Moore, H. L. and Selchow, S. (Eds.) *Global Civil Society 2012: Ten Years of Critical Reflection*. Basingstoke: Palgrave Macmillan.

White, M. (2010) 'At the Student Protests, the Ancient Cry of "Tory scum" Once Again Echoed Out', *The Guardian*, Accessed online at http://www.guardian.co.uk/politics/2010/nov/10/student-protests-tory-demonstrations.

YouGov-Cambridge (2012) *YouGov-Cambridge Report on the Future of Europe*. Cambridge: YouGov-Cambridge, Accessed online at http://www.yougov.polis.cam.ac.uk/?p=1935.

8
Alter-Europe: Progressive Activists and Europe

Geoffrey Pleyers[1]

Subterranean politics as an agency-centred perspective

Below the surface

On 15 May 2011, ten days before the national general election, a crowd took over the Plaza del Sol in Madrid to protest against the lack of alternatives proposed by the two main parties, the centre-left Socialists and the right-wing 'Popular Party'. Inspired by the recent events in Tahrir Square, one of their goals was to implement direct democracy in the plazas and neighbourhood camps and assemblies. Following Madrid's lead, *Indignados* camps bubbled up in all Spanish cities and across various European countries. Then on 17 September of that year, activists set up camp in Manhattan's Zuccotti Park to denounce rising inequalities and the power of the richest '1%' over national policies. In its turn, 'Occupy Wall Street' inspired camps and actions in dozens of US cities and all over Europe, from London to Moscow. These mobilisations captured the attention of the mainstream press, and were celebrated by progressive activists as a much-awaited reaction against the economic crisis. Yet two years on from that day in the Plaza del Sol, the economic crisis and the austerity plans which generated so much indignation remained at the top of the European agenda. Meanwhile, the squares are empty, tents have gone, and most occupiers' assemblies have disappeared. Was it nothing more than an ephemeral outcry?

Another topic practically omnipresent in the mainstream media since the start of the financial crisis – and certainly since 2011 – has been the future of the European Union (EU), most notably the future of the euro. Yet fieldwork and interviews conducted with progressive activists across Western Europe, as part of the 'Subterranean Politics' project, point to a second paradox. While European public intellectuals and progressive media all focus on Europe as the primary space of action with which to counter the crisis, and to the importance of the EU as a key actor (see for example Habermas 2012, and further in Chapter 2), progressive activists have a far less consensual opinion. While a few stress the importance of the European level, many consider Europe neither as a target nor as an important scale of action, and several discount Europe altogether.

To grasp these two paradoxes, we need to have a closer look at what is going on below the surface of mainstream media coverage, highly mediatised events and institutionalised civil society. We need to take *subterranean politics* into account. Our research shows that behind the scenes, vibrant citizens' initiatives are still going on, and indeed were so prior to the events of 2011, but in ways that typically do not correspond to institutionalised civil society, and which only gain media coverage during ephemeral actions. These active citizens develop different cultures of activism and practices, resulting in different stances towards Europe, EU institutions and democracy.

An analytical outlook focused on agency

The concept of 'subterranean politics' refers to an analytical outlook that draws on a 'grassroots agency centred perspective' that has been at the core of the work by Mary Kaldor (2003) and her research teams (see in particular Anheier et al. 2001; Kostovicova and Glasius 2011). Its starting point is to consider grassroots actors as contributors to public debate and, more importantly, to the transformation of the world in which we live. A wide range of studies gathered in the *Global Civil Society* yearbooks since 2001 have shown how the interaction of 'ordinary people', micro-level leaders and grassroots initiatives are 'both far more complex and more agentic than the standard portrayals would suggest' (Kostovicova and Glasius 2011: 2). This agency-centred approach is also the core of the sociology of action proposed by Alain Touraine (1973) and Michel Wieviorka (2009). The former, a French sociologist, underlines that social movements and individual subjects are the actors of the transformation of society, notably through the way they contest and transform central cultural orientations. In this perspective, recent social movements, citizens' mobilisations and subterranean politics in Europe should be considered less as symptoms of an economic crisis than as emerging actors that indicate societal conflicts, attempting to re-politicise austerity policies and debates about the crisis and develop alternative practices that contribute to the transformation of democracy.

'Subterranean politics' is thus less an analytical category than an analytical outlook. It points to various forms of grassroots initiatives, activism and protests that are most of the time barely visible in mainstream media and for outsider observers. This outlook invites us not to limit democracy to institutional politics, parliamentary debates and mainstream media. Political debates, societal changes and democracy are not only happening under the spotlight of global media, through professional politicians and intellectuals. They are also (and foremost) produced in the shadow of everyday life, by 'ordinary citizens' who develop thousands of small but significant debates, initiatives and practices.

Adopting this grassroots, agency-centred perspective and taking subterranean politics into account leads to a different outlook on the two above-mentioned 'paradoxes' concerning progressive activists in Europe:[2]

1. It leads us to consider that the *Indignados* and Occupy were actually only the tip of the iceberg, the visible part of a wide range of citizens' initiatives that oppose austerity policies and that implement concrete alternatives. Even more than the economic crisis, these actors point to a 'crisis of democracy'. They are outraged that citizens do not get to comment when it comes to economic policies. They advocate for a deepening of democracy but also seek to 'live democracy', to implement democratic practices in various sectors of their political and daily life.
2. It leads us to look for the role of 'Europe' in different places, beyond the dominance of the Euro discourse. Strategies, concepts of social change and democracy vary considerably among progressive activists practicing 'subterranean politics'. Some citizens want to build stronger democratic institutions; others no longer trust elected representatives and promote a change that starts at a local level and in daily life. Different cultures of politics need to be distinguished, rather than lumping 'activists' together as one group. From that point one can assess the relationship of these cultures to 'Europe' as a political space: for example, while 'expert activists' may focus on action at the level of European institutions, other cultures of activism may relate to 'Europe' in a different manner, if at all.

Thus the first part of this chapter will provide an overview of *four cultures of activism across progressive activists in Europe*. It doesn't constitute a full map of subterranean politics, but synthesises the logics of action implemented by some of its driving forces. The second part analyses their *stances towards Europe and the EU*. It focuses on the impact of nation, age, cultures of activism and the perception of social agency at a European level. The analysis of these successive factors points to a strong connection between European identity and the sense of agency at the European level. It suggests that, among the people we interviewed, activists who feel strongly European are those who are convinced that it is possible to have an impact on EU policies. Conversely, those who feel politically blocked at the European level do not claim a European identity.

Methodology

This research is based on 37 interviews conducted with progressive activists in France, Belgium, Spain, Finland, Poland and Germany; a focus group discussion organised in Paris with nine activists from different sectors of civil society and networks; and participatory observation in activists meeting and events between January and June 2012. In addition, we build on elements of the focus group organised by the Subterranean Politics project in Brussels on 21 June 2012, which gathered a dozen activists and ten scholars from across Europe. The results are neither exhaustive nor representative. They may nevertheless provide a perspective that helps to categorise some parts of the subterranean politics agenda and set reference points and questions for further research. In order to take into account a possible 'generation or age effect', young activists (22–35 years old) are over-represented in the sample. The analytical perspective draws on previous extensive research on the alter-globalisation movement and on local food movements (Pleyers 2010; 2011).

Our primary concern in the selection of actors has been to go beyond the 'usual suspects' (intellectuals and institutional civil society activists) and classic biases in media coverage (see Tillicule 2007). Mobilisations that gain the most media coverage are not always the most frequent, innovative or significant ones, while journalists often focus on leaders with good communication skills, transnational spaces and happenings that provide spectacular images, rather than day-to-day activism or behind-the-scene advocacy.

Four cultures of activism

This fieldwork research suggests four primary cultures of activism discernible among the progressive sector of subterranean politics in

Europe: 'square movements', 'ecological *transitioners*', 'expert activists' and 'mobilisers'. They consist in coherent sets of concepts of social agency, action and social change (Pleyers 2010) and connect to a specific vision of Europe. Like ideal-types (Weber 1995), they are heuristic tools that may help us to understand some features of progressive subterranean politics in Europe. They exist neither in a pure form nor as isolated practices. Most activists, performances and events mix different logics of action even if one is often dominant.

Square movements' activists: Camps and assemblies

The *Indignados*, Occupy and other 'square movements' brought together thousands of citizens from different backgrounds, many of whom had no previous experience of protest. Inspired by Tahrir Square in Cairo, *Indignados* and Occupy mobilisations emerged partly as a 'generation movement' (Feixa and Nofre 2013), one that has mobilised young citizens belonging to a generation that has grown up in a neo-liberal environment of income insecurity with diminished welfare state, where neither work nor public services can be taken for granted (see Rosenhek and Shalev 2013). 'Our generation has experienced in its daily life what it means to live in a neoliberal world. For us, the crisis is nothing new' (Mike, an activist from Occupy London Stock Exchange (LSX), OSI/LSE focus group June 2012).

Across Europe, *Indignados*/Occupy activists vigorously denounce the austerity politics promoted by the EU and national governments. But, for them, austerity policies are merely symptomatic of a greater problem: namely, the actual and structural limitations of representative democracy. These activists denounce an '*empty democracy*', claiming that the policies that have a real impact on their lives are settled in circles that operate beyond the influence of the ballot box. The 'M-15' movement in Spain, for example, began as a denunciation of a '*democracy without choice*'; Spanish citizens believed that the 2011 general elections did not offer a choice between alternatives, given that the two main parties had no significant differences in their policy approach. Activists also point to the collusion between corporations (and banks in particular) and policy makers: 'We must break the vicious link between capital and the representatives of democracy, who are more eager to defend the interests of capital than those of the voting population' (David, Barcelona, January 2012).[3]

Crucially, *Indignados* and Occupiers consider democracy not only as a *claim* but also as a *practice*. They seek to implement prefigurative activism (see Pleyers 2010) and place experimentations in horizontal and participatory discussion and deliberation processes at the core of their activism (Ganuza and Nez 2013; Glasius and Pleyers 2013). In the first few weeks of the camps, the daily general assemblies of Occupy LSX became efficient enough to disseminate information and to discuss and adopt practical decisions during the first part of the meeting, by then attended by over 200 people (see also Occupy Wall Street 2011), while the second part of the meeting was dedicated to broader political or strategic issues, such as how to reach out to other sectors of the population.

Movement assemblies, camps and neighbourhood meetings become 'spaces of experience', understood as places sufficiently autonomous and distanced from capitalist society permitting actors to live according to their own principles, to knit different social relations and to express their subjectivity (Bey 1991; Pleyers 2010: 37–40). The Occupy camps' claimed objective was to implement collective, horizontal decision-making processes, respecting gender equality.[4] In many cities, including in London, the camp kitchen provided local and vegan food. Libraries were set up where people could freely take books, and a system of free exchange allowed everyone to leave or take clothes and objects. 'Around St Paul's cathedral [Occupy London main camp], I was able to avoid money, universities ... and all the things that people tell me I have to do to have a happy life ... We build spaces where you find freedom of imagination ... ' (Mike, an activist from Occupy London Stock Exchange, OSI/LSE focus group June 2012).

Reflection on the movements' own practices and the development of techniques to increase the open, horizontal, anti-sexist and democratic features of the assemblies remain a major focus for activists.

> I'm now working on a great project, looking at developing alternatives to the traditional methodology of assemblies. We try to move from 'general assemblies' to 'open spaces', a methodology that allows an optimal management of diversity and that has no limits in terms of the number of participants. I'm really excited about this project!
>
> (M-15 activist, Barcelona, August 2012)

By occupying a square and taking part in *Indignados* assemblies, youth and 'ordinary citizens' assert themselves as actors and active citizens against the crisis and the deadlocks of institutional politics. Experimenting with concrete forms of direct democracy is also a personal, and often transformative, experience.

What was interesting in the [Indignados] movement is that we tried to organize ourselves horizontally, to talk, to communicate, to make sure that everyone had a voice and that this voice was as important as any other.... It requires being open, truly open... If we want to get at a point to make a true democracy work, we need to be honest and open with each other.

(Laure, an Indignada in Brussels, February 2012)

Indignados camps and assemblies aimed to provide time and space for every participant to express themselves and take an active part in the camp and movement organisation, notably through long group discussions and the creation of commissions and working groups around specific issues.

Personal subjectivities and histories mix with social and economic claims and with national or global history. Activists' insistence on the consistency between one's actions and values brings a personal commitment at the core of *Indignados'* commitment. *Indignados* and occupiers consider that changing oneself is a fundamental step towards a better world.

I think that things happen much through a change of oneself.... After having been part of the indignados, I don't see people in the same way anymore. I realized that everyone has something to say and I try to care about everyone's opinion, and also about everyone as a human being.

(Anne, focus group in Paris 2012)

The goal of the movement is the development of a new subjectivity and a change that is not only political because capitalism is within ourselves, in our consumption habits, our way of thinking, in the way we connect to other people, in our sexuality, in the way we think about ourselves. It is hence also a spiritual revolution.

(Daniel, Barcelona 2012)

The prevalence of these subjective and expressive dimensions may explain the insistence of direct participation and the avoidance of authority, representation and delegation.

We don't represent anyone. Everyone can come and bring her own ideas, her own expertise, as an individual. Actually, it is really the idea of questioning the authority... There is indeed more focus on the individualities, even though it is a movement that criticizes individualism.

(Cecile, an Indignada in Paris)

Like many alter-globalisation youth camps, the *Indignados* camps in various cities were 'No Logo' camps (Pleyers 2010), where banners and slogans from political parties and civil society organisations (including alter-globalisation organisations) were not welcome: 'It is a movement without pre-conceived labels, that would restrain the field of possibilities' (Cécile, Indignada, focus group in Paris). This reveals the mistrust of these activists not only towards institutional politics, but also towards 'activism as usual'. *Indignados*-style activists in France were characterised by their desire to distinguish themselves from more institutional civil society actors, including trade unions, anarchist networks and the main alter-globalisation organisations. Interviewees considered more experienced activists as 'too hierarchical', 'formal', 'institutionalised' and 'invasive'. This perspective also allowed citizens with diverse opinions to join the camps, which took the role of an open agora rather than a closed community.

However, the path from these very diverse, expressive and informal spaces to longer-term convergences and strategies seemed uncertain for many activists, even very soon after the event.

A general idea able to unite the movement was missing. We said 'Something is wrong', this was the first and fundamental idea. But then, what do we make to fix it? There, there were so many different trends, so many ideas. There were people from everywhere and it couldn't work anymore.

(Augustin, Brussels, 2012)

Like alter-activists' youth camps (Pleyers 2010: 84–86), square camps and assemblies are ephemeral: once they end, groups tend to dissolve and networks unravel. However, in his study of the Freedom Summer participants, McAdam has shown that such an intense experience of political activism during one's youth can transform social identity and political beliefs in fundamental ways (McAdam 1988). An active participation in an Occupy camp represents important moments in which individual lived experience intersects with collective history. It may have a long-term impact on the participants' political stances and commitment towards a more democratic society.

Transition movements and critical consumption

In the last decade, Western Europe has witnessed a rise in actors seeking to implement more sustainable lifestyles, with less consumption and a stronger sense of community. They define themselves as 'objectors to growth and speed' and question the economists' GDP and growth figures and indicators of well-being (Schor 2010). This field of activism ranges from the transition movement (Hopkins 2011) to voluntary simplifiers, local money initiatives, critical consumerism and to local food networks. The latter has developed into a large economic sector in most of the Western world. In both the UK and the USA, networks of 'community supported agriculture' (CSA) provide local food for people and local public administrations (Maye and Kirwan 2010).

While *Indignados* and Occupiers implement prefigurative activism in public spaces and in their movements' camps and organisations, critical consumers and 'local transition activists' focus on prefigurative actions and the consistency between practices and values in their daily life, as behind alternative consumption lies the question and possibility of a radically different society. In the words of Illich (1973: 28), it is a matter of 'moving from productivity to conviviality'. These 'convivial relations' (Illich 1973; Convivialist Manifesto 2013), or community activities, are a key feature of this activism pathway. Creating a stronger local social fabric is now the force at the centre of a multitude of 'conviviality'-minded urban movements, ranging from the 'critical masses' of bicyclists who promote the use of bicycles – and the safe passage of their riders – in cities (Eliasoph and Luhtakallio 2013) to the community gardeners who create small, green areas in disused corners of the city. While some critical consumers and local activists emphasise the political dimension of their commitment, others do not consider their practices as activism: 'I don't see it as activism. It is just a change in our way of life' (a Swedish student, interview 2012).

Rather than the economic crisis, many activists interviewed rank climate change and environmental damages as their main concerns. They consider it a personal responsibility to lower their impact on the environment.

> It is first and foremost a way to refuse playing a game with which I disagree. At least with vegetables, I don't play the game, I don't provide more water to the system.
>
> (Jerome, 23, Paris)

The roots of social change thus lie in a change of one's lifestyle and in alternative practices at the local level. Subjective and personal dimensions are particularly strong in this way of action.

> I do it to feel good with myself. At least I can say that everything that happens, all this pollution, all these environmental disasters, all this waste...well it's not my fault. I am at peace with myself.
>
> (Philippe, Liège, Belgium)

> The idea is not to make efforts. It is not about implementing little changes. It is about desalinating oneself. Once you become better aware of your needs, you simply become happier!
>
> (David, Brussels)

Relationships with state institutions and the need for coordinating players are poles of tensions and a source of permanent debate among these activists and local networks. Some trust that limited institutional support may foster their activities and help local food producers, while others strongly oppose any form of institutionalisation. Likewise, while some foster cooperation with policy makers, others connect their activism with mistrust in institutional politics and conventional activism.

> I trust more in the vote with the credit card than in the vote in the polls. Actually I won't go and vote at the next elections. I don't believe in it anymore. I believe we have to re-build everything starting from the ultra-local level.
>
> (Eloise, Paris)

Many 'transition activists' proudly claim that they go beyond rhetoric and implement concrete alternatives. However, the spread from self-transformation or social change in a limited group to larger-scale transformations often remains a blind spot in the overarching quest for societal change, especially as many of these groups are reluctant to engage in large-scale coordination and institutionalisation.

Expert activists

Committed intellectuals and expert activists have published dozens of appeals (see further Chapter 2), books and articles on the euro crisis and European austerity plans. They develop both rigorous analyses and political statements underlining the irrationality behind the way that both the EU and national governments deal with the crisis, challenge the EU and government experts, and propose concrete alternative measures to the austerity model (see for example the Tax Justice Network, www.taxjustice.net; or the French network 'Les Economistes Attérés', www.atterres.org). As in Habermas' model of deliberative democracy, they trust that rational and well-developed arguments will ultimately be taken into account by policy makers and believe that their activist expertise has already achieved significant results.

> We try to mobilise expertise and apply it in relevant policy and advocacy processes, rather than mobilising citizens to make an outcry: we believe that once we create enough public information, people will mobilise themselves.
>
> (Mita, Tax Justice Network, Finland)

> The EU officials, the businessmen and the lobbyists take our activity into account, even if, in the end, our influence is very limited. But yes, we have an influence.
>
> (Kasia, Panoptykon Foundation, Poland)

Expert activists challenge EU experts by producing a 'citizen counter-expertise'. They aim at countering the power of corporate lobbies, by providing accurate expertise to EU policy makers.

> We must not forget that the European Parliament in Brussels is the capital of lobbies. What is prohibited in Washington is allowed in Brussels.
>
> (Fabian, Paris)

> Lobbyists have taken over the expert role in designing EU policies.... The EU itself doesn't have these competencies within itself, so it looks for competencies where it can...the European commission is open to us, so they listen to us and they've taken up some of our points.
>
> (Mita, Tax Justice Network, Finland)

Expert activists' conception of social change is institutionalised and rather top-down, as it focuses on policy makers, regulations, institutions and redistributive policies at the national, continental and global level. The push towards social change and its sustainability, however, also requires a bottom-up dynamic, with active citizens familiarised with macro-economics and able to promote these alternative policies. Popular education is thus an urgent task, to which expert activists dedicate much of their time.

Mobilisers

'Mobilisers' believe that neither left-wing governments nor expert activists will be able to 'force' a major political change without a strong citizens' mobilisation.

> Social progress has never been obtained only by elections. In 1936 [year of the 'Front populaire' in France], social benefits were obtained not only thanks to the progressive government but because millions of people were striking and demonstrating.
>
> (Ronan, Paris, 2012)

Hence, they focus on building popular mobilisations and mass demonstrations with the potential to shift the balance of power in the institutional political arena and to influence national governments.

> If we want to influence the destiny of a democratic and social Europe, we must create a balance of power with this political system.... We, as a trade union, we try to bring any worker or employee and tell them 'you have something to say or something to do on these big ideological issues, even if you are not a priori an activist'.
>
> (leading Belgian trade unionist, 2012)

> I am convinced that it is the social movements that will make a difference...there are times when the mass of small movements make a large movement.
>
> (Bernard, Paris, 2012)

Through the combination of producing analyses of the economic and political situation and organising actions, 'mobilisers' aim to shape the public space, setting the topics of discussion and policy agenda. They share with 'expert activists' their focus on convincing policy makers and educating citizens. They seek both to give citizens the tools for a better understanding of what is at stake in policy debate and to make them aware that social mobilisation may have an impact on governments' policies. Some have become professional 'social movement entrepreneurs' and play an important role in organising and connecting movements,[5] both nationally and internationally.

Cross-fertilisation

Most activists, performances and events mix different elements from these four logics of action, even if one is often dominant.

Indignados/occupy camps provide a clear illustration of coexistence and cross-fertilisations among these four cultures of activism, blending alternative food initiatives and popular education (e.g. the 'university tent' at Occupy London) with the discussion and elaboration of expert-produced alternatives, the publication of appeals, newsletters and magazines, and organised days of action and demonstrations. And many of these newer camps and movements would not have lasted long without the support of more institutionalised and experienced activists. At the same time, different concepts of social change and of movement organisations amongst activists also lead to misunderstandings and tensions. Many of those we interviewed were very conscious of differences in strategy or on the concept of social change among their peers. Most insisted on the complementarity of different forms of activism.

> There is not a right and a wrong way to do things. There are various ideas of how to transform society, some are pragmatic and other ones are utopian. Some focus on the global and other on local relations. Some are implemented *by* unions and other by associations. In my perspective they are all complementary and shouldn't be opposed.
>
> (Jerome, a local/transition activist, Paris)

Likewise, after the camps in the squares, *Indignados*/Occupy movements have combined their energies and creativity with initiatives closer to the other three trends. Connections and cross-fertilisations occur with local human economy projects (this is particularly the case in Barcelona; see Sánchez 2012), with expert activists and popular education (see for example the magazine *Occupied Times of London*, www.theoccupiedtimes.co.uk) and with more formal civil society organisations. Such cross-fertilisations may contribute to overcoming the ephemeral nature of their camps and the sporadic nature characterising movements rooted in experience, subjectivity, creativity and horizontal organisation.

Where is Europe?

While public intellectuals (see for example Habermas, op. cit.; Kaldor 2012), governments and mainstream media portray Europe as the main scale of action and debate for solving the current crisis, progressive activists' stances towards Europe are far less homogenous. Expert activists do consider European institutions as the main targets of their advocacy and Europe as the fundamental scale of political and social change. Experienced mobilisers stress that the European dimension was far more developed among social movements a decade ago, at the time when European Social Forums gathered dozens of thousands of activists from all over the continent. Europe is surprisingly infrequently referred to by the *Indignados* (and almost absent in debate amongst those located in France and in the UK; see Chapter 7) and very remote from many local activists' preoccupations. Most of the local activists we interviewed didn't have much (if anything) to say on Europe or the EU; they did not consider Europe as a relevant scale of action.

Although this would need to be tested further in extended qualitative and quantitative studies, interviews and fieldwork suggest four main explanatory factors that allow a better understanding of these contrasting stances towards Europe among progressive activists.

1. The four *cultures of activism* described in the first part of this chapter correspond to different stances towards Europe as a scale of action and towards the EU as an institution.
2. *National perspectives*: With the exception of cosmopolitan expert activists, progressive activists' perspectives on Europe are deeply shaped by the perspectives and debates in their home country.
3. *Generation*: Younger activists develop more radical criticisms of the EU, which they often consider 'exclusively neo-liberal', an expression used repeatedly in focus groups and interviews. Age and generation have an impact on the actors' subjectivity, their strategies and their vision of Europe.
4. The analysis of the three previous factors suggests that *the perception of the possibility of social agency at the European level* is the main factor in explaining progressive activist stance towards the EU. The more an activist perceives the EU as a public space open to political debate and civil society arguments, the more they assert a European identity and consider Europe as an important scale of action. Conversely, the sense of being politically blocked at the EU level lead activists to focus their action at the national (mobilisers) or local (*Indignados* and local activists) scale.

Cultures of activism and their scales of action

Expert activists: Europe as the main scale of action and advocacy

The expert activists interviewed denounce EU neo-liberal policies, but maintain a deeply pro-European identity. The European scale and EU institutions are often the main target of their action. They claim to have an impact on EU policies on specific issues.

> We have some experts who have actually advised the European commission on the EU directive on tax, on how to make it effectively tax evasion proof.
>
> (Mita, Tax Justice Network 2012)

The EU is seen both as an opportunity and as a tool that has been used to impose neo-liberal policies, budget cuts and austerity plans. Contrary to many young and Idignados activists, these expert activists do not consider the EU as being structurally neo-liberal but believe, to its detriment, that it has become more so: 'treaty after treaty since the 1980s'. They perceive Europe as the main scale on which activists proposing alternative policies may have an impact, whether to influence European policies or to have an impact on global institutions (e.g. the WTO) and national policies.

Expert activists point out that the EU is often blamed for neo-liberal policies that are actually decided on by national governments. Most expert activists support a stronger European integration, notably in fiscal matters, in order to limit the power of transnational corporations and to get out of the current crisis.

> People say 'We like the EU to give us benefits such as a common currency; a kind of regulatory framework for many products and services in Europe; oversight on human rights; and other basically public goods. But we don't want to contribute taxes to the EU and this'. I see it as a fundamental problem.
>
> (Martin, a Polish-French expert activist, 2012)

'Expert activists' is the category that interacts the most with EU institutions. In general, their organisations are very keen on building European networks and, where possible, opening up an office in Brussels. They have formed a perspective on the EU over decades of interaction, cope with European policies on a daily basis and organise seminars in Brussels. They are familiar with EU vocabulary and norms and speak the same expert language as European civil servants, with whom they met and discuss the grey literature that informs EU meetings and the creation of new norms. Moreover, expert activists organise meetings of European Activists, like the ATTAC-Europe Summer School, which helps to strengthen the participants' European identity.

We invited many European activists of ATTAC to the Summer University to fill the void left by the European Social Forums. We don't have many spaces for discussions at the European level.

(a young French expert activist)

Mobilisers: the national level and cross-national alliances

The question is not as much in terms of having targets and interlocutors at a higher scale as of building a stronger social struggle at the national level, and to do it in different countries at the same time.

(Ronan, Paris)

Mobilisers consider national governments as the primary policy makers. They thus focus much of their efforts on building movement organisations, promoting demonstrations or fostering citizens' awareness at the national scale. The main mobilisations against austerity, including the general strikes in southern Europe and the anti-tax evasion protests staged by UK Uncut, focus on the national level.

At a time of recession and economic crisis, the general mood among most civil society actors, and in particular those of the trade unions, is oriented towards defending their members at the national level rather than expending efforts on adopting a common European position.

This is a very big problem for the trade unions. Germany is a winner of the crisis ... So, the [German] trade unions are not willing to be in real solidarity with other countries.

(Judith, ATTAC-Germany)

Those experienced mobilisers and professional activists who were previously involved in the European Social Forums process have stated their regret that Europe is hardly present in civil society internal debates:

There are movements in every European country, but is there a debate on Europe?

(Bernard, an experienced French activist)

There is indeed a striking contrast between the past few years and the period between 1997 and 2004. Alter-globalisation demonstrations took place at each EU summit during those years, along with the European Social Forum process, fostering the rise of a European movement. Trade unions from all over Europe and the unemployed peoples' network 'Euromarches' were among the first civil society organisations to demonstrate at EU summits.[6] In 2002, the European Social Forum (ESF) in Florence was opened by a march involving one million people, and the following ESFs in Paris (2003) and then London (2004) gathered over 50,000 activists each.

In contrast, despite widespread protest against austerity since 2008, there has been little pan-European action (see Chapter 2). The Greek demonstrations, UK Uncut campaigns, French youth and student mobilisations and the Spanish and Portuguese protests in the squares have all denounced similar policies with practically the same arguments, but without any significant coordination. In 1997, when Renault planned to close its car factory near Brussels, unions organised a 'European strike' in the company's factories in four countries. In November 2012 and February 2013, Mittal successively closed sections of its steel factories, first in northern France and then in Belgium. Trade unions and governments focused on the defence of national workers never managed to develop a coordinated transnational strategy.

Some pro-European mobilisers tried to relaunch a European social movement dynamic by organising an 'Alter-Summit' in Athens in June 2013, but it gathered only 4,000 attendees (see Chapter 2), far from the numbers of the earlier ESFs that gathered over 50,000 activists in 2002, 2003 and 2004. Both the Alter-Summit and 'Blockupy Frankfurt' actions conducted on 1 May 2012 and 2013 had a strong symbolic relevance, as they gathered activists from various European countries and targeted European policies (see Box 8.1, p. 217). The limited size and the impact of these events were, however, insufficient to connect the local and national mobilisations and struggles at the continental level. This decreasing will or ability to coordinate protest at the continental level contrasts not only with the similarity of austerity measures across many EU countries, but also with the rising integration of economic policy across the eurozone.

It is important to note that as 'mobilisers' focus on the national scale, national differences and conjuncture are more important in analysing this category. For instance, in the months before national presidential elections, French activists focus primarily on the national scale. By contrast in Belgium, where they have traditionally invested time and effort in European networks, a pro-European stance has become part of trade unions' and progressive activists' identity (Gobin 2004; Pleyers 2007). In 2013, Belgian trade unions took a leading role in organising the 'alter-summit' mentioned above.

Box 8.1   Blockupy: A pan-European anti-austerity protest in the counter-globalisation tradition?

'You want capitalism without democracy, we want democracy without capitalism'

After a decade of widespread counter-globalisation protests, it seemed strange to many commentators there was not more pan-European resistance as an immediate response to the crisis and to the austerity measures imposed by the EU. As I argue elsewhere, an important reason is to be found in the successful previous containment and control of counter-globalisation movements. However, slowly the picture is changing. Besides the occasional eruption of mass protests on national scale, such as in Greece, Spain and Portugal, the pan-European mobilisation and social movement formation is under way with common protest actions (such as Blockupy in 2012 and 2013, a European-wide strike day in 2012 and protests at the 2013 EU spring summit) and European-wide gatherings (such as the 2013 Alter-Summit in Athens and *Indignados* meetings in 2012 and 2013).

Blockupy is an alliance initiated by German counter-globalisation and anti-capitalist groups, trade unions, Occupy movements and the left-wing party Die Linke. Their aim is to mobilise a one-day blockade of the European Central Bank (ECB) as a protest against what they see as a protagonist of the so-called Troika. The name itself is in fact a combination of blockading, a tactic often used in alter-globalisation protests, and occupying, the chosen tactic of the Occupy movement. The mobilisation poster includes a third symbol: a red flag that refers to the older protest repertoire of the socialist and workers' movements. These are the three tactical repertoires combined in the 2012 Blockupy protests: occupations (for the encampments) on the first day; blockade of the ECB on the second; and a mass demonstration on the third.

Citing confrontations that ensued during previous protests in the context of another decentralised European day of action on 31 March 2012, the city of Frankfurt prohibited all the protests planned and registered in advance by the Blockupy organisers. Time to fight such a ban through the courts was scarce; Blockupy continued to mobilise, using the anti-democratic character of such

Box 8.1   (Continued)

a blanket ban on the public voice of dissent as a factor of support. On the first day of action, thousands of people occupied two central squares in Frankfurt (one of them ironically next to the Paulskirche, where the first German constitution was drafted after the 1848 upheavals). Riot police corralled both squares for several hours until they started to clear them in the early evening. The next morning, 1,000–2,000 protesters participated in the attempted blockades. Operating in small groups, often just drifting around the small streets of the centre and attempting to regroup, they tried to approach the ECB, which had been evacuated and surrounded by fences. The initial plan of approaching the bank from various sides with five themed marches proved untenable, given the protest ban and the large police presence (9,000 officers had been recruited from across Germany). On a number of occasions a group made it to the actual fence, but several hundred protesters were arrested and sent away with banning orders for the city of Frankfurt. However, the demonstration on the last day attracted 30,000 participants and ended without confrontation.

The Blockupy alliance soon decided to launch another attempt to blockade the ECB in 2013. A number of preparatory meetings created the space necessary to take collective lessons from the first mobilisation, adapt some of the tactical elements and enlarge participation. One major adaptation both to accommodate more participants and be less vulnerable to legal prohibitions was to refrain from square occupations and organise a permitted camp in the outskirts of the city. A number of local Blockupy groups started (in Vienna, for example) while several international meetings brought together a larger international network early on in the process of preparation in order to coordinate with other plans for anti-austerity protests (such as those in Madrid). Mobilisation for the 2013 Blockupy action was carefully embedded in a larger choreography of pan-European protests and gatherings that year. Some Blockupy organisers participated actively in the 2013 protests against the EU summit in Brussels, and a caravan made its way from Blockupy to the Alter-Summit in Athens, making various stops throughout Europe to protest and mobilise against EU austerity management.

Several thousand protesters participated on the day of the blockades. Although the ECB was once again protected with huge fence constructions and a massive police presence, protesters managed to reach the fences and encircle them to block all access. The afternoon of the same day was dedicated to a variety of interventions in the city of Frankfurt, symbolising the broader agenda of various involved movements: the airport was targeted because of the collaboration of airlines with deportation of undocumented migrants; fashion stores in the shopping mall for their collaboration with sweatshops and child labour practices. On the following day, however, the legally granted rally of approximately 20,000 people was stopped after 500 metres by police encircling the first part of the rally, arguing that some people were masked. The ensuing negotiations took more than nine hours but by then most people had left. Several press statements, complaints and solidarity demonstrations followed in the weeks afterwards.

The Occupy alliance announced further protests for the autumn of 2014, when the ECB was due to move to their new premises in Frankfurt.

The ongoing process of Blockupy highlights the potential strength – but also the weaknesses – of current pan-European mobilisations. Compared with previous summit protests confronting the meetings of powerful elites, Blockupy shows the potential of moving beyond a merely reactive logic to build up the capacity to intervene in the daily routines of EU institutions through pan-European collective action. As part of the so-called Troika at the centre of EU austerity management, the ECB is moreover a new but appropriate target. Nevertheless, the Blockupy alliance experienced difficulties in making the pan-European mobilisation a real success. Lessons were learned from the first experience, and Blockupy profited from the other ongoing pan-European mobilisation efforts, but to date it has remained primarily a German initiative with limited pan-European repercussions. The other challenge confronting Blockupy concerns their chosen target, and the state and police repression brought to bear on protests aimed at such a powerful institution. It is unclear how the protests will unfold in the future but, whether legalised or not, it seems clear that protesters challenging EU austerity management in the streets of Frankfurt will face a considerable police presence.

Box 8.1   (Continued)

Christian Scholl is a postdoctoral research fellow at the CriDIS Institute of the UC Louvain (Académie universitaire 'Louvain'), author of Two Sides of a Barricade. (Dis)order and Summit Protest in Europe (Albany: SUNY Press 2013) and co-author of Shutting Down the Streets. Political Violence and Social Control in the Global Era (New York: New York University Press 2011).

Occupiers/Indignados: *local, national and global*

Indignados' claims, networks and identities are both rooted in the local context and spawn over the oceans and across the world. However, they focus their actions and most of their energy at the local level. One may consider that occupiers are a new generation of 'rooted cosmopolitans' (Tarrow 2005), who articulate the local and the global in a way that is partly different to that of the alter-globalisation activists.

The *Indignados* and occupiers develop global claims such as democracy and social justice, and have broadcast the resonance of their local and national movements with similar movements in other countries (Glasius and Pleyers 2013). The *Indignados* we interviewed in Barcelona, Paris and Brussels reported being inspired by the example of what was happening in Tahrir Square. In turn, Occupy Wall Street was inspired by both Tahrir and the Spanish *Indignados*, while the Muscovite punk band Pussy Riot was formed to 'Turn the Red Square into Tahrir Square'.[7] The Internet is another 'global' location where *Indignados* and occupy activists develop and defend an open space of expression (Castells 2012; Gerbaudo 2012), call for mobilisation and build tools to empower off-line democratic and horizontal processes.

However, while many profess strong cosmopolitan ideals and are in touch with friends and activists in different countries, they are more rooted in the local and national reality than young alter-globalisation activists a decade ago. *Indignados* activists want their actions and assemblies to be as local as possible and refer to their movement as 'translocal' or 'inter-city' rather than 'international' or 'global'. Occupiers focus almost all their energy at the local level; their assemblies and networks of activists are very committed to local people and issues. And rather than organising transnational meetings to discuss global claims, the protest wave that started in 2011 sites these global claims in a local context (Bringel 2013). The local is seen as the scale where it is possible to implement strong and participatory democracy through horizontal, open and participatory assemblies.

> I'm not sure democracy can work beyond a certain level, beyond the local or city level. Beyond, it is rather about coordination than democracy.
>
> (Sophie, Paris)

The national level is also considered a relevant scale of action by many *Indignados*/Occupy activists (although this was not the case in Belgium), since they denounce the problems of representative democracy that is primarily organised at this scale and demand that national governments change their economic policies. In May 2011, the Spanish 15-M movement ('the *Indignados*') started as a reaction to the absence of political alternatives at the national elections. From 20 June to 23 July, the *Indignados* marched from all cities of Spain to Madrid (see Feixa and Perondi 2013), collecting claims and proposals from the population and illustrating the national character of the movement.

The European scale seems lost somewhere between actions at the local and national levels, and values and resonance at the global. On 15 October 2011 the *Indignados* organised a global day of action, with events occurring in cities across Europe and beyond, and a few protests and actions were 'networked' at the European level. However, these transnational mobilisations are conducted in a decentralised way, coordinated online and by working groups in dozens of cities. While such networked actions have proved efficient in diffusing information and action repertories, they may be less efficient in fostering a European identity and creating a European public space in comparison with the experience of an ESF or activist meeting.[8]

Several of the *Indignados* we interviewed question the importance and legitimacy of the European level. For many, Europe appears as an intermediary scale that has lost most of its appeal or may even be referred to as Occidentalism or 'quasi-racism':

> I care about the global level, the community level, the regional level... but Europe, does it still make sense among all these levels? And even more, isn't it in some way a quasi-racist concept? Why should we care about Europe and not the Mediterranean region?... We have many links with French-speaking Africa for

instance. Why shouldn't we be solidary with them? Why more with the Danes than with the Senegalese people?

(Sophie, a young *Indignada*, focus group, Paris)

I'm always interested in something more global: Europe, the world, the universe...Why shouldn't we include the whole Mediterranean area altogether? Because we exchange many things within this area, as well as with a part of Africa, actually almost all Africa.

(Sofia, Brussels)

Their responses suggest a deep change in the connection between the EU and the cosmopolitan ideal for this new generation of activists. While the EU was once considered to embody a global project and correspond to global citizenship (e.g. Albrow 1996; Beck 2009; Habermas 2012), *Indignados* and young activists question this connection. In the minds of many *Indignados*/occupiers, the EU is no longer the Union embodying a cosmopolitan ideal, but the opposite: a fortress building fences between youth from different continents.

Ecological transition activists: local change

Transition activists maintain that a better society will come from changes to daily life, and that these changes are more important than decisions taken from above by policy makers and institutions.

The idea is to show that it is possible to construct something locally, at a scale where we have the means to act.

(Benoit, Brussels 2012)

First of all, as an individual, you must become aware of your own role in society.... Then you say, 'Well, let's start to rebuild social fabric, connections among people. And let's create social connections by starting at the micro level, precisely to re-create participatory democracy.'

(Martin, Namur 2012)

Many local transition activists share mistrust towards institutions in general, and fear that scaling-up their activities at the national or European level will lead to the institutionalisation that they are trying to avoid. Europe was absent in the discourses of almost all the local transition activists interviewed. Even after persistent questioning on the subject, they typically replied in evasive ways or asserted little interest.

Europe is something I don't know much about.... It's something that may be used and that can bring a lot of nice things. But the problem is that it is very remote from people. I don't feel at all concerned with Europe.

(Augustin, an Indignado from Brussels)

I do not feel European. For me Europe doesn't mean any-thing... I think I would have been open to feel European if there were reasons to do so, but the Europe we are in is exclusively economic and political. I do not feel we are in a cultural Europe, unfortunately.

(Eloise, a young chair of
a local food network, Paris)

At a time when the EU and the euro were portrayed in the media daily as the only actors able to solve the debt crisis, the absence of interest for Europe by these young local activists is particularly significant.

Variations across countries

Among the progressive activists interviewed, the debate on Europe is also *deeply shaped by national contexts*. Activists' visions of Europe, con-cepts of the welfare state and central demands vary considerably from one country to another. As mentioned above, the 'experienced activists' all consider that social movements have adopted perspectives which are more national and less European than those of ten years ago.

The two interviews conducted in Poland, although hardly exhaustive, suggest that activists may have a better opinion of the EU in Eastern Europe, where the EU has contributed to the democratic transition and is still considered as more transparent and accessible than the Polish government and institutions.

I am very often in Brussels and I lobby in the European Parliament. I very much like Brussels because the politicians and the officials there act in a more transparent way. In Poland it is more difficult to get in touch with higher level officials and there is a huge lack of transparency in our democratic process.

(Kasia, expert activist, Poland)

A number of activists from Barcelona also valued the EU's contribu-tion to Spain's democratisation, modernisation and to the decrease of corruption since the 1980s. However, the current crisis may deeply change their perspective, as the EU often appears to weaken national sovereignty and the influence of citizens on their politicians.

> In Spain, we have a vision of the EU with Germany and France impos-ing their will on Spain in a series of austerity politics ... It affects our national sovereignty and decision power of our country.
>
> (Daniel, Barcelona)

Although it was never raised in our questionnaire, the rise of the *extreme right, nationalisms and xenophobia* was mentioned by a majority of interviewed activists, and by all of the 'older' activists. The post-1929 scenario was frequently mentioned by these interviewees, who fear that, once again, a major economic crisis might lead to nationalism and war. They consider that the current austerity policies foster a similar scenario and thus stress the urgency to build up an alternative vision of the crisis and to promote 'another Europe'.

> We have to choose between two alternatives: either we manage to re-build a dynamic for a progressive Europe (...) or we will see an increasing dichotomy between nationalist and xenophobic move-ments, to which we will leave a part of the power to deal with social questions; and a global techno-structure, not European anymore but global, and they will feel even more powerful as they will be able to play on the divisions created by identity movements.... We will have people like Marine Le Pen to amuse the gallery and then serious stuff will be decided between Frankfurt and the City. We have already experienced it in various countries.
>
> (Bernard, an experienced French activist)

Generations

While EU policies suffer an unfavourable image among all categories of progressive activists, both the interviews and the focus group in Paris show a generational divide on the stance towards the EU itself. The older activists we interviewed presented themselves as pro-European activists opposing not the EU itself but its neo-liberal agenda, while on the contrary, most of the young activists were much more radical in their criticisms against the EU – although some, particularly in the 'expert activists' category, testified to a strong European identity.

The way that each generation has experienced EU integration and policies appears to be an important factor. 'Older' activists underline the importance of progressive policies promoted by the EU.

In my case, I had some experience with the EU a couple of decades ago. [As a trade-unionist], I work on health at work-related issues. The EU 1989 directive is very valuable since it has allowed a huge amount of improvements. I know that there is a useful Europe that has been built, a positive Europe. But these days, I don't recognize it at all.

(Etienne, Paris)

As young people are the most impacted by job market flexibility, precarity and budget cuts on education and unemployment benefit, younger activists draw on both this generational experience and the European treaties of the last decade. They thus tend to view the European project as 'entirely dedicated to the imposition of neoliberal policies' and 'free competition' 'since its beginning' (see also Chapter 7).

Most activists over 40 years old, and those who are younger but who fit the 'expert activist' categorisation oppose EU neo-liberal policies but strongly value the European integration process, considering it an opportunity to build a 'Europe of peace and solidarity'. They insist on reminding younger activists of the advantages derived from the EU, notably those derived from the EU's social and environmental standards. Conversely, a generation that has not experienced the divided Europe of the Cold War, nor border controls in the Schengen space, appear to take the practical advantages of the EU and European integration for granted. Young activists may thus not mention the things they value in the EU, whereas allegedly negative impacts and the neo-liberal agenda are brought into focus. To an extent, this testifies to success in some aspects of the European integration project. Several interviews reveal that some young activists, mostly students and those close to the 'expert activist' category, combine a strong European identity with a critical stance towards EU neo-liberal policies.

The previous generation was very reluctant in criticizing Europe because they remember how Europe used to be divided and the consequences it had. For my generation, Europe is a fact. We have travelled and grown up within it. Hence, it is much easier for us than for the previous generation to have a critical position towards European institutions and democracy in Europe.

(Hélène, a French expert activist)

Being European is something already incorporated by young people today ... I have a feeling that young people are European in their mind. For my younger brother, the Euro is not a change; it is normal.

To cross borders frontiers just like that, it is normal for him. It is amazing, he has friends in England, in Germany....

(Cécile, France)

Moreover, young activists appear to have developed both *local and global identities*. *Indignados* and some young expert activists in France, Poland and Spain claim a cosmopolitan identity more oriented towards the global than to the EU: 'We may feel European, but people like me, we think of us as the global citizens' (Kasia, expert activist, Poland). This generation has been referred to as the 'global generation' (e.g. Beck and Beck-Gersheim 2007). Around the world, young activists are using the tools of globalisation to create global movements (McDonald 2006): networking, circulating news via social media, participating in global chats, sharing common cultural references, and using similar protest styles and tactics. While Europe used to be perceived as a first step towards a cosmopolitan identity, young European activists now denounce the harsh migration policies of 'fortress Europe' that oppose their cosmopolitan ideals. This disconnection between the European construction and cosmopolitan ideals may represent a structural factor in the decline of interest in Europe and of a European identity.

Perception of social agency

A structural analysis of the empirical material gathered during this research suggests that the main factor which can help to explain these highly contrasting stances towards Europe is the sense of social agency at the European level. The more activists believe that they may have an impact on EU policies, the more they feel European. On the contrary, those who are convinced that the European institutions pay no attention to civil society arguments and will stick to their neo-liberal agenda, whatever happens, do not feel very European nor do they consider Europe as an important scale of action.

Analysis of the interviews shows a strong connection between the sense of a European identity and the sense of social agency at the European scale. For instance, when asked whether they felt 'culturally European', most activists answered referring to European political citizenship and its democratic deficit or to the (im)possibility of a significant political change at the European level.

I do not believe in Europe... If changing Europe means changing institutions with other institutions which will then be occupied by the same people, it won't change anything.

(Eloise, local food network, Paris)

In fact, I don't take Europe very much into account. I don't know much about it. I don't understand it much either and it doesn't interest me that much. This scale is too big for me. I feel too small to act and affect Europe. [...] So, I feel easily as an actor, but not at the European level.... I see Europe as too big, too untouchable.

(David, transition activist, Brussels)

You can't separate the content of the European model from the promotion of the European idea. I think that if you want to promote Europe you should try to make Europe the vehicle of a sustainable society, the vehicle of new regulation ....

(Wojtek, a pro-European, expert activist)

Likewise, activists closer to a culture of activism which maintains that civil society may have an impact on the EU are also those who assert a European identity. *Expert activists* are convinced that advocacy and good arguments will have an impact on EU policies and claim some successes on concrete issues, and are those who assert the strongest European identity. At the opposite end of the scale, *local transitioners* who believe that no significant change will stem from the EU claim that they don't feel European at all. This withdrawal to the local scale and mistrust in the possibility of change coming from institutions partly results from a feeling of 'being politically blocked at the European level': that the EU cannot be reformed and will remain dominated by neo-liberal policies.

Likewise, when defending their European identity, 'older' activists point to the fact that they have experienced the EU as a means to foster progressive policies and to overcome closed political opportunity structures at the national level. The fact that many young activists do not manifest a strong European identity may be connected to the fact that for the current generation of young protest activists, *Indignados* and local transition activists, the EU has come to embody a 'democracy without choice'. They associate the EU, and in particular the European Commission, with neo-liberal policies and believe it will stick to these policies. This has led some activists to focus on the local level and on cultural changes (*Indignados* and local activists), or to (re)invest at the national scale.

Conclusion: a crisis of European democracy

This research suggests a strong connection between activists' self-identification as European and their perception of Europe as a space of social agency and political debates. To re-politicise Europe and to rethink democracy at that level appears thus as one of the most urgent challenges for the EU and its citizens.

The economic crisis and austerity policies have strengthened homogeneous perceptions of national issues and public opinions. Each country appears to have a clear national position on the crisis and on austerity policies. According to Chantal Mouffe (2012) in her recent essay, the results of this research plead for a re-politicisation of Europe as a public space, and she would rather foster a debate among different visions of Europe. National public opinions are indeed not particularly homogeneous concerning their visions for Europe's future, while the main perspectives on Europe are shared by some of the citizens of each member state. Framed in Ulrich Beck's terms, European policy makers (as well as its citizens) need to get rid of methodological nationalism in order to foster debate on the future of the EU at a continental level.

The case of Europe invites us to raise the broader issue of democracy beyond the nation state. As Martin Albrow (1996) and David Held (1995) suggest, such a democracy remains to be invented and cannot be thought of only in terms of representative democracy and institutional politics. Below the surface of institutional politics and mainstream media, actors of subterranean politics are exploring different cultures of activism and ways to empower citizenship. They attempt to re-politicise debates on the European and economic crisis and to develop alternative practices that contribute to the transformation of democracy, society and our way of living together, whether at a small or large scale. Taken together, they offer concrete ways forward for a multidimensional approach to deal with structural limits of representative democracy and to explore paths towards a more democratic Europe.

Notes

1. Dr. Bartolomeo Conti (postdoctoral researcher at the CADIS-EHESS) and Madeleine Sallustio (intern at the Université Catholique de Louvain) provided efficient research assistance, conducted interviews and fieldwork in both Paris and Belgium and took part in the first round of analysis.
2. It should be stressed that subterranean politics is not limited to progressive activism (as discussed in Chapter 1).
3. This echoes the concerns of Occupy Wall Street activists, where citizens claim that the two political parties are under the control of big corporations and the richest '1%' of the population.
4. This was the stated aim. There has been a lot of self-reflective criticism on how this did not always come to fruition.
5. Tarrow (2005) has underlined the key role of these brokers in the building of transnational coalitions.

6. Since 1997, at the EU summit in Amsterdam. Fifteen years later, Euromarches has lost most of its impetus. The dynamic unemployed network 'EuroMayDay' conducts decentralised and very creative actions all over Europe led by the precariat, making the movement younger, more decentralised, closer to the way of subjectivity and less coordinated at the EU level.
7. Extract from Pussy Riot's first song, 'Release the Cobblestones', November 2011.
8. Some *Indignados* who had previous mobility experience in Europe, however, asserted a stronger European identity: 'I am pro-European and feel completely European but the EU model is completely undemocratic...' (David, Barcelona).

References

Albrow, M. (1996) *The Global Age*. Cambridge: Polity.
Anheier, G., Glasius, M. and Kaldor, M. (Eds.) (2001) *Global Civil Society 2001*. Oxford: Oxford University Press.
Beck, U. (2009) *Cosmopolitan Europe*. Cambridge: Polity Press.
Beck, U. and Beck-Gernsheim, E. (2007) 'Generation global', in Ulrich Beck (Ed.) *Generation Global*. Frankfurt: Suhrkamp, pp. 236–262.
Bey, H. (1991) *T. A. Z. – The Temporary Autonomous Zone, Ontological Anarchy, Poetic Terroris*. New York: Autonomedia.
Bringel, B. (2013) *Brazil within the Geopolitics of Global Outrage*. ISA: Gobal Dialogue.
Castells, M. (2012) *Networks of Outrage and Hope*. Cambridge: Polity.
Convivialist Manifesto (2013) Available in English in an abridged form online at http://lesconvivialistes.fr/?page_id=12.
Eliasoph, N. and Luhtakallio, E. (2013) 'Personal attachment and global climate change: Promoting bicycling', in Helsinki, Los Angeles, and Paris, session Theorizing Context, ASA, New York.
Feixa, C. and Nofre, J. (Dir.) (2013) *#GeneraciónIndignada. Topias y Utopias del 15M*. Lleida: Milenio.
Feixa, C. and Perondi, M. (2013) 'El peregrino indignado: El camino de Sol', in C. Feixa and J. Nofre (Dir.) *#GeneraciónIndignada. Topias y Utopias del 15M*, Lleida: Milenio, pp. 117–140.
Fillieule O. (2007) 'On n'y voit rien. Le recours aux sources de presse pour l'analyse des mobilisations protestataires', in Fabre P., Fillieule O., Jobard F. *L'atelier du politiste*. Paris: La Découverte.
Ganuza, E. and Nez, H. (2013) 'Among militants and deliberative laboratories: The indignados', in Benjamín Tejerina et Ignacia Perugorría (dir.), *From Social to Political: New Forms of Mobilisation and Democratization*. Bilbao: Universidad del País Vasco, pp. 119–134.
Gerbaudo, P. (2012) *Tweets and the Streets*. London: Pluto.
Glasius, M. and Pleyers, G. (2013) 'The global moment of 2011: Democracy, social justice and dignity', *Development and Change*, 44(3), pp. 547–567.
Gobin, C. (2004) La Confédération européenne des syndicats. Résolutions du congrès de Prague et position du syndicalisme belge, Courrier hebdomadaire du CRISP, no. 1826.

Habermas, J. (2012) *The Crisis of the European Union: A Response.* Cambridge: Polity Press.

Held, D. (1995) *Democracy in the Global Order.* Stanford: Stanford University Press.

Hopkins, R. (2011) *The Transition Companion.* Devon: Green Books.

Illich, I. (1973) *Tools for Conviviality.* Glasgow: William Collins and Sons.

Kaldor, M. (2003) *Global Civil Society: An Answer to War.* Cambridge: Polity.

Kaldor, M. (2012) 'Taking on the Technocrats: Paths Towards Another Europe', blog entry, LSE EUROPP (European Politics and Policy), 6 March 2012, Accessed online at http://blogs.lse.ac.uk/europpblog/2012/03/06/national -politics-technocrats-subterranean-politics/.

Kostovicova, D. and Glasius, M. (2011) 'Agency in global bottom-up politics', in Kostovicova, D. and Glasius, M. (Eds.) *Bottom-up Politics: An Agency-Centred Approach to Globalization.* London: Palgrave Macmillan, pp. 1–17.

Maye, D. and Kirwan, J. (2010) 'Alternative Food Networks', in Sociopedia: The ISA Encyclopedia, Accessed online at http://www.isa-sociology.org/publ/ sociopedia-isa/.

McAdam, D. (1988) *Freedom Summer.* New York: Oxford University Press.

McDonald, K. (2006) *Global Movements.* London: Blackwell.

Mouffe, C. (2012) 'An agonistic approach to the future of Europe', *New Literary History*, 43(4), pp. 629–640.

Pleyers, G. (2007) *Forums sociaux mondiaux et défis du mouvement altermondialiste.* Brussels: Academia.

Pleyers, G. (2010) *Alter-Globalization.* Cambridge: Polity.

Pleyers G. (Ed.) (2011) *La consommation critique.* Paris : Desclée de Brouwer.

Rosenhek, Z. and Shalev, M. (2013) *The Political Economy of Israel's' Social Justice' Protests: A Class and Generational Analysis*, Paper presented at the EPCR joint session.

Sánchez, M. (2012) 'Losing Strength? An Alternative Vision of Spain's Indignados, Reflections on a Revolution', 23 June 2012, Accessed online at http://roarmag .org/2012/06/losing-strength-an-alternative-vision-of-the-indignados/.

Schor, J. (2010) *Plenitude: The New Economics of True Wealth.* New York: Penguin Press.

Tarrow, S. (2005) *The New Transnational Activism.* Cambridge: Cambridge University Press.

Touraine, A. (1973) *Production de la societé.* Paris: Seuil.

Weber, M. (1995 [1922]) *Économie et société*, vol. I. Paris: Plon.

Wieviorka, M. (2009) *Neuf leçons de sociologie.* Paris: R. Laffont.

Conclusion: Towards a European Spring?

Ulrich Beck and Mary Kaldor

This book describes the ways in which the European crisis is analysed and perceived by a range of newly emerging political actors. As outlined in the introduction, today's political activists view the crisis as a political one. They are disillusioned with democracy as it currently practised; they are the Internet generation; and, while many of them feel European in a cultural sense, Europe as a political project is 'invisible'.

Our concern in this conclusion is whether a renewed European political project could offer an answer to some of these concerns. Could it provide a mechanism for renewing democracy and restoring the legitimacy of our institutions? Are there prospects for a European spring, for a new social contract for Europe – a new Europe from below?

The European Union was founded not on the logic of war, as were states. It is not a nation-state and not an international organisation. It is a new kind of polity constructed in reaction to the risk of war and now, in reaction, to the risk of economic collapse. Is there a way that the European Union can be reimagined as a political project aiming to construct, restore and/or reinvent freedom and justice in the context of global risk? What kind of Europe could confront issues such as climate change, financial instability and mass surveillance so as to allow individuals and communities to flourish as human beings?

Background

A central tenet of European integration from the beginning was the idea that economic cooperation would lead to political cooperation. The founders of the European Union believed that through what was known as 'low politics', 'high politics' would follow. Economic and social cooperation would bring people together and this would lead eventually to a political union. And during the first three decades following World War II, this argument did appear to have some merit. The so-called Monnet method involved cooperation on infrastructure (coal and steel) and agriculture, in addition to the provision of regional assistance. And small steps were taken in the direction of greater political cooperation.

But after 1989, all this changed. On the one hand, this was the high point of the post-1968 cosmopolitan movements – the era of 'freedom's children'. The coming together of peace and human rights and the end of the Cold War led to a wave of cosmopolitan Europeanism. On the other hand, it was also the coming of the age of neo-liberalism. The same critique of the rigidity, paternalism and authoritarianism of the state developed by 'freedom's children' was used by the right to argue for more markets – deregulation, privatisation and macroeconomic stabilisation. 'Freedom's children' had taken social justice for granted and in reacting against the old Left had opened the space for the new radical Right.

The 1991 Maastricht Treaty can be regarded as a contract between the new wave of pro-Europeans, championed by Jacques Delors, and the new marketers epitomised by Margaret Thatcher. The cosmopolitan pro-Europeans got greater integration and the neo-liberals got the single market and convergence criteria. Economists argue that the monetary union was a big mistake in the absence of political union. But the point was just the opposite – to create a monetary union that would establish material interest in political union. Without a monetary union there would be no momentum for political union.

The logic of the market, however, is very different from the logic of earlier forms of state cooperation. This contradictory union between cosmopolitanism and the market has been played out over the last two decades. On the one hand, Europe expanded to the East and developed its neighbourhood policy largely based on the outward application of the Monnet method, using techniques that had been developed in the process of integration to bring in the outside world, extending 'low politics' to the neighbourhood – and even sometimes beyond.

It developed external policies for crisis management and for development that were similarly organised, albeit often rather bureaucratically, becoming in the process the biggest aid donor in the world and contributing to global debates about climate change, poverty and global security.

On the other hand, the rules of the single market and the euro – the so-called convergence criteria – associated with other neo-liberal reforms led to increased inequality, insecurity and atomisation undermining community and/or cosmopolitan politics. What is more, internal security and surveillance, especially on the borders of the expanded Europe, contributed to growing mistrust within societies.

Thus, in today's Europe, economic and political logics are pulling in opposite directions. It is true that monetary union dictates the need for political union and that everyone understands this at both elite and non-elite levels, which is one of the primary reasons for distrust. But the consequences of monetary union and the neo-liberal agenda with which it was associated are, at one and the same time, undermining what is known as the permissive consensus and greatly weakening the legitimacy of European elites.

It is true that material interests could force political cooperation. That is the only way to save the euro. But the 'high politics' of the European Union is still absent. National elites lack popular support and the therefore the capacity of European politicians to push through the policies they favour is rapidly disappearing. The fate of the technocratic prime ministers, Mario Monti and Lukas Papademos, who were imposed upon Italy and Greece, illustrates the end of this permissive environment.

The growing together of Europe has always been a process that occurs *vertically* – from the top down – between European institutions and national societies. While there have been all sorts of 'citizens' programmes', the questions of how individuals experience Europe, and in what kind of Europe they want to live, have never played any serious role in social science or political analysis. Scientific Europeanisation then means, on the one hand, the formation of supranational institutions (public bodies, the European Commission, financial union, etc.) and, on the other, the repercussions of this supranational institution-formation on national societies – for example, the adjustment of national norms and institutions to European guidelines. *Vertical* Europeanisation becomes confined to the integration of the nation states at the level of institutions. There are no European-born citizens. There are only national-born citizens. How national citizens become European citizens is an open question. In this view, the house of Europe is empty of people. Nobody lives there. And the absurdity of this view is that nobody notices!

The lived experience of Europe

Everywhere in Europe young people are becoming aware that, although the culture of their native country is certainly important and constitutive of their identity, it is not sufficient for understanding the world.

Young people want to become acquainted with other cultures because they sense that cultural, political and economic questions are closely embroiled with globalisation (see for example chapters 7 and 8).

According to this analysis, young people experience European society as a 'double sovereignty', as the sum of national and European opportunities for development. Contrary to what is often expected, they do not describe their identity as an independent European identity. Nobody is only a European. Young Europeans define themselves in the first instance in terms of their nationality, often second as global citizens and then as Europeans. In this sense, young people experience a cosmopolitan Europe in which national differences and antagonisms mix and are becoming increasingly blurred.

Why is this individual experience of a lived Europe practically absent in the current controversy over the euro crisis and the European crisis? It is because of this top-down institutionalisation and because of the association of the European Union with the single market. The European Union is experienced as a neo-liberal bureaucracy.

This is why Europe faces a profound political crisis. The protests and demonstrations, the new political initiatives and the new parties that we call 'subterranean politics' are not necessarily a reaction to austerity. They were and are about a profound loss of trust in current political elites – a belief that these elites are locked into financial and media interests and unable to act on behalf of the public good, and a sense that representative democracy is no longer about participation, but about reproducing that elite.

The problem is that in the absence of a bottom-up emancipatory cosmopolitanism, a project of European solidarity, that lack of political trust can easily be manipulated by xenophobic, eurosceptic and exclusivist parties of various stripes. Parties like UKIP, the True Finns, the Dutch Freedom party, New Dawn and similar parties are making electoral inroads in nearly every European country. And the mainstream parties, preoccupied by short-term electoral considerations, tend to pander to the sentiments expressed by these parties instead of voicing the longer-term public interest.

So how can Europe escape this downward spiral?

More freedom through a cosmopolitan Europe

Europe is not a national society and cannot become a national society; it is composed of democratically constituted national societies. If there is to be a renewed European project, European 'society' must rather be conceived as a 'cosmopolitan society of national societies'. The task is then to find a form of European Union that, by virtue of its communal strength, legally protects every individual in every national society and thereby encourages the emergence of a cosmopolitan, common sense. Indeed, this generation has already become, in one way or the other, a *Homo cosmopoliticus*.

Less uncertainties through a social Europe

The European society of individuals is at the same time also shaped by risk capitalism, which on the one hand dissolves prevailing moral milieus, forms of belonging and of social security, and generates new risks on the other.

Individuals should be able to feel that not all of the risks of the world, and especially not those of banks and states threatened with bankruptcy, are being dumped onto their shoulders, but rather that something exists which deserves the name 'European Community', because it takes the renewal of social security in these unsettled times as its programme and guarantees it. Then the concept of 'European Community' would stand not only for the experience of freedom and for the maximisation of risk and not only for the epicurean Europe that its citizens currently enjoy – but also for a *social* Europe!

Any new social contract designed to win over individuals to the European cause must answer the question: how can we reconceptualise the realistic utopia of social security so that it does not end, as it does at present, in one of two dead ends – either the defence of national welfare state nostalgia or the reforming zeal of neo-liberal self-sacrifice? How can we square the circle of elevating European politics to the level of transnationality, while at the same time winning national elections?

More democracy through a Europe of the citizen

The foundation of a new social contract for Europe is not, as Rousseau believed, a *volonté générale* (common will) that transcends individual interests and is absolute.

Rather, it is the recognition that old institutions that were assumed to be eternal are collapsing, and that there are no ready-made answers to key biographical and political questions in a Europe of individuals – and that this is not a defect but rather enables a surplus of freedom.

European society, understood in this way, is a laboratory of social and political ideas, the like of which exists nowhere else. What counts in large-scale politics, as in individual lives, is uncovering alternative futures and thereby, in a spirit of curiosity and experimentation, overcoming the dread of the past and responding effectively to the risks of the present.

The European project – enemies becoming neighbours – is in danger of failing. Many Europeans feel like Helmut Kohl, who said of the current German chancellor: 'That lass is destroying my Europe!' They can no longer endure the cultural hegemony of the eurosceptics and are demanding: stop your whining!

At this decisive moment, Helmut Schmidt, Jürgen Habermas, Herta Müller, Senta Berger, Jacques Delors, Richard von Weizsäcker, Imre Kertész and many others are calling for a transcendence of a Europe of empty pieties, Europe without Europeans, and for the foundation of a down-to-earth Europe, a Europe of citizens, a Europe from below – not only in word but also in deed, by 'doing Europe'.

Their idea is that a voluntary European year should allow everyone, not just the younger generation and the educational elites, but also retirees, the employed and the unemployed, to realise a part of Europe from below, in another country and in another language area (see *Manifesto 'We are Europe!'*[1]). This would not be work geared to securing the immediate essentials of life, but a mode of action aimed at political participation and structuring that creates connection and cohesion in the Europe of the citizen.

A European spring?

The malaise of Europe is rooted in the fact that we have a Europe without Europeans. What is missing, the Europe of the citizen, can only develop from below.

How can we awaken Europe's and the world's social and environmental conscience and shape it into a Europe-wide, indeed a worldwide, political protest movement that unites irate Greeks, unemployed Spaniards and the middle classes who are staring into the abyss – forming the political subject to implement the social contract?

Who could trigger the European spring? Those who form the new underclass; those who cannot afford health insurance; those whose retirement benefits were cut; those who have to take out loans in order to be able to study. It is not the superfluous, nor the outcasts, nor the underclass, but individuals from the middle of European society who will protest in the public squares of Europe, as they have already done in Athens, Madrid, Rome and Frankfurt.

What could be the source of the power of the European movement? The euro crisis has stripped neo-liberal Europe of legitimacy. The result is an asymmetry of power and legitimacy. There is a surplus of power and a dearth of legitimacy on the side of capital and the states, and a dearth of power and high legitimacy on the side of the protesters. This is an imbalance that the European movement could use to press home its core demands – for example, for a global tax on financial transactions – in the enlightened self-interest of the nation states and against their own narrow-mindedness, and for Europe. An exemplary, legitimate and powerful alliance between protest movements and the avant-garde of the nation-state architects of Europe would implement this Robin Hood tax, an alliance capable of making the political quantum leap into a world in which state actors would emerge to act transnationally within and beyond national borders.

And there is a final argument. What is happening in Europe is not just a European problem. The conflict over Ukraine, for example, exhibits a clash of two worldviews of the national, namely, that of Russia's aggressive ethno-nationalism (symbolised by 'rolling tanks' in the Crimea) and that of actually existing cosmopolitanism (symbolised by 'lack of investment'). Both images of the national have their 'weapons', though each follows a different political logic.

We do not live in an age of 'cosmopolitanism' (as a philosophical idea) but in an age of 'cosmopolitisation' (as a fact). And here it becomes clear that 'cosmopolitisation' does not create world citizens. On the contrary, it creates scepticism concerning Europe and anti-European resentment. But this is also a reason why Vladimir Putin's maxim 'Everywhere where Russians live should also be Russian territory' meets with sympathy.

While globalisation is dissolving borders, people are searching for new ones. This is why it is crucial to distinguish clearly between 'cosmopolitanism' (in the sense of normative philosophy and theory from Immanuel Kant to Jürgen Habermas) and 'cosmopolitisation' as a historical process of upheaval that in reality gives rise to existential, more or less conscious, publicly reflected interdependencies across all national, territorial, cultural and religious boundaries: the distant other is in our midst.

Putin's aggression is not only frightening the West. It is also unifying it, and people realise the difference between an aggressive ethno-nationalism and the notion of a 'cosmopolitan nation' (Beck and Levy, 2013) a cosmopolitan Europe which could make possible the kind of cosmopolitanism that the world needs. In other words, more peace from a European spring.

Note

1. http://manifest-europa.eu/allgemein/wir-sind-europa?lang=en.

References

Beck, Ulrich (2013). *German Europe*. Cambridge, UK/Malden, MA: Polity Press.
Beck, Ulrich (ed.) (2014) *Ulrich Beck – Pioneer in Cosmopolitan Sociology and Risk Society*. Cham/Heidelberg/New York/Dordrecht/London: Springer.
Beck, Ulrich and Daniel Levy (2013). 'Cosmopolitanized nations: Re-imagining collectivity in world risk society', *Theory, Culture & Society* 30(2): 3–31.

Index

Printed and bound by CPI Group (UK) Ltd, Croydon, CR0 4YY